D-Day
Spearhead Brigade

We who are left, how shall we look again
Happily on the sun or feel the rain
Without remembering how they who went
Ungrudgingly and spent
Their all for us loved, too, the sun and rain?

Wilfrid Wilson Gibson

D-Day Spearhead Brigade

The Hampshires, Dorsets & Devons on 6th June 1944

Denis Bounsall DCM, having received his Legion d'Honneur

Dedication

The perspective of history often adds a gloss of reassuring certainty that was entirely absent at the time. Seventy-five years after the event, the world rightly remembers D-Day – the beginning of the successful liberation of North West Europe – as a colossal victory. But, for the soldiers who crossed the storm-tossed, stomach-churning Channel on the night of 5th/6th June 1944, success was far from assured. Within a few hours, some, like the poor American infantry on Omaha Beach, would encounter horrors that surpassed their worst nightmares; others would find it less of an ordeal than they had expected. But that morning, as he stared from his bucketing landing craft at the approaching French coast, each of them knew there was a good chance that he would be killed or maimed, or that the Allies might be driven back into the sea.

Landing on the Normandy beaches early in the morning of 6th June 1944 demanded iron resolution and stalwart courage. This book, the story of the men of one of the British army's spearhead brigades that day, salutes their courage and their sacrifice. It is dedicated to all who landed – or tried to land – on D-Day, and especially to 231 Malta Brigade's most distinguished surviving D-Day veteran, who has contributed his own vivid memories:

Denis Bounsall, DCM, Chevalier of the Legion d'Honneur,
of A Company, 1st Battalion, The Dorsetshire Regiment,
who fought in Malta, Sicily, Italy, France, Belgium and the Netherlands.

Published in May 2019 by Semper Fidelis Publications

Copyright © Christopher Jary 2019

ISBN 978-0-9929033-7-4

The right of Christopher Jary to be identified as author of this work has been asserted by him in accordance with the *Copyright, Designs and Patents Act 1988.*

A CIP Catalogue record for this book is available from the British Library.

All rights reserved. No part of this book may be reproduced in any form or by any means, electronic or mechanical including photo-copying, recording or by any information storage and retrieval system, without permission from the author in writing.

Typeset in Freight Text Pro / 11pt by BluemoonPrint, Bristol

Produced in the United Kingdom by BluemoonPrint, Bristol

Contents

	Sponsors	xi
	Order of Battle 21st Army Group: 6th June 1944	xiii
	Acknowledgements	xv
	Introduction	xix
Chapter One	People, preparations and plans	1
Chapter Two	D-Day: 0330–0800 hours	40
Chapter Three	D-Day: 0800–0930 hours	71
Chapter Four	D-Day: 0930–1200 hours	96
Chapter Five	D-Day: 1200–1500 hours	110
Chapter Six	D-Day: 1500–1630 hours	124
Chapter Seven	D-Day: 1630–2359 hours	138
Chapter Eight	Unfinished business: D+1–D+3	149
Postscript	What lay ahead: D+4 to VE-Day and beyond	171
	A note on medals	197
Appendix One	1st Battalion, the Hampshire Regiment Order of Battle 6th June 1944	199
Appendix Two	1st Battalion, the Dorsetshire Regiment Order of Battle 6th June 1944	200

Appendix Three	2nd Battalion, the Devonshire Regiment Order of Battle 6th June 1944	201
Appendix Four	1st Battalion, the Hampshire Regiment Roll of Honour 6th–9th June 1944	203
Appendix Five	1st Battalion, the Dorsetshire Regiment Roll of Honour 6th–9th June 1944	205
Appendix Six	2nd Battalion, the Devonshire Regiment Roll of Honour 6th–9th June 1944	207
Appendix Seven	47th (Royal Marine) Commando Roll of Honour 6th–9th June 1944	209
Appendix Eight	The Royal Armoured Corps Roll of Honour 6th–9th June 1944	211
Appendix Nine	The Royal Artillery Roll of Honour 6th–9th June 1944	212
Appendix Ten	The Royal Engineers Roll of Honour 6th June 1944	213
Appendix Eleven	The Royal Army Medical Corps Roll of Honour 6th June 1944	214
Appendix Twelve	Gallantry Awards won by 231 Malta Brigade and by Officers and Men of Supporting or Associated Units 6th-9th June 1944	215
Appendix Thirteen	Special Army Order	218
	Bibliography	219
	Unpublished sources	221
	Index	223

Maps

Map 1	231 Malta Brigade's landing on Gold Beach: what was planned	xxii
Map 2	231 Malta Brigade's landing on Gold Beach: what happened	xxiii
Map 3	The 2nd Devons on D-Day	102
Map 4	The 1st Dorsets on D-Day	110
Map 5	The 1st Hampshires on D-Day	114
Map 6	The 1st Dorsets' objectives inland	118
Map 7	1st Hampshires capture Le Hamel East	126
Map 8	The Beach-head captured by 231 Malta Brigade on D-Day	147
Map 9	The Devons capture the Longues Battery on D+1	149
Map 10	47 (Royal Marine) Commando's capture of Port-en-Bessin on D+1/D+2	153

Sponsors

The production of this book was made possible only by the generosity of our Sponsors, whose names are listed here in appreciation and with thanks.

Charles Ackroyd	Dennis Collings	John Gaye
Nick Andrew	Connaught Trust	Robin Gilbert
Jeremy Archer	Mick Cook	Bob Gillam
Nigel Atkinson	Tony and Maureen	Jon Gliddon
Sandy Bagshot	Coombes	Geoff Goater
Dudley Barnett	Charles Cooper	Mick and Diana Gould
Tony Barron	Malcolm Corbidge	Stan Groves
Toffer Beattie	Paul Creech	Rex Gudge
Ian Bell	Patrick Crowley	John Hamblin
Stuart Blake	John Curl	Anthony Hannah
Denis Bounsall	Gordon Curtis	Don Hanney
David Bredin	Michael Curtis	Bobby Hanscombe
Geoff Brierley	Paul Davis	Hants and IOW Territorial
Alan and Daphne Brown	Mike Davis-Sellick	Trust
Mike Bugler	James Dewar	Happy Harman
Michael Bull	Horace˚ and Joyce Dibben	Eddie Harris
Bill Bullocke	Pam Dicker	EG Harris
Pat Burgess	David Dixon	Bill Hart
Gerald Burnett	Dick and Joan Eberlie	Mike Hawkins
Derek Burt	Joe Edkins	Dee Helmore
Trevor Burt	Andrew and Debbie	Peter Helmore
Jesse Carr-Martindale	Edwards	George Hendrick
Gary Carter	Adrian Esdaile	Pat Hendrick
Les Carter	Exeter Branch Devon and	David Hingle
Michael Carter	Dorset Regt Assocn	Neville Holmes
Peter Chilton	Dan Fraser	Peter Hughes
Ken Chivers	Robin Fraser	Philip Hull
Ian Clark	Tim Gallego	Ant Hurst
Ken Coles	Geoff Galpin	Bill Hutchings
Roger Coleman	Sue Galpin	Peter Huxham

xi

Geoff Hyde	Julia Mee	Terry Smith
Mick Jarrett	Mo Mee	Southampton Branch Royal
Christopher Jary	John Mellin	Hampshire Regt Assocn
Lois Jary	Peter Metcalfe	David Southwood
Tony Jeapes	Charles Miller	Diana Speakman
Graham Jefferies	Minden Dorsets Gp	Ian Speakman
Christopher Johnson	Harry Moore	Nick Speakman
Vicky Johnson	Catherine Mott	Nigel Spink
Hugh Keatinge	Richard Murray-Peters	Martin Stanley
Keep Coffee	Diana Nelson	Rory Steevenson
morning Gp	Geoff Nicholls	Robert Steptoe
Bryan Kelly	Ken Noble	Bill Stevens
Edward Kemp	Mike Osborne	Ian Taylor
Hugh Kent	Mick O'Shea	Robert Taylor
Jonathan King	Dennis Pannett	Derek Thomas
Norman King	Colin and Jean Parr	Tony Thornburn
Michael Kinney	James Porter	Laurence Thornton-
Colin Lane	Poundbury Wealth	Grimes
Michael Lane	Management	Richard Caesar-Thwaytes
Colin Lauder	John Powell	Bill Tong
David Laughrin	Robin Price	Richard Toomey
Tony Laurie-Chiswell	Adrian Pryce	John Travell
Lindsay Lawrence	Victor Pullman	Tony Trevis
Mark Layton	Purbeck Branch Devon and	Andy Triggs
Trevor Leaton	Dorset Regt Assocn	Mike Tuck
Ailsa Lee	Andrew Ravenhill	Peter Turner
Alex Lee	John Raymond	Adrian De Villiers
Nick Lee	David Read	Nick Wall
Roger Lidgley	Robert Rees	Greta Wall
Gerald Long	Mike Richardson	Trevor Webb
Roger Lowans	Bob Roberts	Debbie Wilkinson
Peter Lush	Bin Roy	Cedric Williams
Tim Lush	Charles Ryan	Bruce Willing
Caroline McCann	Nigel Salisbury	Douglas Winstone
James McCarthy	Fiona Santry	Allan Wood
Sarah McCarthy	Ken Shipton	Peter Wood
Terence McCarthy	Penny Singlehurst	

* Sadly, Horace Dibben died soon after sponsoring this book. A proud Dorset, who served in Hong Kong and Korea and once famously played a Japanese soldier in a re-enactment of the Battle of Kohima, he will be remembered for his kindness, the ever-present twinkle in his eye and the warmth of his friendship. I always felt happier for seeing Horace.

Order of Battle of 21st Army Group: 6th June 1944

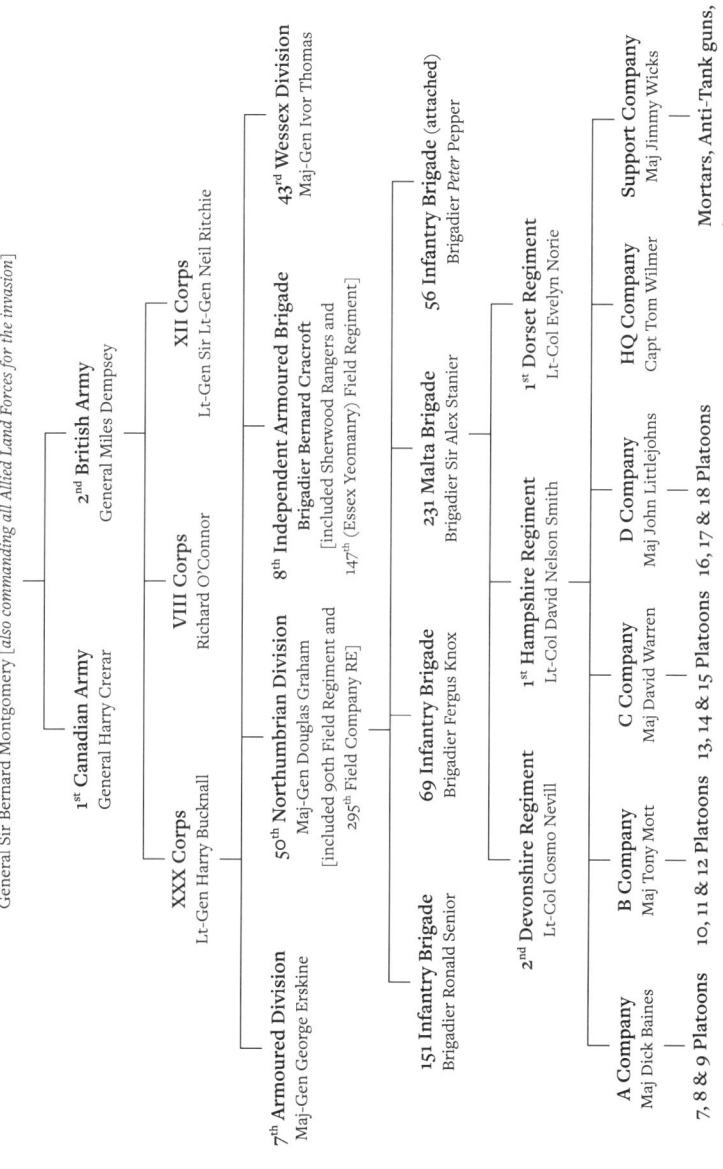

21st Army Group
General Sir Bernard Montgomery [*also commanding all Allied Land Forces for the invasion*]

- **1st Canadian Army** — General Harry Crerar
- **2nd British Army** — General Miles Dempsey
  - **XXX Corps** — Lt-Gen Harry Bucknall
    - **7th Armoured Division** — Maj-Gen George Erskine
    - **50th Northumbrian Division** — Maj-Gen Douglas Graham
      [included 90th Field Regiment and 295th Field Company RE]
      - **151 Infantry Brigade** — Brigadier Ronald Senior
      - **69 Infantry Brigade** — Brigadier Fergus Knox
      - **8th Independent Armoured Brigade** — Brigadier Bernard Cracroft
        [included Sherwood Rangers and 147th (Essex Yeomanry) Field Regiment]
      - **231 Malta Brigade** — Brigadier Sir Alex Stanier
        - **2nd Devonshire Regiment** — Lt-Col Cosmo Nevill
        - **1st Hampshire Regiment** — Lt-Col David Nelson Smith
        - **1st Dorset Regiment** — Lt-Col Evelyn Norie
          - **A Company** — Maj Dick Baines
          - **B Company** — Maj Tony Mott
          - **C Company** — Maj David Warren
          - **D Company** — Maj John Littlejohns
          - **HQ Company** — Capt Tom Wilmer
          - **Support Company** — Maj Jimmy Wicks
            Mortars, Anti-Tank guns, Pioneers, Bren gun Carriers
          - 7, 8 & 9 Platoons
          - 10, 11 & 12 Platoons
          - 13, 14 & 15 Platoons
          - 16, 17 & 18 Platoons
  - **VIII Corps** — Richard O'Connor
  - **XII Corps** — Lt-Gen Sir Lt-Gen Neil Ritchie
    - **43rd Wessex Division** — Maj-Gen Ivor Thomas
      - **56 Infantry Brigade** (attached) — Brigadier Peter Pepper

xiii

Private Childs, Anti-Tank Platoon, 1st Dorsets, having just been wounded on D-Day (Geoff Hebden)

Acknowledgements

On 5th October 2016 – the day before my 60th birthday – I was due to give a talk in the Library of the Keep Military Museum to a group from the University of the Third Age. The talk was about the Devons, Hampshires and Dorsets during the Siege of Malta, and I was just about to start when the Curator told me that downstairs in reception was the sister of Private Ken Leach. Ken was from Poole and had served with the 1st Dorsets throughout the siege. He had landed with them in Sicily and Italy and again on D-Day, and he had served for many years after the war right up to the time of the troubles in Northern Ireland. On Malta he had won a Military Medal for bravely continuing to fire his Bren gun after Private Francis Smith, from Lyme Regis, had been killed beside him by a Messerschmitt fighter which was strafing their small boat.

Ken's sister had never been to the Museum before but by pure chance she had come at exactly the right moment. She and her family were able to join us, where they heard for the first time how Ken had won his MM. This is one of the nicest things about writing books of this kind. Families of the men in the story come bobbing up. They are always helpful, interested and very pleasant, and their photographs and memories play an important part in bringing these stories to life. Several – not just from the three regiments but from others as well – have helped enormously.

An equally delightful aspect is the production team we have created. This is the sixth book Nick Speakman and I have produced. None would have happened, and my life since 2012 would have been much the poorer, without him. It is our second book to include research by Laurence Thornton-Grimes, James Porter, Andrew Edwards and Ian Taylor. Every one of them played a major part in producing this book but Ian, despite my protestations, modestly prefers his name to appear here rather than on the cover. I gave up arguing because I value our friendship, but I still think he's wrong!

This book describes a day on which lots of things happened, many of them simultaneously and in different places. Structuring the story in a way the reader can take it in and retain it presents a challenge to a writer. Without maps it would be impossible. Once again – for the sixth time! –

we are grateful to Peter Turner, who has drawn all ten maps to show who was doing what, with whom, where and when. I hope his maps and my text will enable you to form a picture in your mind of what happened on this cataclysmic day in history.

At the Keep Military Museum, all three members of staff have been very helpful. John Murphy has again located and assembled all the photographs for us. Because, in a book primarily about people, photographs are important and numerous, John's contribution has been considerable. Laura Gardner has helped often with research and ideas for publicising the book while our Curator, Chris Copson, has kindly provided access to the Devons' and Dorsets' archive and collection. Chris's opposite number, Colin Bulleid, at the Royal Hampshire Regiment's Museum in Winchester, has found all sorts of first-hand accounts and photographs from his Museum's archives and again shared them generously with us. Susannah Jarvis, Colin's Deputy, has also unearthed some very helpful first-hand accounts written by Hampshire veterans of D-Day.

Martin Stanley, Barry Paine and James Porter have each read through the draft and made some invaluable suggestions for improvements. It is a better book as a result. Peter Helmore and Rex Lovell have once again provided some very helpful information. Roger Coleman, himself a lifelong Royal Hampshire, not only read the draft and made helpful suggestions but also contributed his own boyhood memories of seeing the D-Day armada setting forth on 5th June 1944.

Elise Ann Wheeler, aboard MS *Azura*, deployed her impressive IT skills to enable me to send bits of the draft of this book home from the other side of the Atlantic. Without her, this feat would have been quite beyond me.

In my home we celebrate 6th June every year because it's my wife's birthday. I have never written anything without a great deal of advice and help from Lois, and this book is no exception. Ben Clark of BluemoonPrint has again brought his usual professionalism to seeing the manuscript through production to create the handsome book that is in your hands now. It is always a joy to work with him.

Posthumous thanks must go to two very naughty Dorsets. Nineteen-year-old Private Terry Parker of 18 Platoon kept an utterly illicit diary while Captain Geoff Hebden (who was old enough to know better) broke all the rules by taking his camera with him. His unique photograph of his Platoon aboard their landing craft is on the back of the dust jacket and several others add reality to this book while Terry Parker's diary entries lend an emotional immediacy that touches the heart. I am in their debt.

Like most histories, *D-Day Spearhead Brigade* draws on lots of other books, which are listed in the Bibliography. Three, however, stand out in my view and together have provided a central resource to which I have referred time and again. First among equals is Simon Trew's *Gold Beach*, which combines academic precision with a professional understanding of the subject. Simon has also very kindly allowed me to use some of his own photographs of the battlefields. Tim Saunders's *Gold Beach-Jig* is an ex-soldier's outstanding battlefield guide while Andrew Holborn's *The D-Day Landing on Gold Beach* brings a fresh, scholarly rigour to the events of the day. I am deeply grateful to all three, and very conscious that this book, although viewing the subject from a different perspective, nonetheless stands on their supportive shoulders.

Photographs have come from all over. Ken Chivers and Rob Fraser once again came on one of our reconnaissance trips to Normandy, Ken driving, Rob navigating and both taking several of the photographs that appear here. It would have been much less fun and much harder work without them. Five photographs have been purchased from the Imperial War Museum. Two – of two Queen's officers, Tony Mott and *Dick* Whittington – were kindly provided by Guzman Gonzalez of the Surrey History Centre through the good offices of our mutual friend Kirsty Bennett. The wonderful photographs of the AVREs and flail tanks were obtained with the enthusiastic help of Kate Thompson of the Tank Museum at Bovington. Marc de Bolster helped by obtaining permission from Terry Cousins's family to use his photograph while Sue Gasquoine kindly sent me two photographs of Denis Bounsall from New Zealand. Pierce Noonan of Dix, Noonan Webb very kindly provided the photograph of Sergeant Bob Palmer of the Essex Yeomanry.

Among the families of men mentioned in this book who have provided photographs or memories are: Annette and Christopher Bowstead (daughter and son of Denis Bowstead MM of the 90th Field Regiment); Leslie Carter (nephew of Vic Carter MM of the Dorsets); David Christopherson (son of Stanley Christopherson DSO MC and Bar of the Sherwood Rangers); Hugh Loxdale (nephew of Hugh *Bubbles* Duke MC and Bar of the Devons); Joe Edkins (son of David Edkins who was wounded on D-Day advancing inland); John Farrar (son of Jonah Farrar and nephew of Arthur Farrar, both Hampshires); Nigel and Annette Hayes (son and daughter-in-law of Willie Hayes MC and Bar of the Dorsets); Colin Lauder (son of Jack Lauder, one of the first Hampshires to land); Mark Layton, and Caroline and Sally née Layton (son and daughters of Gordon Layton, who was badly wounded at the radar station); Stuart Mason-Elliott, Penny Singlehurst, Diana Nelson and Fiona Santry (nephew and nieces of Graham Mason Elliott who died of his wounds); Adrian Norman (son of Alan Norman who was another of the first Hampshires to land); Tim Parker (son of Terry Parker, the 1st Dorsets' illicit diarist); Paul Scaife (son of Bert Scaife DCM who turned the battle at Le Hamel); and Dave Dudley Ward and Sue Sargent (son and daughter of Tim Dudley Ward of the

Hampshires' Assault Pioneers). It was a joy and a privilege to encounter them all and to hear a family view.

Finally, my special thanks to the only veteran of 231 Malta Brigade to have helped directly with this book. Last year, I wrote to ninety-seven-year-old Denis Bounsall DCM in Auckland, New Zealand, asking if he had any memories of 6th June 1944. He replied with twelve pages of vivid memories and, throughout this book's writing, he has been my constant, enthusiastic supporter. When he read it recently in draft, his response – reproduced on the dust jacket – gave me more pleasure and pride than any praise from any critic could ever do. On 2nd March 2019, shortly after renewing his passport and driving licence, Denis and his friends celebrated his ninety-eighth birthday with fish and chips on the beach. He hopes to attend the book launch in Dorchester in June. In this, as in many other respects, he is an example to us all. If this story rings true for Denis, my friends and I have achieved our purpose.

Christopher Jary
Frampton, Dorset

Introduction

At two hundred yards all parts of the body are distinctly seen. At three hundred yards the outline of the face is blurred. At four hundred yards no face. At six hundred yards the head is a dot and the body tapers.

In *Men at Arms*, the first book of his *Sword of Honour* trilogy, Evelyn Waugh reproduced the *patter* of an NCO instructor teaching recruits how to judge distances. Beyond three hundred yards individual soldiers start to become unrecognisable.

So it is with books. The distant perspective of a history of 21st Army Group would encompass a million men, a tiny proportion of whom, most of them generals, might emerge as characters in the story. Even a book about a single infantry division would have to tell the story of 18,000 soldiers. But one about the three battalions in an infantry brigade concerns only 2,500 men – the population of a town even smaller than Beaminster. While readers of a book about a brigade on a single day can keep in mind the various activities of its composite units at any one time, the writer can also zoom in on the story of individual officers and soldiers of all ranks. So writing this book about the men of 231 Malta Brigade – Hampshires, Dorsets and Devons – on D-Day was a practical and an attractive proposition.

The passage of time creates its own distance. Writing this book ten or twenty years ago, I would have been able to find plenty of men who landed on D-Day and many more who knew them well. Sadly, that is no longer the case. As the years pass, interpreters of what happened become more and more reliant upon written sources. Happily, however, enough people recorded their vivid memories for there to be plenty of evidence of events. This book contains the personal recollections of eighty-three survivors who landed either with or beside 231 Malta Brigade on 6th June 1944. Their memories often allow us a glimpse of the characters of many of the participants – especially of the witness providing each piece of testimony. In many cases that testimony is so powerful and so vivid that it needs no elucidation.

A book of this kind requires many of the same ingredients as a novel: plot, pace and character. 231 Malta Brigade's story on D-Day is a cracking one, with a gripping plot and a real sense of progress, and with setbacks, tragedies and triumphs enough to maintain anyone's interest. The history of any military formation is essentially a story of people, and there were many interesting characters in 231 Brigade. Having written several books about the Dorsets, Devons and the Brigade, I already knew some of the principal players in this drama. Many of the men who landed on D-Day had served on Malta and appeared in *Yells, Bells & Smells*, a good proportion of the Dorsets featured in my last volume of their Regimental history, while all the Devons and Dorsets who won awards figured in *Devotion to Duty*. And I have known some of the Hampshires from my boyhood from stories told by my father, who was a proud Hampshire.

Unlike those in a novel, the events and characters in a history cannot be adjusted to suit the writer's purpose. No novelist would ever allow so many characters to appear, all doing different things at about the same time and in the same place – often in the wrong place! This, though, was the confused reality of Gold Beach on the morning of D-Day. I have made every effort to structure the story to make it easier to take in, but I cannot streamline events or exclude important characters in order to make life easier for me or my readers. We each have a duty to the men who were there to try to get as close as possible to how it was and what they were like. Any depiction of them must not only ring true, but *be* true to the men described. Where I feel I can, I have tried to give an impression of their characters, but I have neither invented nor enhanced what can confidently be deduced from the record. I am proud to be allowed to tell their story, and I hope this impression of them does them justice.

They seem to me good men to know. Too many of them died – if not on D-Day, then later. Their losses in the Normandy battles were horrific. The 1st Dorsets' War Diary in the archives at the Keep Museum includes two orders of battle, listing the Battalion's officers and showing their role within the unit. One is for 1st June 1944, the next for 1st July 1944. Of the thirty-seven names on the June list, only nine appear on the July one. The name of only one officer – Captain Arthur Harris – remains among the twenty names of officers in the rifle companies. The American breakout in the west and ultimate victory in the three-month campaign in Normandy were bought with the blood of British and Canadian infantry.

I have made no attempt to sanitise or soften the often brutal reality of the human cost that was paid to liberate Continental Europe. Telling the tragic end to the story of familiar names who had already endured the siege of Malta before landing on Sicily, then Italy and finally on D-Day, found me on several occasions sitting at my computer with tears in my eyes. The loss of the youngsters who supplemented and then replaced these veterans was no less poignant.

The use of names raises questions for an author writing seventy-five years later about a past where they did these things differently.

Christian names (now called first names and used ubiquitously) were reserved principally for family use. Men and boys called each other by their surnames, sometimes preceded by a rank or Mr. And yet friendships were as close as they are today – perhaps, in a platoon or company in battle, even closer. And so nicknames proliferated. Many of the men in this book had nicknames which were as much part of their identity as any name given by a loving parent beside the font. These were the names used in the mess, barrack room or trench, in discomfort, danger and even in death. *Bubbles has bought it* carried a weight of grief and affection that *Major Duke has been killed* would have lacked. And few of his friends and comrades would have known that his family called him *Hugh*. I have tried to preserve this special, battalion identity by introducing these young men first with their family names and thereafter by using the names they were called by their friends.

I have defied conventional regimental seniority (Devons, Hampshires then Dorsets) by putting the Hampshires first throughout this book. In the story of D-Day I think this is right. They landed first (closely followed by the Dorsets), had the hardest fight and lost the most men (again followed by the Dorsets). Few, I hope, will disagree that, on 6th June 1944, the 1st Battalion of the Hampshire Regiment earned their place on the right of a very distinguished line. At Appendix 13 is the Army Order of 28th November 1946 which, recognising the Regiment's proud record throughout the Second World War (in which D-Day was one of the highlights), announced that it had been granted the title *The Royal Hampshire Regiment*.

In his addresses to troops and civilians before D-Day, Monty repeatedly said: *What really matters is the man inside the tank, and the man behind the gun. It is the man that counts.* This book is in that spirit. It is first and last about the men who landed on Jig Sector of Gold Beach on D-Day. The strategy, tactics, weapons, equipment and everything else are all secondary to the men who began the liberation of North West Europe. The generations who have followed and will follow – in France, Belgium, the Netherlands, Denmark, Germany and Great Britain – owe them a debt none of us can ever fully repay. It was clear last July, when my friends and I visited the Mairie in Asnelles, that the people there have not forgotten the many young lives the Hampshires, Dorsets and Devons gave to free their town and their country. Nor should we.

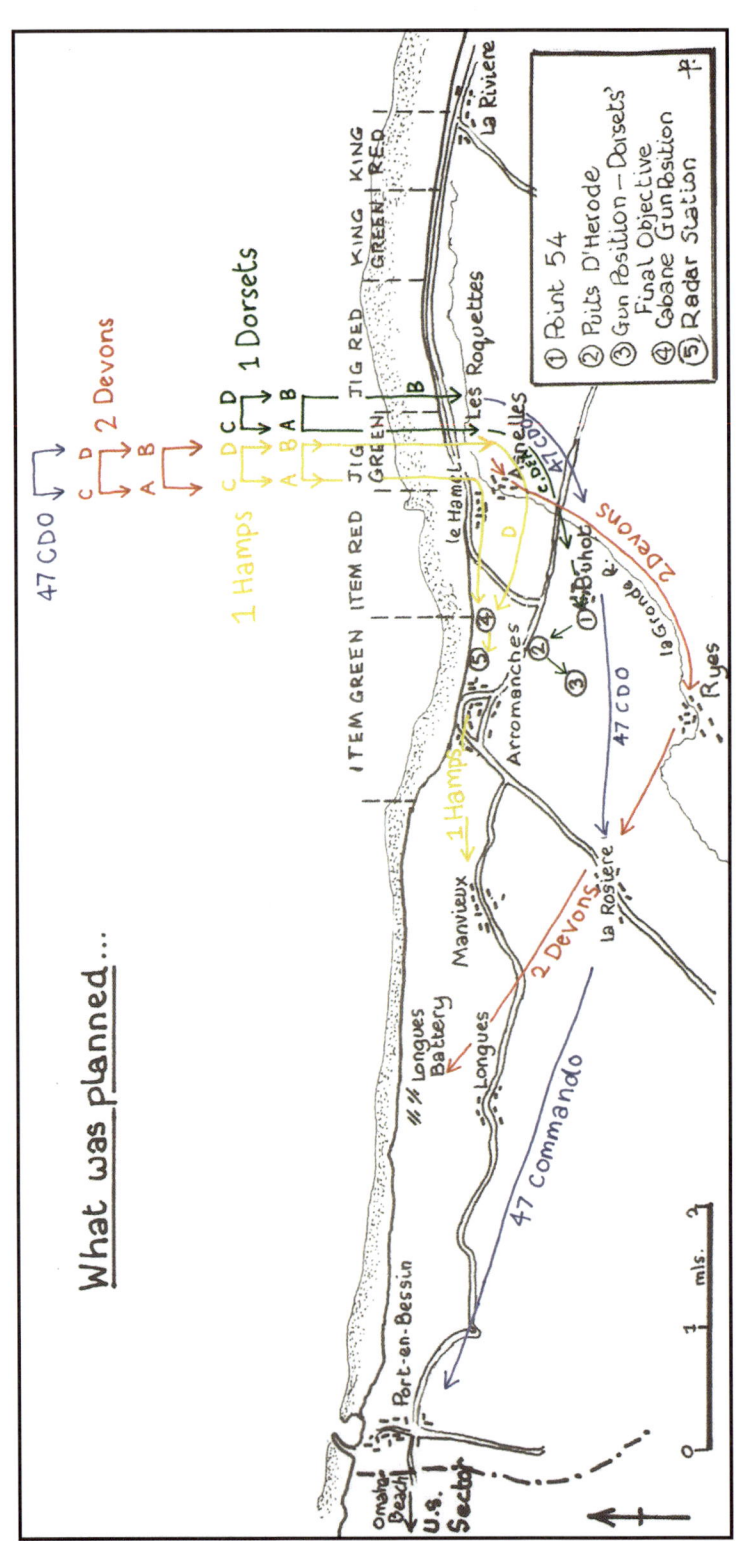

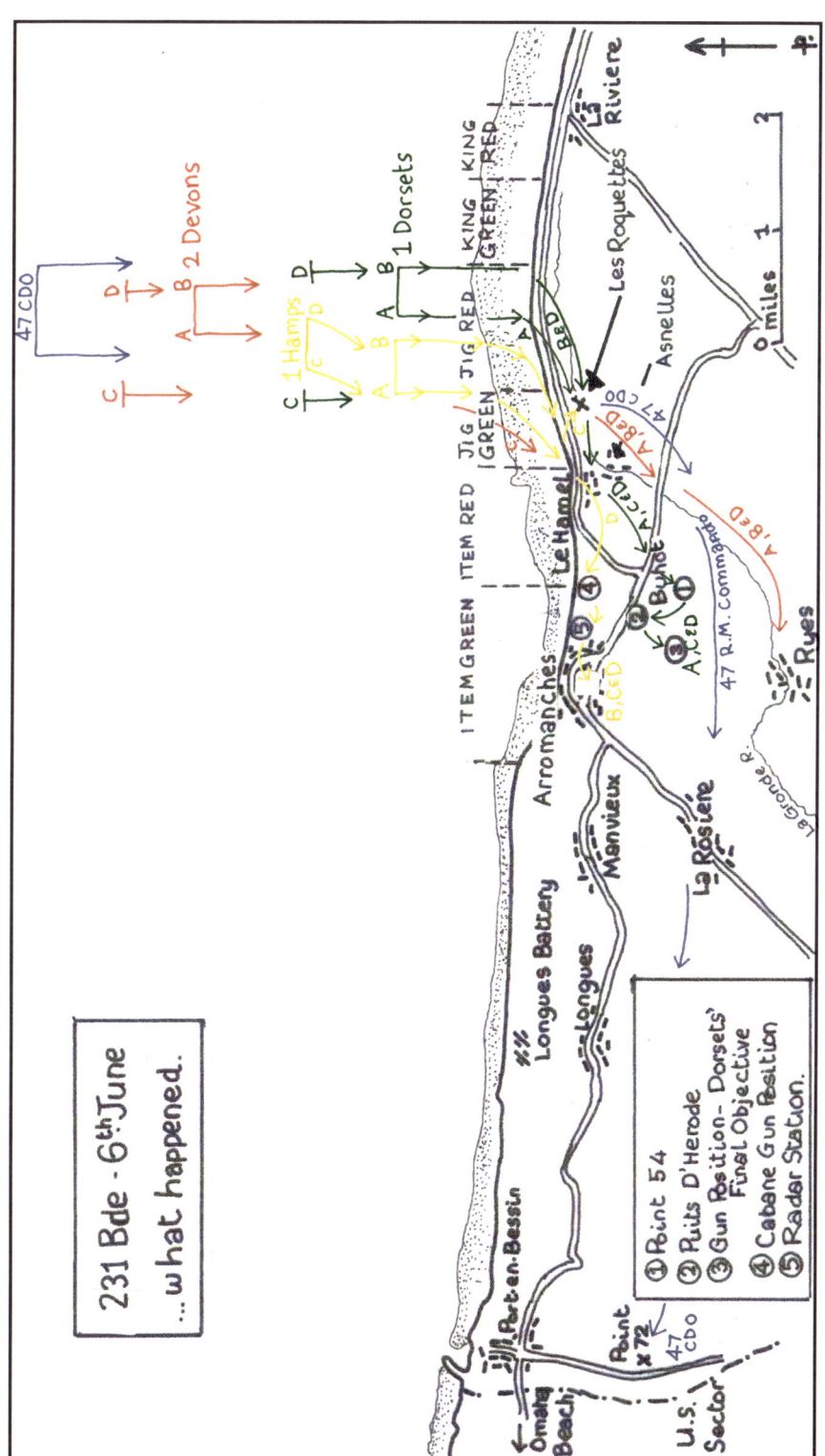

Looking east along Gold Beach from the lane to Les Roquettes

CHAPTER ONE

People, preparations and plans

The beach

They landed at low tide, wading through the bitingly cold, choppy water onto a darkened shore. All around was silence except for the constant sloshing of the waves, and the night air was heavy with the smell of salt and seaweed. The waving beam of a searchlight moved apparently at random across the sand, illuminating a patch here, then another patch there, before moving on again. Operating that searchlight was a German soldier, and there were others, closer to where they were now, guarding and patrolling the beach.

The Sergeant set off at once across the sand, followed first by the young Officer and then by the Corporal. They moved swiftly and silently, thanking God with each step that this was a sandy beach without scrunchy pebbles. The sudden flare of a match revealed the position of a sentry, just forty yards ahead of them. Too far away to see the tip of his cigarette as he drew on it, but still much too close for comfort.

As they crept closer, a six-man patrol appeared and the three men lay doggo as the enemy passed. Just ahead loomed the tall shape of a twelve- or fifteen-foot pole with a strange bulge at the top. There was another over there, and another. In the Sergeant's haversack was a long length of string, a magnet and a wooden staple. By attaching the staple close to the bulge – the mine – then threading the string through it, they could retire to a safer distance, haul the magnet close to the mine and see what happened next. If it exploded, the mine was magnetic; if it didn't, it wasn't. During their two weeks' training at Dover this had become a simple and familiar procedure. Here, within spitting distance of the enemy, it seemed less straightforward.

An accident spared them the trouble. The Sergeant inadvertently caught the mine a crack with his metal mine detector. After a nerve-jolting metallic clonk, nothing happened. No explosion and no response from the Germans all around them. A welcome silence resumed. They had achieved their object – to determine what sort of mines were attached to these poles. They had recognised them, from their days in the desert, as Teller anti-tank mines 1942. All that remained was to pace out the distance between the poles. While they were doing this, the searchlight swung towards and across them, but still no response came from the enemy.

Turning back to the boat, the Officer was horrified to see, clearly delineated against the phosphorescent sea, the Sergeant-Major and his squad of eleven Commandos who had come to protect them, the waiting motor boat and even the distant shape of the motor torpedo boat that would take them back to Dover. It seemed impossible that he and his team had not been similarly silhouetted for anyone further up the beach, but still the Germans had not seen them.

Back on board the MTB, the Officer and his Sergeant were separated. Their orders were to report their findings individually without having first discussed them with each other. In Dover next morning each was treated to a large breakfast before being driven at speed – still separately – up to the War Office in London. Here each was interviewed by General Sir Bernard Montgomery's Chief of Staff, Freddie de Guingand. Monty himself joined them and listened very carefully to their descriptions of what they had found on the beach.

They learned too that, of the four teams despatched to the Normandy beaches, theirs had been the only one to succeed in its mission. One had been unable to land because of the rough sea while the other two had been captured by the Germans.

The findings of this three-man reconnaissance patrol two weeks before D-Day prompted Monty to discuss the problem posed by the German mines and obstacles with Admiral Sir Bertram Ramsay, the Naval Commander-in-Chief. After their discussion, the plan for the landings was changed. Instead of landing at high tide, when the submerged Teller mines would blow huge holes in the landing craft, they would land on a rising half-tide, allowing the landing craft to spot and avoid the mines. Although this would considerably increase the size of the beach the troops would have to cross, it greatly reduced the chances of their being blown up before they reached the shore.

The young subaltern who led this operation on 15th May was Lieutenant John Stone of the 274th Field Company of the Royal Engineers. A twenty-one-year-old product of Weymouth Grammar School and Cambridge, he was already a veteran of North Africa, Sicily and Italy. For his gallantry on the French beach he was later awarded a Military Cross. His Sergeant, a Scot named Forbes Blyth Ogilvie from the same Field Company, was awarded a Military Medal. They, their Corporal, and their supporting section of Commandos, had all earned the gratitude of every man who would land in Normandy on 6th June 1944.

Monty and the Second Front

Since 1942 the Americans had been pressing for an Allied invasion of mainland Europe. So had Stalin, who thought a second front in the west would relieve the pressure on his forces in the east. But 1942 had also seen the disastrous raid on Dieppe, when 6,000 mostly Canadian troops launched a division-sized attack on the French port. The result, which cost sixty per cent casualties among those who landed, achieved practically nothing. For an invasion to succeed, it would need to be planned and executed on an unprecedented scale. In 1942 such an operation was far beyond the capacity of the British, Canadian and American armies. It might have been achieved in 1943 but, once the decision to invade first Sicily and then Italy had been taken, it had to be shelved until 1944.

In the spring of 1943 planning had begun under Lieutenant-General Sir Frederick Morgan, but it was not until November that Roosevelt and Churchill decided who should command the invasion. General Dwight Eisenhower was appointed Supreme Commander with Montgomery as Land Forces Commander for the invasion. Once the battle in Normandy had been won, Monty would revert to commanding the British and Canadian 21st Army Group and the American armies would return to American command.

Among the tens of thousands who played their part in putting 231 Malta Brigade on the beach near Asnelles on the morning of 6th June 1944, foremost is Bernard Montgomery, who planned and commanded the invasion and whose influence permeated 21st Army Group. But his influence had begun fifteen months earlier when he had spotted the potential of an obscure brigade which had spent most of the war defending tiny Malta.

The 1st Malta Brigade then contained four battalions – the 2nd Devons, the 1st Hampshires, the 1st Dorsets and the 3rd King's Own Malta Regiment, made up of keen Maltese Territorials. During one of the longest sieges in history, they had endured the heaviest bombing then recorded, the threat of invasion, blockade, starvation, heat, malnutrition and intense boredom. They had built runways, repaired bomb-damaged roads, runways and buildings, serviced fighters, provided airfield anti-aircraft defence and guarded coastal shipping with their machine guns, and trained hard – both to defend the island against imminent invasion and for future offensive operations elsewhere. Their far-sighted Brigadier, Kenneth Pearce Smith, had even prepared them to lead an invasion of Sicily.

At the end of the siege, in March 1943, Monty had visited Malta and had seen for himself the Brigade's impressive state of readiness. The stalwarts of the King's Own Malta Regiment stayed put on what remained of their island, but Monty had other plans for the Devons, Hampshires and Dorsets. Instead of sending them off to recuperate, he sent them for intensive training in Egypt and ordered them to spearhead the invasion of Sicily in July. For a man whose habit was to trust only those he knew, this was an unusual departure and a rare tribute to the Brigade. He did, however, revert to type by replacing their Brigadier with Roy Urquhart, one of *his own chaps*. Dissatisfied with the original American plan for the invasion of Sicily, Monty entirely recast it, giving the Malta Brigade a leading role.

The campaign in Sicily was short-lived but hard-fought. On 10th July the Brigade, now renamed 231 Malta Brigade and wearing the Maltese cross on their sleeves, landed from rough seas at Marzamemi on the south-eastern tip of the island. In this operation they established the pattern they would follow in both their subsequent assault landings: the Hampshires and Dorsets provided the assault companies with the Devons in reserve. After initial brave but sporadic resistance, the Italians crumbled. The Germans did not and, as the Brigade advanced north-westwards, fought a series of vicious defensive battles as they withdrew through a succession of Sicilian hill villages. It was under the scorching Sicilian summer sun – first in the landings and then in battles such as Vizzini, Agira and Regalbuto – that the Brigade learnt their trade as infantrymen. By the end of the campaign, they had earned their Army Commander's respect, just as long-established units of the Eighth Army had won it during the long march from Alamein to Tunis.

After the briefest of respites, Monty gave the Brigade the special task of landing in early September on the toe of Italy. As an independent brigade, they would land at Pizzo, ahead of Monty's main force, and speed his advance north to join the Americans at Salerno. Despite more rough seas, which caused a chaotic landing in which no one seemed to land in the right place or in the correct order, the Brigade shook itself into shape and successfully beat off a German counter-attack before meeting the advancing units of Eighth Amy and clearing their path forward.

In November 1943 the Malta Brigade returned to the United Kingdom as part of 50th (Northumbrian) Division. Soon afterwards, Monty was appointed to command the British and Canadian Army Group and to plan and execute the invasion of North West Europe. He decided at once that the division he wished to lead the assault was 50 Div and that 231 Malta Brigade should be one of the Division's two spearhead brigades on D-Day. Monty was therefore personally responsible for choosing our three battalions to lead the Normandy invasion.

He was also responsible for transforming the plan he had inherited for the largest amphibious operation in history into one that promised success. Despite having been fighting without a break in three major campaigns for the past seventeen months, he threw himself into this huge task immediately and wholeheartedly. Arriving in England on New Year's Eve, on first sight of the plan that night he unerringly put his finger on its principal flaw, writing: *The initial landing is on too narrow a front and is confined to too small an area*, and asserting that, for the invasion to succeed, it was essential for *one British army to land on a front of two, possibly three, corps. One American army similarly.* He enlarged the whole enterprise, recasting the plan to involve many more troops landing on a much wider front in order to seize a more substantial and more readily defendable beachhead. In the following five months he oversaw the production of a workable plan and toured the country, making sure that his influence was felt throughout the armies which would carry it out and even in the factories manufacturing the necessary weapons and equipment. Alamein had been a triumph, but this was his finest hour. Undiplomatic, bossy, egotistical and at times downright rude, Monty single-mindedly forged the weapon – and the plan for how it should be wielded – which would ensure Allied success on the beaches and in the fields of Normandy.

231 Malta Brigade

To those unfamiliar with the eccentric inclusivity of the British Army's county regiments, to append a brigade of Devons, Dorsets and Hampshires to a Northumbrian Division of Durham Light Infantrymen, East Yorkshires and Green Howards may seem perverse. But these unlikely juxtapositions often worked remarkably well. Later, when casualties in Normandy really began to deplete the strength of fighting battalions, the 1st Dorsets would absorb an entire company of Durhams who fought very happily as Durham Dorsets. After all, the General commanding the Northumbrian Division was Major-General Douglas Graham, a lowland Scot from the Cameronians! A decorated veteran of the First World War, Graham had commanded the 51st Highland Division at Alamein, earning a DSO. His Division's rapid advance to Sfax in Tunisia had won him a Bar to the DSO before, injured in a jeep accident in October 1943, he had been brought home to the UK to recuperate. He recovered in time to take command of 50th Division and to prepare for the invasion.

Commanding 231 Malta Brigade was a Welsh Guardsman. Brigadier Sir Alex Stanier, now forty-five, had been commissioned a month before his eighteenth birthday. He had looked so young when reporting to his Battalion in France that his new Commanding Officer called him *the infant Samuel*; for the rest of his army career he remained *Sammy* Stanier. Despite his youth, in October 1918 he had won an MC leading an advance at St Vaast. In 1939 he had been asked to raise a 2nd Battalion of Welsh Guards, which he took to Boulogne in May 1940. He had won a DSO in a fierce two-day defence of the port which cost his Battalion many casualties. Their survivors were some of the last troops to leave Northern France. More recently, training in the UK, he had lost an eye in an accident with a grenade. One of the last commanding officers to leave France in June 1940, *Sammy* Stanier would be one of the first to return four years later to fight his first battle as a brigade commander.

Brig Sir Alex 'Sammy' Stanier DSO MC

The three battalions in the Brigade had come together by chance. No one in blitzed, besieged Malta in early 1941 had made a conscious decision to group them because they came from three adjacent counties on England's south coast. But it was a happy chance because, despite their proud distinctions, they were county regiments of similar character and standing. All had emerged from the First World War with high honours, and all three – the 2nd Devons, the 1st Hampshires and the 1st Dorsets – were Regular battalions who had served in India between the wars. On Malta the Devons and Dorsets had worked well together and, when the Hampshires joined them from Egypt in February 1941, they completed a very effective and cohesive infantry brigade.

In March 1944 each of the three battalions had at least one officer who had served in Brigade Headquarters in Malta or Sicily: David Nelson Smith of the Hampshires, Franc Sadleir of the Devons, and Bob Tucker of the Dorsets. Sixteen or more of the commanders or seconds-in-command of companies in the three battalions had served together in Malta, where they had got to know each other very well. Having served and fought together for so long, this shared experience, and the trust and easy relationships that flowed from it, would be central to success.

Their casualties in Malta, except during the heaviest of the bombing in 1942, had been relatively light. The Sicily campaign had been much costlier but had lasted only six weeks, and they had fought only one battle in Italy. As a result, the Brigade that returned to England in November 1943 retained the character of the pre-war Regular Army. The passage of time brought some changes. Some older officers, NCOs and soldiers were transferred to less physically demanding roles than the infantry. Some who had been private soldiers in 1939 were now junior NCOs, while the subalterns of 1939 were now mostly captains and majors. Some recently recruited soldiers and junior wartime officers had taken their places, leavening the Brigade with some young men who, but for the war, would not have joined the army. In the First World War these distinctions had sometimes been more obvious: wartime officers were occasionally referred to disparagingly as *temporary gentlemen*, while the higher standard of training of pre-war Regular soldiers had marked them out in a unit. In the Second, these distinctions – if felt at all – were less marked, and wartime officers and soldiers were absorbed into the healthy mix that created and maintained a good battalion. Given what was to befall them in the campaign in Normandy, this was a very good thing indeed.

Each battalion had several officers from other regiments within it. Designated to act as the Dorsets' Unit Landing Officer on D-Day was Captain Charles Whittington, a long-serving Territorial officer of the Queen's Royal Regiment, known for obvious reasons as *Dick*. The Dorsets' Intelligence Officer, thirty-year-old Donald Youngs, was a married lawyer who had been commissioned into the Royal Norfolk Regiment. Leading 12 Platoon was twenty-one-year-old John Whitebrook, an officer of the King's Shropshire Light Infantry, whose remarkable Platoon Sergeant – William Evans – was nearly thirty-five. Sergeant Evans had served in the late 1920s and early 1930s in Egypt and Hong Kong with the South Wales Borderers and joined the 1st Dorsets on Malta in September 1939. More recently, he had won an MM for patrolling in Sicily, and a Bar in Italy for knocking out a German armoured car with grenades.

Within the Brigade, the close relationships between the three regiments bordered on the incestuous. Leading 16 Platoon in the 1st Dorsets was a Hampshire: Lieutenant Joe Bradbury. Commanding a platoon in the Devons was another Hampshire, Lieutenant Edward Smith. Commanding one in the Hampshires was Leonard Paul (known as *Peter*) of the Devons. Among their forty officers, the 1st Hampshires had two Dorsets: twenty-one-year-old Lieutenant Jack Lauder commanded a platoon in A Company while Major Charles Martin was the Battalion's Second-in-Command. Martin was the younger of two brothers from Rampisham in Dorset whose parents had separated when both boys were very young. John and Charles were very close and had been delighted when, in the middle of the siege of Malta, they were able to meet. Charles was there with the 1st Dorsets when John, then a pilot in Royal Air Force, flew in. It was the last time they had been able to get together. Since then Charles had been awarded a DSO for leading the first company to land on Sicily and, in the Battle of Agira, capturing a German machine gun post single-handed. A proud Dorset, he had his doubts when the Brigadier appointed him to be Second-in-Command of the Hampshires. He wrote to John: *It is a bit of a wrench leaving the old Dorsets after all these years, but as the Brig himself picked me from all those eligible in the Brigade, one feels rather pleased and prepared to do something in return.*

Maj Charles Martin DSO, Second in Command, 1st Hampshires

The effect of this intermingling of regiments was almost entirely beneficial. Sydney Jary, a subaltern of the Hampshire Regiment who led a platoon of Somersets from 31st July 1944 until VE Day, later wrote: *To me, a very junior and young officer from another regiment, the reputation of the 4th Battalion, The Somerset Light Infantry, was important. Above that was the reputation of D Company and, paramount, that of 18 Platoon. I was proud to wear their badge and conscious also that, as a representative of the Hampshire Regiment, high standards were expected of me.* This loyalty cut both ways. As the survivors of his Battalion marched past him on parade at the end of the campaign, Lieutenant-Colonel Christopher Lipscombe took the salute. His Adjutant remarked to him: *It's a pity so many of them aren't Somersets.* The Colonel replied: *They're all Somersets to me, Tim.*

Important though this subtle web of loyalties was, still more important was the shared battle experience of the officers, NCOs and men within the three battalions. The scattering of 1914-18 war ribbons which had adorned the chests of several senior officers and warrant officers in Malta days had largely disappeared. By D-Day only two would remain: Sir Alex Stanier and Regimental Sergeant-Major *Jimmy* Burgess of the 1st Hampshires, who had won a Military Medal at Ypres in 1917.

Many Dorsets had pre-war operational experience in Palestine and India, and a significant number of Hampshires had achieved what was known as *the Hampshire hat-trick*. Having served on the North West Frontier from 1935 until 1937, some members of the 1st Battalion fortuitously spanned the period covered by two distinct India General Service Medals, qualifying for both. They were then posted in 1938 to quell the Arab Revolt in Palestine, where they earned their third campaign medal in four years: the purple-and-green-ribboned General Service Medal with the *Palestine* clasp. In 1944 a Hampshire soldier did not have to have been a real old sweat to have achieved these distinctions, and there were several officers and men of ten years' service with all three ribbons on their chests.

The new commanding officers of the three battalions, David Nelson Smith, Evelyn Norie and Cosmo Nevill, all appointed in March 1944, were of a new generation. None had commanded a battalion in battle before and only one was an officer of the Regiment he commanded: David Nelson Smith, now commanding the 1st Hampshires, was thirty. Commissioned in 1934, Lieutenant-Colonel David Nelson Smith had served in Waziristan, Palestine and Egypt before becoming Staff Captain of 1st Malta Brigade during the siege. Having won a Military Cross at Agira in Sicily, he had been Second-in-Command when the Hampshires had landed in Italy. Now he was about to achieve what was every Regular infantry officer's principal ambition: to command a Regular battalion of his own Regiment in battle. His company commanders were his contemporaries and he knew most of them well. Dick Baines, commanding A Company, John Littlejohns, commanding D Company, and Jimmy Wicks, commanding Support Company, had all served alongside their new CO as young subalterns in Waziristan and in Palestine. Baines had been wounded at Dakai Kilai in December 1936. Littlejohns had recently taken over D Company from Captain David Edkins[1], who had led it in Sicily and Italy. Now, because of Littlejohns's seniority, Edkins became its Second-in-Command.

All who had served with the 1st Hampshires for eighteen months or more shared memories of the relentless bombing at the Safi air strip on Malta, and the dusty heat and the precipitous rocky slopes and head-

---

1. David Edkins had transferred to the Hampshire Regiment from the Bedfordshire and Hertfordshire Regiment in 1943. His son Joe later continued the tradition of 231 Brigade by enlisting in the Royal Hampshire Regiment before accepting a commission in the Devonshire and Dorset Regiment.

Lt-Col David Nelson Smith, MC,
CO 1st Hampshires

Maj Dick Baines,
OC A Company

Maj Tony Mott,
OC B Company

Maj David Warren MC,
OC C Company

Maj John Littlejohns,
OC D Company

Maj Jimmy Wicks,
OC Support Company

splitting detonations of 88mm shells at Agira on Sicily. David Warren, originally commissioned in the East Lancashire Regiment and now leading C Company, had fought on Sicily and in Italy, where he had won the MC. But two officers – Captain Cecil Thomas, Second-in-Command of B Company, and Lieutenant *Horace* Wright, commanding 16 Platoon in C – shared a very different experience. Both had fought with the 2nd Hampshires at Tebourba, Tunisia, in December 1942. Tebourba was a defensive action in which the Hampshires, greatly outnumbered and outgunned by the new German Tiger tanks, had held their position for much longer than seemed possible. Guernseyman Major Herbert Le Patourel and the unflappable Cecil Thomas had both been recommended for the Victoria Cross. Le Patourel's recommendation was successful while Thomas's instead earned him a Distinguished Service Order for leading almost suicidal bayonet charges. The bespectacled, deceptively heroic *Horace* Wright had won his MC rescuing wounded under fire. *Horace* had been captured but escaped when Italy surrendered; he was mentioned in Despatches for making his way down Italy – in defiance of idiotic orders from senior British officers – back to the British lines and back into the war.

Left: Capt Cecil Thomas DSO, B Company, 1st Hampshires
Right: CSM William Mayne DCM, B Company, 1st Hampshires

Commanding B Company was Tony Mott, a thirty-one-year-old officer of the Queen's Royal Regiment, whose battle experience had been in Waziristan during the early years of the war. Fighting there with his Regiment, he had been mentioned in Despatches for his bravery. As we have seen, Cecil Thomas was Mott's very experienced and dazzlingly brave Second-in-Command. Two of Mott's platoon commanders – Lionel Bawden and Charles Williamson – were older than average. Bawden, a married man from Portsmouth, had no battle experience. At thirty, Charles Williamson was three years older, single and had been commissioned in November 1942. Within eight months he was fighting in Sicily, where he won a Military Cross. The baby among the Company's officers was twenty-year-old Graham Mason Elliott from Botley. He was a very large baby indeed. Tall, powerfully built and with a passion for shooting and fishing, he was the son of a brigadier, a product of Canford School and an enthusiastic soldier. Originally commissioned into the cavalry, he had been transferred to the Hampshires. Their Company Sergeant-Major, William Mayne from Bexley, had already proved himself in battle, winning a Distinguished Conduct Medal at Agira in Sicily, where he took over two platoons who had lost their officers. Wounded in Italy, he had now recovered and was back with the Battalion. Colour Sergeant Eastburn, like his Company Commander, was not originally a Hampshire; he was a Regular soldier from the Green Howards.

Across all three battalions, the pattern was similar. Company commanders and seconds-in-command mostly had battle experience; platoon commanders tended to be younger and, although some had fought before, many had not. D-Day would be their first experience of battle.

The Dorsets' new CO, Evelyn Norie, had originally joined the RAF as a pilot but later transferred to the Army. An officer of the King's Own Royal Regiment, he came to the 1st Dorsets having served on Monty's staff. Three of Norie's four rifle company commanders had fought in Malta, Sicily and Italy. The fourth, Tony Jones commanding A Company, had served in Palestine before the war, then on the staff of the 1st Division in France; he had since fought in North Africa attached to the 8th Durham Light Infantry and then in Sicily and Italy with his own Regiment. Pat Chilton of B Company had won an MC in Sicily while Bobby Nicoll, just past his thirtieth birthday and commanding C Company, was a thoroughgoing professional who had been Battalion Second-in-Command for some time. Willie Hayes of D Company, a keen cricketer and humourist, had joined the Dorsets as a second lieutenant early in their time on Malta. Commanding the Carrier Platoon on Sicily, he had even managed to see the funny side when his Colonel ordered him to deploy his vulnerable Bren gun carriers near Etna to counter-attack German tanks. Denis Bounsall DCM, an experienced, discerning and gallant soldier in A Company, wrote in a letter at Christmas 2018: *The 1st Dorsets were very fortunate to have company commanders like Majors Nicoll, Chilton and Hayes. They were outstanding, and the men regarded them with respect and affection in equal measure.*

People, preparations and plans

Maj Tony Jones,
OC A Company

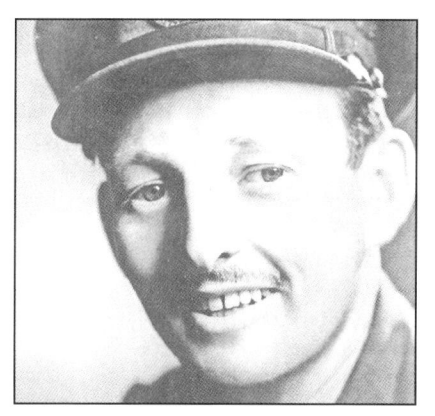

Maj Pat Chilton MC,
OC B Company

Lt-Col Evelyn Norie,
CO 1st Dorsets

Maj Bobby Nicoll,
OC C Company

Maj Willie Hayes,
OC D Company

Commanding the 2nd Devons was Cosmo Nevill, a Royal Fusilier who had won both the Sword of Honour and the King's Medal as a cadet at Sandhurst. Tall and impressive, he joined the 2nd Devons after many years in India and from a staff appointment, in which he had earned an OBE. All the commanders of the Devons' four rifle companies – Franc Sadleir, Mike Howard, Hugh Duke and John Parlby – had fought in Malta and Sicily. Franc Sadleir had been appointed MBE for his work on the Brigade staff in Malta and mentioned in Despatches for his bravery on Sicily. Mike Howard had won a Military Cross during the short battle in Italy. Known as *Bubbles*, Duke was a boyish favourite throughout the Battalion. On Sicily he had been very upset about a wounded donkey and enlisted the help of Jock Russell, a stretcher-bearer, in tending its wounds. Later, when Duke was himself badly wounded, he had refused treatment until everyone else had been tended. He had been recommended three times for the MC during the six-week campaign on Sicily and now wore the ribbon and silver rosette of the MC and Bar. He and John Parlby had both been mentioned in Despatches on Malta.

These officers, bolstered by warrant officers, NCOs and soldiers of similar experience, made a strong brigade team. The battles on Sicily had shown the mettle of several remarkable men. In A Company of the Dorsets, Bandsman Denis Bounsall had won a Distinguished Conduct Medal rescuing wounded under heavy fire at Agira. In the same battle, Private Sam Thompson of C Company had been recommended for a DCM for his bravery. When his Corporal was wounded, he took over and captured a machine gun position, an anti-tank gun and fifteen German prisoners. His DCM was downgraded to a Military Medal, but his fellow Dorsets knew his worth. Thirty-three years old, he had served five years in India in the mid-1930s and had rejoined the 1st Dorsets in 1939. Also in C Company was Corporal Len Bunning MM from Kentish Town, who had also led his platoon when his platoon commander, sergeant and section commander were all killed at Agira. These few examples are drawn from the ranks of the Dorsets, but each of the other battalions had NCOs and men of similar calibre and experience. We shall meet several of them in the course of D-Day.

People, preparations and plans

*Maj Franc Sadleir MBE,
OC A Company*

*Maj Mike Howard MC,
OC B Company*

*Lt-Col Cosmo Nevill OBE,
CO 2nd Devons*

*Maj Hugh Duke MC and Bar,
OC C Company*

*Maj John Parlby,
OC D Company*

Supporting gunners and tanks

In battle, the relationship between the artillery forward observation teams and the infantrymen they supported was a close and very important one. Providing their artillery support were two regiments, each equipped with twenty-four Sexton self-propelled 25-pounder guns. The 90th (City of London) Field Regiment, commanded by Lieutenant-Colonel Ian Hardie, were veterans of Iraq, Tunisia and Sicily, while the 147th (Essex Yeomanry) Field Regiment, commanded by the Oxfordshire cricketer Lieutenant-Colonel Robert Phayre, were still unblooded. Organisationally, 90th Field Regiment were part of the 50th Division while the Essex Yeomanry belonged to the 8th Armoured Brigade and were attached to the 50th Division for D-Day.

The armoured regiment that would support the Brigade through much of the campaign was the Nottinghamshire Yeomanry, known universally as the Sherwood Rangers, who were also attached from the 8th Armoured Brigade. On D-Day their three Squadrons, A, B and C, would be under the command respectively of the 2nd Devons, 1st Hampshires and 1st Dorsets. Veterans of the Eighth Army, the Sherwood Rangers had fought their way from Alamein in October 1942 to Enfidaville in May 1943, winning a reputation for gallantry and panache. Many of their squadron and troop leaders and tank crews were desert veterans with impressive battle experience. During the campaign in North Africa there had lingered some social and professional distinctions between the pre-war Yeomanry officers, who still mourned the loss of their horses, and some of the less affluent wartime officers who had been professionally trained more recently in modern armoured warfare.

Having won a DSO as a Brigade Major in France in 1940, Lieutenant-Colonel John Anderson of the 5th Inniskilling Dragoon Guards had served in North Africa and Italy before recently taking command of the Sherwood Rangers in England. The Regiment's Second-in-Command, Major Michael Laycock, was a brother of the Commando Robert Laycock. Hot-tempered and fiercely loyal to the Yeomanry, Mike Laycock had won an MC at Alam Halfa, two months before the Battle of El Alamein. Leading A Squadron was Major Stanley Christopherson, a Wykehamist whose easy social manner enabled him to span any gulf with pre-war Yeomanry officers. His gentleness belied a shrewd tactical brain and an unremitting fearlessness; he already wore the Military Cross and Bar, and further honours lay ahead. Christopherson's Second-in-Command was the poet and artist, Keith Douglas, who had recently completed his sharply observed book about the Regiment, which would be published as *Alamein to Zem Zem*. A prickly young Oxford graduate, Douglas was the product of a broken marriage who had spent his school, university and army days in the company of contemporaries from richer and more stable family backgrounds. Having been trained as a wartime officer of the Royal Armoured Corps, he was often impatient of pre-war officers with greater social confidence but less technical understanding of their tanks; but he seldom questioned their courage. Commanding B Squadron, Major John Hanson-Lawson was a wartime officer, commissioned in the 24th Lancers, while C Squadron was led by one of the original Yeomanry officers from 1939, Old Etonian Stephen Mitchell. A troop leader and a second lieutenant at the start of the war, he was now a very experienced squadron leader who had won his MC at Wadi Zem Zem in January 1943.

Left: Maj Stanley Christopherson MC and Bar, A Squadron, Sherwood Rangers
Right: Capt Keith Douglas, A Squadron, Sherwood Rangers

Training and preparation

When the three battalions of 231 Malta Brigade returned to England in November 1943, the Hampshires had assembled in Suffolk, and the Devons and Dorsets in Essex. For the 1st Hampshires and 1st Dorsets, both of whom had served many years in India before the war, this was after a very long absence: the 1st Hampshires had left England in 1920. The 2nd Devons' absence had been shorter. They had been in Aldershot until the summer of 1938, when they had been sent to Malta for a short, largely ceremonial tour of duty in a tranquil backwater, but the Mediterranean ambitions of Mussolini and Hitler had decreed otherwise. Now, soldiers who had not been home for five, ten even fifteen years were quickly sent on leave.

During the Brigade's few weeks in Essex, Lieutenant David Holdsworth's young bride, Diana, followed the drum and set up house there. Recently commissioned, David had been able to join the 2nd Devons, with whom his twin brother Mike, a Captain, had recently returned from Malta and Sicily. Before the war, Mike had gone to Sandhurst while David had joined the Police Force and become an Inspector. Now, slightly to Mike's consternation, the twins were in the same Battalion. Diana Holdsworth rented a cottage at Wethersfield, where the Mawdesley family next door made the young couple and their friends very welcome. On 13th March, one of the daughters of the family, seventeen-year-old Jane, became engaged to *Bubbles* Duke, the commander of C Company in the Devons. It seemed a time for putting down roots. During their time at Wethersfield, two of Duke's fellow officers, Franc Sadleir and Arthur Eteson, married their fiancées, Ruth and Elizabeth.

Left: Capt Mike Holdsworth, D then B Company, 2nd Devons
Right: Lt David Holdsworth, D Company, 2nd Devons

Coming home must have been a delight, even though all knew that they were doing so to take part in what was then known as the Second Front. At this stage, the 50th Division was due to play a supporting part in the invasion but, as we have seen, Monty's appointment rapidly promoted them to a leading role with 231 Brigade in the front row as the very first infantry to land on D-Day.

Since Monty's arrival the pace of change had accelerated, starting at the top. Major-General Douglas Graham had succeeded General Sidney Kirkham in command of 50th Division. On 24th February, the day after a visit from the King, the Brigade had learnt of the appointment of Sir

Alex Stanier as their new Brigadier. In March the three greatly respected Commanding Officers of the battalions – *Cupid* Valentine, Bill Spencer and Broke Ray, each of whom had led his battalion with great skill and courage – had been succeeded by younger men: Lieutenant-Colonels Cosmo Nevill, David Nelson Smith and Evelyn Norie. Nevill was thirty-six and Norie thirty-seven, while Nelson Smith was seven years younger. All three were recent graduates of the Staff College.

In early March the battalions took part in Operation *Bullock*, which introduced them to some of the beach obstacles they were likely to meet across the Channel. These included the Teller mines on wooden poles encountered on 15th May by Lieutenant John Stone and his beach party, and *hedgehogs*, which were six-pointed iron calthrops[2], shaped like giant throwing jacks. Designed to rip the bottoms out of landing craft, *hedgehogs* were sometimes fitted with explosives to create even greater damage.

Two weeks later the whole Brigade was sent to the Combined Training Centre at Inverary, near the head of Loch Fyne. Here they trained in techniques for amphibious landings which, until they attended this course with its array of specialised equipment, they had thought they knew all about. They saw LSIs – Landing Ships Infantry – that would take a whole battalion of infantry across the Channel before they boarded the landing craft to take them the last few miles to the shore. LSTs – Landing Ships Tanks – carried fifteen to twenty tanks or self-propelled guns; their bows swung open and a ramp was lowered to allow the tanks to board and disembark. LCTs – Landing Craft Tanks – held three or four tanks and could take them right up to the beach. The most weird and wonderful were LCT(R)s, a variant on the LCT, which carried instead of tanks up to 5,000 rockets with which to bombard coastal targets. But the vessels of most direct interest to the infantrymen were the LCAs – Landing Craft Assault – which would ferry a platoon of infantry the last few dangerous, decisive miles from ship to shore.

On Thursday, 16th March, Private Terry Parker of D Company of the 1st Dorsets, just shy of his nineteenth birthday, recorded in his diary: *Spent nights on big ships carrying LCAs.* Next day, he wrote: *In the morning were let down into sea to make dawn attacks. It was all very interesting but too much of a grim purpose behind it.*

The Brigade also encountered *Funnies* or AVREs (Armoured Vehicles Royal Engineers). One of many lessons learnt from the disastrous assault on Dieppe in 1942 was the need for specialised armour to perform particular tasks on and beyond the beaches. Collectively known as *Funnies*, they were from the 79th Armoured Division, which was commanded by

---

2. A calthrop was an ancient weapon made of upward-pointing nails or spines designed to damage the feet or hooves of advancing infantry or cavalry.

Fascines on an AVRE (Tank Museum)

A Petard AVRE (Tank Museum)

A Duplex Drive (DD) Sherman at sea (Tank Museum)

Major-General Percy Hobart, Monty's brother-in-law. Flail tanks (usually Shermans and sometimes known as Crabs) beat the ground ahead of them with metal chains revolving on a cylinder, exploding mines to clear paths through minefields. Fascines could be carried on any tank, and consisted of a large roll of paling designed to fill gaps and make terrain passable for tanks and other vehicles. These rolls were so large that the tank commander had to climb on top to see where he was going! Bobbin tanks carried a reel of material that could be unwound to make soft ground passable. Some AVREs were fitted with a spigot mortar, called a Petard, which propelled a forty pound bomb, known as a flying dustbin, up to ninety yards. Churchill tanks fitted with flame-throwers were called Crocodiles. The strangest of all were the DD – Duplex Drive – Sherman tanks which could be launched three or four miles from shore and, with their watertight canvas skirts, could simply swim into battle, firing as they swam.

The Brigade's supporting field artillery had also adopted tracks. Half the batteries were now equipped with the Sexton: a 25-pounder mounted on the adapted chassis of a Sherman tank. The infantry's Gunner support would now be able to follow the battalions more rapidly – without awaiting transport – more closely and in more difficult country.

The sophistication and number of these astonishing gadgets made 231 Brigade's landings in 1943 in Sicily and Italy seem antiquated, and underlined the unprecedented scale and importance of the enormous operation in which the Brigade were about to take the lead. Meanwhile, the exercises demonstrated that, despite their experience, they still had a lot to learn. It was here they heard that, once again, the Hampshires and Dorsets would lead the landings with the Devons in reserve.

Major *Speedy* Bredin, who had served with the 1st Dorsets in India and in the early days in Malta, rejoined the Dorsets just in time for this course. A well-known regimental character, he became Second-in-Command to Colonel Norie. He later recalled that, after a period of lectures, craft training and 'dryshod' exercises, the Brigade progressed to more ambitious waterborne exercises, notably Exercise *Newton Bay* and Exercise *Ardno. The last named, carried out on 22nd March, was a Brigade exercise, designed roughly to approximate to our operational task.*

Two days later the Brigade moved to Hampshire. The 2nd Devons moved to a camp near Beaulieu which was still being constructed and was not due for completion until 15th April. Cosmo Nevill recalled: *The cookhouses were unfinished, there were no hot water facilities, no baths, no drying rooms and no duckboards. The last two items became all important because it rained persistently for three days after our arrival, and the mud was indescribable. Finally, there was no NAAFI. ...in spite of acute discomfort, we settled down to make the best of it.*

Training was a difficult problem. We were told that there would be at least six weeks available in which to get fighting fit and ready for the great day. The training areas were, however, few and very small; rifle ranges became progressively more difficult to obtain as more troops poured into the area. Many of us learnt for the first time that the New Forest meant literally forest, excellent for camouflage purposes, but useless for training troops in the finer points of assault landing.

Sergeant *Ginger* Wills of the Devons remembered: *The tents, when we first saw them, were delightful and snug. Each had four camp beds and a small solid-fuel stove. Unfortunately we were told to remove the camp beds and the stoves and keep ourselves warm by having another six men in each tent. Our American hosts were flabbergasted.*

The camp was hidden in thick woods, tents were camouflaged and no washing lines or clothing were allowed outside. Very quickly the walkways became quagmires...

All ranks were confined to camp for security reasons but many were able to use their West Country knowledge of fieldcraft to find ways of getting through the perimeter barbed wire to slink off for a drink in various pubs. The locals knew we were there, of course, and they could guess why, but not where we were going, or when. In these circumstances security was maintained – for we didn't know where or when either.

Cinema performances, in huge marquee tents, were nightly and before each cinema show there was a record-request programme lasting for about forty-five minutes. A disc jockey had an easily accessible stack of records and would endeavour to satisfy requests shouted from the waiting audience.

Battery Sergeant-Major Jack Vilander Brown of the Essex Yeomanry, whose self-propelled guns would be supporting the Brigade on D-Day, had a better experience in his camp at Beaulieu. *They were marvellously well run, the arrangements, everything, were absolutely fantastic. Everything was in the right place at the right time, everything was there.*

We were in there for quite some while and we thought things might be getting near when we were told to send any surplus kit home. We were issued with French money, with Dutch money, with Belgian money and Italian money. I remember thinking at the time, God, we can't be going to Italy.

Trooper Joe Minogue, a member of a flail crew in the Westminster Dragoons, recalled that at Beaulieu *the only thing we had to do was waterproof the tanks, get all the guns and ammunition ready and make absolutely sure that anything mechanical was going to work when we wanted it to work. It was really rather a boring period in some respects, because unless you were on guard you were stuck in this pine forest with absolutely nothing to do. ...at one stage, just for a bit of diversion, people set fire to the NAAFI tents. That was really the only excitement available...*

...I think everybody who was involved in the invasion was afraid. Later one learned that basically this is what war is about: it's really two groups of very frightened men facing each other. But we didn't talk to each other about our particular fears.

As tank men I think we had two main worries. One was the danger of being trapped inside a tank that was on fire and the other, because we were soldiers and used to being on land all the time, was a fear of water. I really think we were more terrified of being drowned in that damned tank than anything else. One thing we did do was get a hacksaw and cut about thirty pounds worth of very valuable metal from inside the turret of our Sherman tank so that, if there was any danger of drowning, the two of us in the turret could grab the driver and co-driver and pull them to safety. We really were scared of going down the ramp of the landing craft into deep water so that the whole tank would be submerged and we would just be drowned.

Also involved in these exercises were the men of 47 (Royal Marine) Commando, who would land behind 231 Brigade on D-Day and whose task would be to capture Port-en-Bessin, between Arromanches and Omaha Beach. Commanded by Lieutenant-Colonel Cecil Phillips, theirs was a new unit which had formed on 1st August 1943 at the Dorset Regiment's barracks in Dorchester.

During April, the *Smash* exercises enabled the Dorsets to return to their home county. Sir Alex Stanier remembered marking *Dorset villages to represent Normandy objectives; for instance, Corfe Castle was Ryes, as it was precisely the same distance inland as our furthest objective on D-Day.*

Major Bredin recalled how these exercises *consisted of assault landings on Studland Bay, north of Swanage. The conditions produced, and the plan of action, were as close as possible to our actual task on the big day. Then, early in May, we again put to sea and carried out Exercise Fabius. This was a landing on Hayling Island by the whole of 50th Division, and all the follow-up portions of the force were involved. These included the beach-groups, which were essential for the build-up and maintenance of the fighting troops in the bridgehead. The weather was rough and it was tricky work re-embarking on the LCIs (infantry landing craft) at the end of the exercise, and DUKWs had to be used (one of the follow-up brigades of the Division had the misfortune to lose some officers and men drowned while trying to get ashore). Generally speaking, Fabius was more of an administrative exercise in contrast to the 'Smashes' in which, among other things, a good deal of live ammunition, from bombs and rockets to small arms, was used.*

Two of the *Smash* exercises included moving from the marshalling area at Southampton, a sea voyage round the Isle of Wight to equal the length of crossing the Channel, and the landing on a replica of the West Wall with full naval and air support and live ammunition.

Officers of the 1st Bn. Dorset Regt. at Fawley Camp. near Southampton prior to Normandy invasion. Late Spring 1944.

Back Row.	Centre Row		Front Row.	
Lt. Bradbury +	Lt. Shambrook	w	Capt. Watt (R.Ch.D)	
" Robjohn w	" Morris		" Whittington	w
" Neale	" Mayes	+	Major Hayes	w
" Thomas w	" Ellis	w	" Nicoll	
" —	" Webb	w	Lt.Col. Norie	+
" Hannah	" Whitebrook	+	Brig. Stanier	
" Hamilton w	Capt. Harris A.L.	w	Major Bredin	
" Stade w	" Hebden		Capt. Browne,(M.C.)	w
" Scott w	" Royle	w	Major Jones	+
" Windebank +	" Luff		" Chilton,(M.C.)	w
" Dibben w	Lt. Hatchard (Q.M.)		Capt. Harris R.E.	+
	" Weekes		" Lassman (R.A.M.C.)	

Absent from Photograph.
Capt. Tucker +
Lt. Lancaster +
" Youngs (I.O.) +

+ Killed } during campaign
w Wounded

Colonel Nevill remembered: *Many mistakes were made and many lessons were learnt.*

The [Devons'] *Adjutant, Captain Tyrrell Holdsworth[3], and the acting Second-in-Command, Major John Parlby, produced landing tables with the utmost regularity to which amendments were seldom needed. Major Franc Sadleir and Major Bubbles Duke, commanding A and C Companies respectively, carried out numerous loading trials of the vehicles which would accompany us in the assault. Frequent conferences were held to discuss what each man should carry; as each battalion in the assault had a different task to perform, we were allowed considerable latitude in this respect. The all-important factor was not to carry too much, especially as we had to cover nine miles rapidly after landing, and fight at the end of it.*

The Devons' veteran Quartermaster, *Titch* Labett, was posted away and his successor, Lieutenant Harry Shinn, inherited a task that required liaison with Royal Tank Regiment and Royal Army Service Corps officers on the Brigade Staff. It also involved testing and accepting or discarding new devices which were constantly being offered to assault battalions to assist them in their task.

Alarmingly, during these last four weeks, members of all three battalions who had trained in Egypt before the Sicily landings began to develop the symptoms of malaria. According to Major Willie Hayes of the Dorsets, this was because the supply of malaria tablets, which they had all been taking, had dried up. As a consequence a number of very experienced soldiers, including Hayes himself, were hospitalised. Sergeant Jim Bellows of the Hampshires was concerned about the effect this might have on the Brigade's professionalism because these experienced men were often replaced by recent recruits. Lieutenant Jack Lauder of the 1st Hampshires played down his malaria to ensure that he would lead his platoon on D-Day. Lance-Corporal Denis Bowstead (known as *Danny*), a Royal Corps of Signals wireless operator with 90th Field Regiment, was given a choice. If he went to hospital, he might be posted anywhere on discharge. If he stayed with his Regiment, he would remain with them for the invasion. He stayed.

Although being chosen to lead the invasion implied a great compliment, unsurprisingly it was not universally welcome. Monty's visits to units in 50th Division received a mixed reception, especially from the veterans of North Africa, Malta and Sicily. During May the Division recorded 1,000 cases of Absence Without Leave. In the 1st Dorsets the offenders included two highly respected, decorated and battle-experienced NCOs. Understandably, many experienced soldiers thought they had earned a break and, at last in reach of their families perhaps for the last time, some of them took it illicitly.

---

3. There were three officers in the 2nd Devons called Holdsworth. Mike and David, as we have seen, were twin brothers; Tyrrell was unrelated to them.

Almost all returned to fight with their units. The two Dorset NCOs were treated gently, retaining their rank to land on D-Day, when both excelled once more. As one would be killed on D-Day and the other soon afterwards, it was perhaps as well that each had enjoyed one last, illegal trip home.

On 10th May Cosmo Nevill, David Nelson Smith and Evelyn Norie were called to a secret conference, where Sir Alex Stanier outlined the plan for the Brigade. From now on, the three commanding officers would spend a great deal of time studying maps and aerial photographs and reviewing new information that was constantly arriving. The outline plan for each battalion would be approved before the orders for the Brigade were finalised. This, as Cosmo Nevill explained, was to ensure that *all difficulties and problems were dealt with before and not after the orders had become firm.*

Conference followed conference, he remembered; *the CO and the Battalion Intelligence Officer* [Captain Bill Wood] *were to be seen daily, coming and going, tightly clasping weighty brief cases as if their lives depended on their security, which in fact they did.*

Monty assembled all commanding officers and their seconds-in-command in a cinema in Southampton and gave them a lucid and inspiring outline of the plan, its importance and their part in it. Nevill, who had high standards having served with Bill Slim, was profoundly affected by the spirit of the talk while his new Second-in-Command, Guy Browne, remembered it as *a spellbinding performance* in which he heard for the first time about the Mulberry harbour, which would be towed in pieces across the Channel and assembled off Arromanches, and PLUTO (Petroleum Lines Under The Ocean). They filed out of the cinema *completely, supremely confident.*

But even with almost total dominance in the air and a huge invasion force, Allied success was by no means a certainty. General Eisenhower and his senior commanders were reviewing the plans, intelligence reports and the weather constantly as the day approached. His Deputy, Air Chief Marshal Sir Arthur Tedder, had originally been commissioned into the Dorset Regiment before the First World War. Now his old Regiment would be one of the first to land. When Eisenhower himself visited 231 Malta Brigade, he impressed everyone with his friendly, relaxed competence. What they did not know was that, in his pocket, he carried a short, handwritten, courageous statement he had secretly prepared for possible future use.

Our landings in the Cherbourg-Havre area have failed to gain a satisfactory foothold and I have withdrawn the troops. My decision to attack at this time and place was based upon the best information available. The troops, the air and the Navy did all that bravery and devotion to duty could do. If any blame or fault attaches to the attempt it is mine alone.

2nd Devons Officers, May 1944
Front row (*left to right*): *Capts J D Symes, M Holdsworth, Majs F G Sadleir MBE, J R H Parlby, Lt-Col C R Nevill OBE, Col The Earl Fortescue OBE MC, Majs G R Young, M W Howard MC, H V Duke MC*, Capt T A Holdsworth*
Middle row (*left to right*): *Lts R W Murphy, R A Pethick, R C Davey, Capts A D Eteson MC, J T A Lloyd, Lts H Heap, F A Pearson, W Kemeys-Jenkin, D F Riordan, J D Campbell MC – note one officer here is unnamed*
Back row (*left to right*): *Lts H R Whalley, D Holdsworth, F H Pease, J G Morris, C J Candlin, J C Coles, E Gamble, E E Mead, H D Shinn, K J Bull*

In these last busy days old friends visited to wish the battalions well. The Devons were delighted to see their Lord Lieutenant, Lord Fortescue, who inspected them and brought with him the good wishes of their King and their County. The Royal Hampshire Regiment's history records a touching incident. *On 24th May, just before the camp was sealed, the Battalion marched past the Colonel of the Regiment, after a field firing exercise at Dibden Purlieu. The Regimental Band had come down for the occasion and led the march past. It was pouring with rain, but when General* [Sir Richard] *Haking saw that the men were coming past without greatcoats or groundsheets the grand old soldier took off his own raincoat and ordered Major Jeffery, who was with him, to take off his coat as well. This was General Haking's last appearance, and this salute, from the 1st Battalion of his Regiment about to go into battle, was the last he was to receive on a ceremonial occasion.* A veteran of the Burma Campaign of the mid–1880s, Sir Richard had commanded a brigade at Mons. In May 1944 he was eighty-two years old. He died a year later, having lived to see his Regiment emerge from a second world war with its reputation greatly enhanced.

Major Bredin remembered seeing *a good deal of our affiliated squadron [Stephen Mitchell's C Squadron] of the Sherwood Rangers... The Gunners of the 90th Field Regiment were unfortunately too busy most of the time – what with trying to get the self-propelled guns into LCTs and, having succeeded in doing that, trying to fire them from the moving craft.*

Tony Mott remembered: *We were briefed at Beaulieu Abbey on 25th May. ...officers were told the real place-names; other ranks were given code-names, such as Odessa and Albany. I was not sure where the Cotentin Peninsula was, so was not much wiser than the others.*

On the orders of the Commandant, the Hampshires' camp was sealed earlier than planned, before Colonel Nelson Smith's promise (that every man would have a chance to see his wife or girlfriend) had been fully honoured. Twenty men of A Company used a Bangalore torpedo[4] to blast their way through the wire and out of camp. Sergeant Jim Bellows remembered:

There was hell to pay, questions were asked but there were no answers. Within twenty-four hours all the men who had broken out returned. The CO had the lot in front of him and their excuse was that he had broken his word by sealing down the camp without giving them a chance for a final drink and to see their wives and girlfriends. The CO said he was as surprised as they were when the camp was sealed. The Camp Commandant had done it as a practice and not informed the CO and for this action he got a very severe rollicking. Now the CO had a problem – if he disciplined the deserters they would face a court martial and he would lose twenty, fully trained men. D-Day was imminent so he did a Solomon. He said if every man promised they would do their best on D-Day there would be no charges, so everyone promised. Lieutenant-Colonel Nelson Smith gave a sigh of relief, as did the defaulters.

The Devonshire Regiment's historian records that at this time: *The granting of leave was always a problem. Nevill was acutely aware that a large proportion of his command had never received a reasonable allocation of leave so he took particular care to grant as many weekend passes as possible. This – some thought hazardous – policy culminated on Saturday 27th May when, to the consternation of the Divisional HQ staff, he sent his whole Battalion off for the weekend and it is clear that even he waited for the dawn of Monday 29th,* the date set for the whole of the allied invasion force to be caged in, with some apprehension. Given the Division's horrific AWOL figures for May, this was a courageously trusting decision on the part of the Devons' Colonel. It was justified. The Regimental History affirms: *In the event, only two men failed to return.*

Diana Holdsworth remembered: *we all lived each day as it came.* When the Brigade had moved to Hampshire, she had again followed the drum and

---

4. A Bangalore torpedo is an explosive charge in a series of connected metal tubes; it can be pushed through barbed wire to explode and clear a path for infantry.

now rented a cottage on the Beaulieu estate. Here, she and her husband David entertained some of his friends from the 2nd Devons. *I was surprised to see one of these tough young men* [Major Franc Sadleir, commander of A Company] *gazing with real pleasure at a large bowl of primroses, and another day he gently fingered the furry leaves of some opening sticky buds which I had arranged in a jar. Turning, he said to me 'They are like tiny hands, aren't they?'* His wife was in Devon expecting the son that he did not live to see.

In the last day or two before the camp was sealed off, the Holdsworths gave a final supper party for some of the Devon officers. *It was a light-hearted party with much laughter and the foolish jokes of the young who were determined not to think of the future. It was a tremendous piece of play-acting and we all enjoyed it. We had our coffee and Cyprus cigarettes in the drawing room while Bubbles* [Duke] *told us about his twenty-four-hour leave. He had spent it visiting his fiancée, Jane, who lived next door to Little Thatch* [in Wethersfield, Essex]. *Jane was working near Cambridge – on arrival at Cambridge Bubbles discovered that the only way to visit Jane was to hire a car. The only car available was an enormous Rolls Royce; naturally Bubbles had taken it.*

He told us how his beautiful, auburn-haired Jane had firmly and loyally ignored the officer in the large Rolls Royce who was trying to pick her up until suddenly she had recognised him and leapt into the car. He was a great raconteur but from his conversation that evening it seemed as if he had known he wasn't coming back.

On Sunday 28th May Padre Skinner of the Sherwood Rangers set up his altar beside Captain Keith Douglas's Sherman tank. After ordering his crew to tidy up the area and helping to fold blankets to use as kneelers, Douglas stayed to receive communion. Later that day he attended evensong in the church at Sway, the village where the Regiment was in camp. After the service Douglas and Skinner walked together in the New Forest and Douglas confided his conviction that he would not survive the campaign that lay ahead. Years later Leslie Skinner recalled their long talk. *He was not morbid about it. He could talk of and even make plans for the days when the war was over and, having done so, come back again to this feeling that it was unlikely he would survive. We walked and talked together, only separating as dawn was breaking.*

This sense of premonition dominated the last poem Douglas completed before embarking for Normandy, which ends:

> The next month, then, is a window
> and with a crash I'll split the glass.
> Behind it stands one I must kiss,
> Person of love or death
> A person or a wraith,
> I fear what I shall find.

The plan

The aim was for the 50th Division to grab a chunk of the coast from La Rivière in the east to beyond Port-en-Bessin in the west. Beyond La Rivière the Division would be able to link up with the Canadians landing to the east around Courselles who in turn would link up with the British 3rd Division landing to their east on Sword Beach. In the west, beyond Port-en-Bessin, the 50th would link up with the Americans on Omaha Beach. They would thus create one long beachhead from Vierville in the west to the area north of Caen in the east which was to be captured by the British 6th Airborne Division. Their airborne assault would begin first, starting soon after 0001 hours on D-Day.

For D-Day 56 Brigade was placed under command of 50th Division. The assaulting infantry on Gold Beach therefore consisted of four brigades and 47 (Royal Marine) Commando. The Commando was 420 strong and made up of five troops of about sixty, a heavy weapons troop and a small section of Bren gun carriers.

For planning purposes Gold Beach was divided into sections named according to the phonetic alphabet of the time: *Item, Jig, King, Love* etc. Most of the action would take place on Jig Sector (Le Hamel and Asnelles) and King Sector (La Rivière). Each sector was then divided in two – Green (starboard or right for the troops who were landing) and Red (port or left). The plan was for 50th Division to assault the beach with two brigades *up* (i.e. leading): 231 Malta Brigade in the west, assaulting on Jig Green beach stretching from Le Hamel to east of Asnelles, and 69 Brigade assaulting on King Green and King Red beaches west of La Rivière. Between the two landing beaches, Jig Red sector was avoided because of two disadvantages: strips of clay, in which heavy vehicles like tanks would bog down, and beyond it marshland which was difficult to cross.

Each brigade would land with two battalions *up*. In 231 Brigade the two assault battalions would be the 1st Hampshires and the 1st Dorsets while 69 Brigade's assault companies would be the 5th East Yorkshires and the 6th Green Howards. Each of the four assault battalions would lead with two companies *up*, followed soon after in a second wave by the two other rifle companies. The reserve battalions – the 2nd Devons in 231 Brigade and the 7th Green Howards in 69 Brigade – would land about forty minutes later.

H-Hour would be 0725. First ashore, five minutes before H-Hour, would be the Duplex-Drive (DD) swimming tanks. On Jig Sector, these would belong to B and C Squadrons of the Sherwood Rangers. Launched from their landing ships 6,000 yards out, they would engage shore targets during their run in. On landing they would drop their skirts (flotation screens) and provide armoured support for the infantry assault companies. B Squadron would support the Hampshires, and C the Dorsets, with A following ninety minutes later to support the Devons.

At H-Hour would come breaching teams, twenty AVREs (Armoured Vehicles Royal Engineers) manned by Sappers of 82nd Assault Squadron, and thirteen flails, crewed by Troopers of the Westminster Dragoons, whose job was to clear exit lanes across and off the beach. More Sappers, the 145 officers and men of the 73rd Field Company, would arrive on foot to clear the mines and obstacles from below the shoreline and the beach. There would also be frogmen from the Royal Navy and Royal Marines Landing Craft Obstacle Clearance Units to perform the same task in deeper water. The Centaurs and Shermans of Colonel Peskett's 1st Royal Marines Armoured Support Regiment would follow.

At H+7 the four assault infantry companies would land: A and B Companies of the 1st Hampshires (on the right) and of the 1st Dorsets (on the left), bringing with them their Gunner forward observation teams. Landing with them would come more Sappers, from the 295th Field Company. Thirteen minutes later C and D Companies of both battalions would follow.

At H+25 the battalions' tails – battalion headquarters, headquarters companies and Gunner battery commanders – would land.

At H+35 some Crocodile (flame-thrower tanks) and armoured bulldozers would arrive.

At H+45 A and B Companies of the 2nd Devons would land, followed ten minutes later by C and D Companies.

At H+60 the supporting batteries from the 90th and the 147th (Essex Yeomanry) Field Regiments would land, having been engaging shore targets since starting their run-in ninety minutes earlier.

At H+90 A Squadron of the Sherwood Rangers would land from their LCTs together with a range of other tracked vehicles belonging to the Gunner regiments and the infantry battalions. A Squadron would support the Devons.

At H+120 47 (Royal Marine) Commando would land.

Once ashore, the Brigade would not function conventionally as a brigade in battle. Instead, the plan gave each of the battalions and 47 (Royal Marine) Commando separate but complementary objectives. Although not under command of the Brigade, for the purposes of D-Day and seizing a cohesive beach-head behind Gold Beach and west to Omaha, the Commandos were playing a part little different from that of a fourth battalion of infantry.

The 1st Hampshires were to turn west along the coast, capturing Le Hamel and Asnelles, a gun position at Cabane and a radar station on the cliff between Asnelles and Arromanches, and then taking Arromanches itself and two strongpoints at Tracy sur Mer and Manvieux. A Company were to take Le Hamel East and B Company Asnelles, then C Company were to push through A, capturing Le Hamel West. D Company were to advance inland before hooking back to the coast to take the enemy gun positions at Cabane. B and C Companies would take the radar station and then the whole Battalion would clear Arromanches and capture the two strongpoints to the west.

The 1st Dorsets' objectives were to break out of the beach and to capture three high points inland behind Arromanches: Point 54 beside Buhot, and two gun positions at Puits d'Herode and 500 yards west. A Company were to seize a strongpoint on the beach and B Company to capture and defend the farm buildings beyond the beach at Les Roquettes. A, C and D Company were then to advance inland, where C Company would take Point 54, and D and A would capture the two positions at Puits d'Herode and beyond. Once the beachhead was secure, B Company would move to Ryes to relieve the 2nd Devons.

The 2nd Devons were to thrust south to capture Ryes, then take La Rosière and the high ground to the west before moving, via Fontenailles, to capture Longues and the large shore battery there. Their last task was to advance west to link up with the Americans who had landed on Omaha beach.

47 (Royal Marine) Commando were to move rapidly to La Rosière before attacking and capturing Port-en-Bessin, the furthest objective and closest to the Americans on Omaha.

Landing from H+150, Brigadier *Peter* Pepper's 56 Infantry Brigade (including the 2nd Essex, 2nd Glosters and 2nd South Wales Borderers) would follow the advance of the Dorsets and Devons and extend the bridgehead to Bayeux and beyond. Landing on King Sector, the Durham Light Infantrymen of 151 Brigade would similarly follow and extend the advance of the Yorkshire troops of 69 Brigade.

They studied maps, photographs and models of the beach and the area behind it. The going would be difficult. Apart from the rows of man-made obstacles and minefields, parts of Gold Beach were known to have a thick clay surface in which vehicles, including tanks, flails and AVREs, would easily bog down. Behind the beaches were low, grassy sand dunes, in which no wheeled vehicle could move. Behind that on the eastern side of the beach was a marsh, which extended nearly half a mile inland. Jig Green sector, from Les Roquettes to the west of Le Hamel, was defended by a series of concrete emplacements and pillboxes. A minefield, five rows deep, extended the length of the beach and encircled the strongpoint at the farm of Les Roquettes, which had two gun emplacements and five machine gun positions. There was another strongpoint on the beach north of Les Roquettes, which was also surrounded by mines and wire.

Allied intelligence – garnered principally by RAF photographic reconnaissance aircraft and members of the local French Resistance – was impressively detailed. A Company of the 1st Dorsets, for example, were able to study photographs of the beach in front of Les Roquettes and were thoroughly briefed on the size and nature of the concrete strongpoint that was their objective, the extent of its protective wire, the likely positions of mines and even the strength of the German unit occupying it.

Some intelligence came from unofficial sources. When Colonel John Anderson of the Sherwood Rangers heard where they were to land, he remembered that his wife had spent several pre-war holidays on that beach. He then found that she had a holiday snap of the partly submerged wreck which his Regiment were to look for to fix their correct landing place.

Composite oblique pictures (constructed from RAF aerial photographs) gave a good impression of the seaside villages and the country beyond in which they would be operating. David Warren, commanding C Company of the Hampshires, recalled briefing after briefing as the plan was cascaded down to company and platoon commanders in the Battalion. *The aerial photographs were so clear and so varied that on D-Day no difficulty was experienced in finding the various points and routes to objectives. Obliques of the beaches and of the underwater obstacles, taken from a very low altitude, were extremely useful if visualising the defences, whilst those of Le Hamel were most helpful in picturing what the place looked like from the sea. There were also vertical pictures, on some of which a defence overlay* [showing the German defences] *had been inserted.*

Intelligence could, however, lead them astray. The 2nd Devons, who were to advance three miles south to Ryes, were briefed to look out for a riverbed that would lead them the whole way. This tiny stream was known locally as the Gronde Ruisseau (ie a stream of the local River Gronde). Somehow in some of the planning this became translated to the Grande Rivière (ie the large river). This error was to cause confusion and amusement in equal measure.

The stretch of coast the Brigade would try to seize had long been defended by a low-grade German division, the 716th, consisting of elderly, young and less fit soldiers. They were less well-equipped than the divisions held back from the coast, which would close in to counter-attack any invasion. Since Rommel had assumed responsibility for the defence of the Germans' Western Wall, a great deal of work had been done to strengthen the defences. Since the spring the 716th had been supplemented by higher grade troops from the 352nd Division. As a consequence, on D-Day the Malta Brigade would encounter stronger defences manned by better troops. In Normandy there were also a great many *Ost Truppen*: Russian or Central or Eastern European prisoners of war who had been formed into units within the Wehrmacht. No one could predict how fiercely such men would fight for their erstwhile enemy against soldiers who were once their allies.

Behind the coast, the landscape would feel very familiar to West Country soldiers, especially those from Dorset. Its hills, open fields and sea views closely resembled the country just inland, east and west from Weymouth and Dorchester: an incongruously beautiful place in which to fight a bloody battle.

Embarkation

On Tuesday 30th May, when an almost entire battalion of Hampshires drove through the streets of Southampton in their lorries, the civilians took no notice at all. For the last few weeks large numbers of troops had been moved backwards and forwards to the docks. No one could know that this, at last, was the real thing.

Colonel Nevill of the 2nd Devons wrote later: *At 1030 hours... of 31st May the Battalion assault group, complete with all representatives of the supporting arms, fell in for the last time at Pennely Camp. The move in MT* [motor transport] *from the camp to Southampton went without a hitch. We were driven straight to the quay alongside which HMS Glenroy was lying ready to receive us. Tea was served to all ranks in the shed while the Adjutant handed the many forms and detailed lists to the Embarkation Officer.*

As the CO [Nevill wrote his account in the third person] *was about to go on board he was met by the Brigade Commander who said, 'I have got here photos which will delight your eyes. The RAF are apologetic about them, saying that of course it is only their first bombing of the place; they hope to do much better later.' He then produced two photographs of the Longues battery, showing the results of the first precision bombing which had taken place on the 29th. We could hardly believe our eyes. The whole area looked a mass of craters. The photographs were passed rapidly round the ship and the atmosphere was 'Well, if the RAF bomb every position like that, the whole party will be a complete picnic.' We no longer felt so anxious about Longues.*

The Devons' Second-in-Command, Guy Browne, remembered that: *Most officers and men were full of confidence; some – a few – less so. Strangely, one of these was Bubbles Duke. He had a sort of premonition that all would not go well with him... he seemed just a bit depressed...*

While the Devons boarded HMS *Glenroy*, the Hampshires boarded the Landing Ships *Empire Arquebus* and *Empire Sword* and the Dorsets

Empire Spearhead and *Empire Crossbow*. Brigade Headquarters embarked on the frigate HMS *Nith*. This was the start of the Royal Navy's massive Operation *Neptune* to land the Allied armies on the Normandy beaches. The ships transporting the whole of 50th Division formed Force G, whose destination was Gold Beach.

Major David Warren of C Company of the 1st Hampshires recalled that the period on board the LSI *gave opportunities for one or two craft manning exercises but little else of interest.*

The men were kept occupied to a certain extent by briefing and, in spite of very limited deck space, by ten minutes' daily PT for each serial. Lectures and quizzes were organised by the platoon commanders and indoor games were used a great deal by the men, whilst parcels of books, containing grades of literature to suit all tastes, were greatly appreciated. A ship's canteen, opened daily at a set time, had a large variety of wares for sale, although… no beer was available.

Sir Alex Stanier remembered Winston Churchill, accompanied by Ernie Bevin (then Minister of Labour), visiting the troops on board the ships. "Will we get our jobs back?" shouted one soldier.

Having been treated for the recurrence of his malaria, Major Willie Hayes, commanding D Company of the 1st Dorsets, was released from hospital just in time to join his Battalion. Later he recalled how, on board ship waiting for days to put to sea, he had to deal with the anxieties of some of the men in his Company. One worry he remembered was: *'We hear the Germans will set the sea alight with oil and petrol. This is your problem, Sir!'*

The other was that when we reached the beaches there would be a bevy of French girls in very small bikinis lying on the beach to keep the soldiers dallying there. 'Don't worry about this one, Sir', they said. 'We'll each grab a girl, giving you two, and they will carry our kit for us so that we will be off the beaches quicker than ever.'

But the men seldom shared their real worries. One of Hayes's soldiers, nineteen-year-old Private Terry Parker from Cardiff, confided his anxieties to his illegally kept diary.

On board Empire Spearhead waiting to land in France. 'Bomber' [Lieutenant Turlogh Lancaster, commanding 18 Platoon] *is in his element. Giving a couple of us lessons in French. The crew are marvellous to us. The sea is full of ships, LSTs, LCT, LC5, Rocket Ships, everything imaginable. We know definite it is the real thing this time. I feel pretty scared about it now. I'm worried stiff about Mother. If anything happened to me it would just about kill her. I wish everything was alright with Jess. I'd feel a lot better if it was. Still, there's one less to worry about me if…!*

…Checked all our equipment and ammunition. Wonder how many Jerries I'll get with mine. Wrote a load of letters home. More scared than ever, but excited.

For the Brigade's third assault landing, the wind, rain and waves had conspired for the third time to make their job as difficult as possible. After they had been five days afloat and having been briefed to land on 5th June, on the 4th the operation was postponed for another twenty-four hours. This was depressing news for all concerned but, for the crews of the two midget submarines in position off the Normandy coast, it signalled another day of dismal claustrophobia sitting on the seabed praying that their oxygen supply would last out.

Major Tony Mott, commanding B Company of the Hampshires, remembered: *We stayed on board, not knowing when the great day was to be. On Sunday 4th I got a hint from the Padre who was fixing Sunday services and said that a voluntary service would be well attended on the day before going into action. The service was excellent, with only assault troops and the LCA crews there, popular hymns and a sermon saying that there is no such person as an atheist in a slit trench. ...we were disappointed to learn that due to the weather it had been put back twenty-four hours. Nevertheless, we ate our pre-D-Day dinner of turkey and Christmas pudding.*

On Monday 5th the weather was a bit worse, overcast and a gale. At about 9am the message came: 'Tomorrow is D-Day' and everyone's spirits soared. The troops were really keen on their job and it was great to have people like that to take into action. Dick Baines [commanding A Company] *and I went in an LCA to the Empire Arquebus to see the CO for a last-minute tie-up. In the evening I assembled B Company and let them into the picture of where we were really going. ...There were messages from Monty and Ike to read out.*

Spirits were also lifted by the news that Rome was now in Allied hands. David Warren remembered *operational maps were issued and LCA were loaded with all heavy equipment. All arms and personal equipment were placed on the seats in the LCA, only the Mae West being retained by the individual. This was carried out to ensure that the assault would take place even if the LSI were sunk. To provide a waterproof cover over and above the operational gas cape and ground sheet, an extra gas cape was issued to all troops for use as a waterproof during the passage to the beach. These were to be dumped on the beach for subsequent collection.*

Twenty-five-year-old Lance-Corporal *Danny* Bowstead from Battersea, serving in Tactical Headquarters of the 90th Field Regiment, was given a piece of paper showing his landing as H+15. He was greatly relieved, thinking that he would not be landing until more than two weeks after the initial landings. He then discovered that the +15 meant minutes, rather than days. He would therefore be one of the very first of his Regiment to land.

Private Terry Parker's illicit diary

That day Terry Parker wrote in his diary: *All off. Weather too bad. 'Spitter'* [the Platoon Sergeant of 18 Platoon of the 1st Dorsets – probably Sergeant Arthur Horlick] *looks worried. I believe he's got a premonition of something. Landing tomorrow. I wonder how many on this ship won't see tomorrow night. I wish it were a month from now. God watch over me.*

Tony Mott recalled: *The build-up of the armada had been incredible. We had been anchored in the Solent for six days and there seemed to be no room for more ships... but day after day more ships had come and taken up their station. I went up to the cable deck at about 6pm to see us sailing and to see the last of England and the Isle of Wight for – perhaps – ever.*

Willie Hayes of the Dorsets also recalled when the armada finally sailed: *My ship, no doubt like the rest, had quite a list as we were all on deck on one side taking our last long look at our country. There was utter silence. How reverent fighting soldiers can be. We communicated our own personal and deepest feelings with our own mother country. So quietly off to bed – no thought of any last minute briefing. I shall never forget that evening.*

Walking on the cliffs near Bournemouth was seven-year-old Roger Coleman. Now in his early eighties, he remembers: *My mother worked at Pioneer Corps Records in a hotel on the cliffs in Bournemouth. One evening she came home and told me we were going for a walk. From our home to the cliffs was about a couple of miles and she then said, 'Look at this'. In front of*

37

me, stretching as far as the eye could see from the Isle of Wight round to the Old Harry Rocks, were lines and lines of ships all moored and seemingly to the horizon. A sight I have never forgotten.*

Colonel Cosmo Nevill later described the Devons' departure on HMS *Glenroy*. At 6pm on June 5th, Force G (50 Div) weighed anchor and sailed west down the Solent. There was no hooting of ships' sirens, no cheering crowds, which in the last war so inspired the departure of the 29th Division from Mudros harbour for the assault on Gallipoli. It was just like another rehearsal. The ships moved quietly off in their allotted places. The Divisional Commander's ship *Bulolo* led the field, followed by the Brigade Commander's frigate HMS *Nith*. We were third.

As we rounded the Needles, the evening sun shone on a perfect setting. The green fields of the Isle of Wight looked very calm and peaceful. In the distance out to sea two immense fleets could be seen moving eastwards up the Channel. These were two more divisions linking up for the assault; truly a noble sight. Above in the sky, squadron after squadron of the RAF flew to and fro giving complete air cover to the immense undertaking. All on board must have felt the greatness of the occasion.

The invasion force, consisting of about 4,000 ships, concentrated south-east of the Isle of Wight, and then moved in the general direction of Le Havre. [This concentration area was known in Operation *Neptune* as *Piccadilly Circus*. It was here that each of the Forces – Force G for Gold Beach, Force J for Juno Beach and Force S for Sword Beach – assembled and set course for their landing area.] *At 1am the force changed direction due south for the approach to the Normandy beaches.*

Aboard HMS *Nith*, Brigadier Stanier recalled sailing with the ships carrying his Brigade. *We could not communicate on the way over as it was essential to maintain wireless silence until just before the landing. We just had to hope and pray that we would all meet up at the other end. Half my staff were in another boat in case of casualties. That is to say, the Brigade Major, the Signals Officer, an Artillery representative and a Liaison Officer. With me was the Artillery Commander from the Essex Yeomanry, a staff officer with a wireless set and my Liaison Officer, Lieutenant Charles Hargrove, Royal Fusiliers, who was to act as my interpreter since my French was virtually non-existent. I also took with me the BBC commentator, Howard Marshall. Despite the improved weather forecast, it was pretty rough. Strangely, I never felt the slightest bit seasick. I slept extremely well for a few hours, knowing there was nothing more I could do till the battle started.*

---

5. In 1954 Roger joined the Royal Hampshire Regiment, became Regimental Sergeant-Major of the 1st Battalion and was commissioned, retiring as a Captain. Maintaining the regimental ecumenicalism of 231 Malta Brigade, he also served as Company Sergeant-Major of C Company of the Devonshire and Dorset Regiment.

Cosmo Nevill *awoke at about 3am and went to the bridge to see if anything was happening. There was nothing unusual in our progress, the outline of neighbouring ships could be seen, all moving at a steady twelve knots. The Channel did not look particularly smooth, but the night shadows on the water tended to exaggerate the height of the waves. In the distance, to our right and left front, there were signs of battle; star shells and incendiary bullets were constantly flashing in the sky, but we were still too far away for the noise of battle to be heard. This activity we presumed to be caused by the American and British airborne landings taking place according to plan.*

CHAPTER TWO

D-Day: 0330–0800 hours

Before dawn

Having slept fitfully, the family awoke very early. The Allied bombing had driven them from their house, and Madame d'Anselme, her seven children and two neighbours had taken shelter in a newly dug trench in the garden. They had been glad of its protection. Their house, overlooking the beach at Asnelles, had been hit, its windows smashed and its roof and walls damaged. Years later, Madame d'Anselme remembered: *...somewhere between three and four o'clock, two of the children took advantage of a pause to go back to the house to fetch something. One of them seized the opportunity to climb onto the garden wall to see what was happening. There was a German gun just the other side of the garden wall. Suddenly he shouted excitedly.*
 'Mummy! Mummy! Look, the sea – it's black with boats!'

In the face of huge waves, 50th Division's voyage to Gold Beach had been uncomfortable and hazardous. A substantial proportion of the landing craft had been forced to turn back and one had capsized. Of the eighteen craft whose role, immediately before the landings, was to fire mortar bombs to clear lanes through the beach obstacles, six had sunk, reducing their collective firepower by a third. Although the sea was rough, the meteorologists' forecast had been correct: the 6th had brought a break in the storm and the troops would land in dry weather, a light north-westerly wind and temperatures in the mid- to upper fifties Fahrenheit. In the morning the skies would be cloudy with some sunshine; by afternoon they would be blue. The break would last for a few days. Nevertheless, a Force 4 wind and high waves were going to make landing on Gold Beach a rougher proposition than on any of the other beaches.
 Aboard a Landing Craft Tank was Sergeant Bert Scaife, commander of one of the Armoured Vehicles Royal Engineers. Twenty-four years old, he had been an ironmonger's apprentice in York before joining the Royal

Engineers. A few weeks earlier he had married his fiancée, Charlotte, and they had enjoyed a three-day honeymoon in Blackpool before he had to return to 82nd Assault Squadron in time for D-Day. His voyage had been particularly unpleasant.

The landing craft did not cut through the heavy seas like a normal ship, but would ride up with the swell, and then drop with a sickening thud that shook everything and everybody, making the tanks and AVREs move, and rattle the chains securing them, and at times we were very worried about their security.

Towards the end of the trip, one member of my crew was so ill and seasick he had to be restrained from going overboard. (May I say here that as soon as we landed he recovered and did his part extremely well.) As morning approached and the light improved we saw a sight we shall never again see. Apart from the destroyer screen, we were among the landing boats, and when we looked back and to the side there was an enormous armada of all types and sizes of ships as far as it was possible to see; a very moving sight indeed.

Among the first of the great armada to arrive within artillery range off the coast was an LCH (Landing Craft Headquarters). Aboard was Major *Speedy* Bredin, whose task, once the preliminary bombardment was completed, was to advise the Deputy Senior Officer of the Assault Group about the naval fire support to be provided for the infantry ashore.

Also among the armada assembling offshore was HMS *Glenroy*. Aboard her was Sergeant *Ginger* Wills, a Devon veteran of Malta, Sicily and Italy. D-Day was his sixth wedding anniversary. He recalled that: *Few of us slept well that night and, at about 0330, we were roused for breakfast, which consisted of almost-cold liver and onions and a lukewarm mug of tea. Then we assembled in our pre-determined positions to load into our landing craft.*

As a member of the reserve battalion, Wills would not land for nearly five hours. But other servicemen were already getting into position. Leading Seaman Wally Blanchard of the Royal Navy was a frogman in the Landing Craft Obstacle Clearance Unit (LCOCU). *I was ashore before 0400 in the morning. I immediately started work. I think the tide was making fairly well. There was a diver working below me and I had what is known as snorkel gear if I needed it, but I worked virtually on the surface. There's a pier at Arromanches and I was working to the seaward side of that, our craft was tied under it, and I went about my business. You had to be able to blow those charges but not before the bombardment started. Some of the bombardment, we think, was designed to land on the beach defences themselves and on the sand. Obviously some of them would fall in the water but that was a chance that had to be taken.*

Blanchard and his comrades from the Royal Navy and Royal Marines were responsible for clearing the mines and other defences at depths of between four feet six inches and ten feet. There were four teams of ratings and Marines operating on Gold Beach; two of which (each of one officer and ten men) were in Jig Sector. Closer to and on the beach, the same task would be undertaken by Sappers of the 73rd and 295th Field Companies, but their work would not start until just before and when the infantry landed.

Reveille, wrote Major Tony Mott of B Company of the Hampshires, *was at about 4 and I had a good wash and a fair breakfast before the lengthy process of dressing up in full war kit.*

In addition to my clothing, I carried: steel helmet, Mae West, binoculars, compass, Sten gun with 180 rounds, two Bakelite grenades and two HE [high explosive], map case, entrenching tool and a small pack containing 24-hour ration, flask with medicinal whisky, gas cape. Also we had two containers of three two-inch mortar bombs to drop at the top of the tide. Other ranks were liable to include Bangalore torpedoes, ladders or tapes… and soon-disposed-of assault kit.

There was not much chance to say goodbye and wish people luck. Dick Baines [commanding A Company] was very cheerful as he had won a bet about D-Day and was all set to empty his flask on sending up the success signal.

D-Day dawns

At 0525 HMS *Nith*, carrying the Headquarters of 231 Brigade, reached its correct position and dropped anchor. At about this time the assault companies of the 1st Hampshires, and 1st Dorsets boarded their landing craft with about one platoon per boat.

Tony Mott *went below to the troop decks at 0530 and, to my joy, CSM Mayne, who had been laid low with malaria for the last day or two, was pronounced fit enough to come ashore, though he was to travel by LCT. I expect he regretted this as he had a sticky voyage, with several casualties in his craft. While we were waiting there was a crash and a rattle and the ship shook. That had frightened me on a previous exercise. It was the anchor being let down.*

Major David Warren of C Company remembered: *It was rather a grey morning and I suppose we got into the landing craft at about 0530 because we had to get the landing craft lowered into the sea and circle about while we formed up in our flotillas. And it was just about first light, soon after first light, when I think we passed the cruiser HMS Ajax, a six-inch-gun cruiser, and she let go just as we were near her. Very heartening if you were going the same way. We bumped around in the landing craft while we formed up for the run-in and I recollect that we'd had tea and rum put in for people to drink as we were going in. But a lot of people were feeling seasick and I think tea and rum was not the best thing.*

As part of the second wave of the assault, C Company would endure another two hours of stomach-churning waves before they landed.

Meanwhile, they witnessed the beginning of the naval bombardment. At 0545 the Brigade Intelligence Officer of 231 Brigade noted in the War Diary that most of the destroyers offshore were now firing. Twenty-two 4.7-inch guns aboard the five destroyers, HMS *Jervis, Grenville, Ulysses, Undine* and *Urania*, opened up on the German defences on the Jig sector of Gold Beach. At about 0600 the shore battery at Longues, which was the Devons' ultimate D-Day objective, fired on HMS *Bulolo*, the Headquarters ship of 231 Malta Brigade. The cruiser *Ajax* immediately returned the fire with a vengeance.

Left: Empire Crossbow from an LCA (Geoff Hebden)
Right: 1st Dorsets Anti-Tank Platoon aboard LCA (Geoff Hebden)

Just below the shoreline, Leading Seaman Wally Blanchard and the other divers had been waiting for the moment the ships began firing. The tide was coming in at a rate of one foot every ten minutes and they could feel the water deepening. *The bombardment duly opened and we duly started blowing charges. The Germans would mistake them, we hoped, for the bombarding ammunition coming in. We didn't succeed in doing all of it.* Nonetheless, in the course of D-Day Blanchard's colleagues would clear 2,500 obstacles and their bravery would win them three Distinguished Service Crosses, one Military Cross and six Distinguished Service Medals[6]. Although several of their number would be wounded, only one would lose his life.

---

6. The Distinguished Service Cross (DSC) and the Distinguished Service Medal (DSM) were the Royal Navy's equivalents of the Military Cross and Military Medal.

We were six or seven miles out, recalled Tony Mott, *and had one and a half hours for the run-in. Our LCAs were in line ahead with A Company's to starboard... Then we threaded our way between craft of all sorts, all slowly approaching the coast, until we picked up our ML* [motor launch], *with all sorts of secret devices, which calculated to the exact spot, where we could not go wrong. Everything was ominously quiet.*

A flight of LCTs moved forward to launch the swimming DD tanks of the Sherwood Rangers' B and C Squadrons. Lieutenant Ian Wilson, a Sapper officer heading for the beach, remembered *seeing one LCT beside us discharging its DD tanks... and we saw six tanks, one after the other, disappear from view.* Happily, casualties were few but all four members of Lieutenant Wharton's crew (Troopers Hewlett, Lowe, Geen and Jackson) were either drowned or killed by machine gun fire swimming ashore. Concluding that the sea was much too rough to launch them as planned, they decided to launch the remaining thirty DD Shermans later and – at greater risk to their Royal Navy crews – much closer to the shore.

At 0630 several squadrons of American bombers droned over to destroy the beach defences and coastal batteries. The roar of the combined naval and aerial bombardments was mind-numbing and, where it hit German strongpoints, it left many of the defenders dazed and bewildered. Even those who were not on the receiving end of it remembered the barrage for the rest of their lives as the loudest noise they ever experienced. Second Lieutenant Gordon Layton, a nineteen-year-old platoon commander in D Company of the Hampshires, remembered that, as soon as his men had boarded their landing craft, *everyone was seasick and remained so as we eventually headed for the shore. I recall the deafening noise of bombs, shells and explosions, indeed so loud I for one was deafened and couldn't hear much.* The clouds, however, impaired the accuracy of the USAAF's bombing, which fell between three miles and 300 yards from the beach. Although the American airmen had considerable success on the eastern end of the beach (where the East Yorkshires and Green Howards were about to land), the defences on the Jig Sector and around Le Hamel survived almost unscathed.

At 0640 the Brigade War Diary recorded the first enemy shell landing near their ship and the shooting down of an Allied aircraft. By this time they could see the coast very clearly and the landing beaches were quite distinct.

Ten minutes later, aboard their LCTs, the Gunners of the 90th Field Regiment began their run-in shoot, controlled by Majors Wells and Girling and Captain Morris. Their targets were the German defences on the east of the Brigade's landing beach. Their forward observation officers were with their battalions: Captain Vine with the Hampshires, Captains Cook and Bishop with C and D Companies of the Dorsets.

Colonel Hardie, commanding the 90th, would land with Colonel Norie's Battalion Headquarters of the 1st Dorsets.

Acting as reserve control for the Essex Yeomanry, Major Christopher Sidgwick suddenly found himself in the hot seat when the motor launch which was to have controlled the Regiment's run-in shoot did not arrive. Sidgwick immediately ordered his own craft much closer to the beach to enable him to direct his Regiment's fire. He thus found himself well in advance of the leading wave of the assault and exposed to heavy fire of all types from the shore. Unfortunately, without the equipment that had been aboard the motor launch, he was unable to direct fire as planned on to the defences at Le Hamel. Instead, his fellow Yeomen's guns were directed to follow those of the 90th Field Regiment, firing upon the east end of the beach. From his close vantage point, Sidgwick watched the fall of his guns' first salvo before correcting their fire. The defenders at Le Hamel thus entirely escaped the Royal Artillery's preliminary bombardment.

The guns' run-in shoot began when they were still between 2,000 and 3,000 yards offshore. Sergeant-Major Jack Vilander Brown of the Essex Yeomanry described the scene. *Everybody opened up, the noise was horrific; it was ear-shattering. It was bad enough our people firing, but there were rocket things on either side, there were capital ships, destroyers dashing backwards and forwards... it was, well, we'd never experienced anything like it.*

That run-in shoot, you know, those guns got so hot the blokes could hardly handle them. Grease was running out of the breech blocks and the cartridge cases were being thrown over the side. We fired 150, 200 rounds – as soon as one's gone, you put another one in – and the noise, well! We didn't have time to be afraid, you don't get time to think.

During their run-in shoot, which would continue until H-5, the Essex Yeomanry fired 3,800 shells.

At 0710 50th Divisional Signals broke wireless silence on all nets and *communication was established all round very quickly and with very little interference.*

Nearing the shore with his fellow Hampshires, Tony Mott recalled: *We passed the rum jar round at 0715 just as the LCT (Rockets) were getting ready to fire. They were close to us and when they loosed off their salvoes we could see the rockets sailing into the air, often two of the batch colliding and exploding. They made a harsh crack as they went off; as each salvo was fired the craft disappeared from sight in a haze of smoke. After firing they turned away, their part in launching the Second Front over.*

Lieutenant Jack Lauder was also heading for the beach with his platoon from A Company of the 1st Hampshires. *Something seemed to have gone wrong. Where were all the bombs and shells, which were supposed to land on our objective before we reached the shore? Not a bomb or shell burst had we seen so far in our area. Suddenly, whoosh! – the rocket craft to our right* had fired its projectiles: at least they should do some damage; but no, they'd miscalculated... the rockets landed in the sea. We were now close in shore.

The rockets proved of limited value. Many fell in the sea and some are reported to have fallen among the LCTs landing the breaching teams.

Short of the beach, the frogmen of the Landing Craft Obstacle Clearance Unit were still clearing the obstacles and weapons in the water. It was a race against time. The first landings were only ten minutes away. Lieutenant Hargreaves, leading one such team, remembered:

We were dropped into our craft from an LSI at seven o'clock in the morning, and went hell-for-leather for the beach, and arrived hoping to find the front row of obstacles on the water's edge, and not in the water, but discovered some two or three feet of water over them. We left our craft and got to work at once on posts with mines secured to the tops of them, specially constructed wooden ramps which were mined, and steel hedgehogs with mines and anti-aircraft shells on top of them, and we were subjected the whole time to quite a hot fire from rockets, shells, and bombs.

We must have been about four hundred yards from the beach when the firing first started, and they didn't forget to inform us that they knew we were coming. When we finally got on the beach we discovered that we were being systematically sniped, not only with rifles but also by odd bursts of machine-gun fire – a most unpleasant experience but one that we soon got used to.... The weather was very much worse than anyone would have expected in June, and we had the greatest difficulty working in a very heavy surf. It was hard going and we soon got pretty tired, but in the meantime the obstacles were slowly but systematically destroyed...

Harold Hargreaves was awarded the Distinguished Service Cross for his bravery on D-Day.

Enter the Sappers

Because the Sherwood Rangers' DD tanks had been unable to land, the Sappers were first to arrive on the beach and had to land without armour to defend them. The 73rd Field Company disembarked on foot with the Churchill AVREs of the 82nd Assault Squadron and the Sherman flails of B Squadron of the Westminster Dragoons.

Lieutenant Ian Wilson, leading a beach clearance party of the 73rd, remembered his Company had to *clear six wide lanes through the beach obstacles... on the front of the Hampshires... each platoon was divided into two demolition teams of twenty-four men, each man carrying twenty-four pounds of high explosive and igniters sets as he waded or swam ashore as well as personal weapon, small kit and forty-eight hours' ration.*

...The specialist armour was to clear the exits off the beaches and was grouped into LCT-sized lane clearance teams. Additional stores, mine detectors, spare explosives and lane markers were loaded into folding boats to be towed ashore by the second tank of each LCT; the boats also held some rum which was left from the morning issue because soldiers were too seasick to drink it. The idea to use boats was a last-minute one, never practised in training.

The LCTs assigned to the Hampshires' beach made their run in abreast some four minutes ahead of the first wave of assault landing craft. The tide was exceptionally high because of the weather conditions and the first row of obstacles was awash. All LCTs beached in rather deeper water than had been experienced on exercises. Only in one case was disembarkation without incident, and that was slightly in the wrong place and in exceptionally deep water. Several stores boats had their canvas sides ripped open, one demolition team had to change to three other landing craft to reach shore. One half-team only started demolition as planned.

Arriving on the beach with Wilson's Company were six breaching teams, which were divided into W and Y Squadrons, of three teams each. W Squadron on Jig Green East was commanded by Captain Harold Stanyon of the Westminster Dragoons while Y Squadron on Jig Green West was led by Sapper Major Harold Elphinstone. Each of the six teams included four AVREs and two flails from the Westminster Dragoons. The six LCTs were commanded by Lieutenant-Commander Arnold Nyburg of the Royal Naval Volunteer Reserve (RNVR). Most of them were caught by the coastal current and beached too far east.

Aboard Commander Nyburg's own LCT 2025 was Bert Scaife's Troop Leader, Captain Ken Wilford. Before he could disembark, he was wounded when a 77mm shell hit the LCT, wedging an AVRE on its ramp. The landing craft became jammed side-on on the beach. None of the men or vehicles aboard were able to disembark for six long, dangerous hours, during which Nyburg won a Distinguished Service Cross.

Beaching beside LCT 2025 at 0725 was LCT 2027, commanded by Lieutenant Jack Booker RNVR, who remembered his landing craft being *hit several times by shellfire, two of which shot away our starboard winch and wire. Fortunately, we got our cargo ashore without serious problems, due, to a great extent, to our anchor winch controller. Stoker Mountain stood by his winch, totally unprotected from bullets and shrapnel, slowly easing 749* [his landing craft] *up to the beach during the half hour or so it took us to off-load our tanks. I am pleased to report that Stoker* [William] *Mountain was later awarded the DSM (Distinguished Service Medal) for his cool conduct while under fire. There were no casualties among my crew but sadly a corporal of the Royal Engineers was killed in the tank hold.*

In the next few minutes the troops landing on Jig Green would discover that the German defences were still intact. Le Hamel had been missed successively by the American Eighth Air Force's bombing, the Royal Navy's bombardment and the rockets fired from the LCT(R)s. Finally, the problems Christopher Sidgwick's craft encountered controlling the Essex Yeomanry's run-in shoot had prevented his Regiment from shelling the Le Hamel end of the landing beach. As a consequence, the German positions were undamaged. Among them were a 77mm gun at Le Hamel East and a 50mm gun at Le Hamel West, both heavily encased in concrete. The 77mm enjoyed a commanding field of fire north and east across the beach while the 50mm dominated the west side of Le Hamel. Machine gun and mortar positions also remained, and the defences on or beside the beach were supplemented by guns and mortars further inland, including those at Meauvaines and Cabane. For the next eight hours the German defenders would exact a high price from the invaders.

The other five LCTs delivering the tanks of the Sappers and Westminster Dragoons beached further east. They suffered less from German fire, but they still had to contend with damage caused by the rough seas, vehicle malfunctions, the boggy clay strips on Jig Red and the marshy ground just behind the beach.

Landing from LCT 2026 were Sergeant Bert Scaife and his crew. *The team consisted of my AVRE leading, and laying a matting carpet to carry the tanks over the soft beach, followed by a crab flail tank to flail a track through the minefield between the beach and the road, followed by an AVRE carrying our OC [Officer Commanding],* Major Elphinstone, *who was in command of the three teams to the right of the line; after him came a second crab flail tank and then another AVRE, this one carrying a fascine...*

As the final approach was made we came under shellfire from guns that had not been knocked out by either the aerial bombing or the warships' shelling, and some of the shells were dropping rather too near for our comfort. We were soon too busy to notice though, as we prepared for touch down, getting the holding chains ready for quick release, starting the engines and warming up and making sure the Roly Poly was ready to roll... As the ramp went down we moved forward and the Roly Poly worked well and we managed to lay the mat up the firmer beach. We then blew the charge to get rid of the waterproofing screen and I could then see most of the beach obstacles set to delay and destroy us.

Among the flails and AVREs aboard LCT 2026, the gears of one jammed in reverse and it had to be abandoned, while a Bobbin AVRE could not lay its carpet over the sand because the frame had been twisted and the charges had failed to blow out the release pins. One fascine had to be abandoned on the beach because its release mechanism malfunctioned.

Jack Booker's LCT 2027 had disembarked Lieutenant Greene's AVREs, but one Bobbin AVRE was hit and a Roly-Poly (designed to make the clay strips passable) failed. The Fascine AVRE received a direct hit. Twenty-six-year-old Lance-Sergeant Eli George, a married man from Dagenham, was killed and his driver, Sapper Rawlinson, wounded.

A few minutes earlier, Trooper Joe Minogue of the Dragoons had been astonished by the firepower of the rocket ships bombarding the beach. Aboard Jack Booker's landing craft, he waited his turn to disembark.

We saw the first couple of tanks go off, then the third one. We were the fourth tank off the landing craft and we were very, very apprehensive… about this business of being in the water. I think the driver of the tank was a bit more apprehensive than the rest of us because he blew part of the waterproofing a little bit before he should have done and we all thought, 'Oh, this is it, this is the end of it.'

Anyway, we plugged on and to our great relief we found the water was well away from us. I was the gunner and I only had a forward view but I could see that the three tanks in front of us were not doing too well. The first tank had stopped because its commander [Sergeant George] *had been killed, the second tank had been a bit too close to him and had slewed to the right and hit a clay patch in the beach and the tank behind him had had a hit in the side, which had set it on fire. I saw the crew busily scrambling out. This didn't do a great deal for our confidence.*

The German 77mm gun had claimed its first two victims (Commander Nyburg's LCT and Sergeant George's AVRE) in the first few minutes after H-Hour. The strength and accuracy of the German defences are vividly illustrated by the experience of the Royal Marines' 1st Armoured Support Regiment, who landed at about this time with four Centaurs (each armed with a 95mm howitzer) and a single Sherman tank. The rough seas had depleted their numbers when four of their landing craft were forced to return to port; the weather had also precluded their engaging any targets during the run-in. Once on the beach, the Sherman was hit twice and its crew wounded or burnt, two Centaurs had their tracks blown off and a third was hit, happily without casualties among its crew. By the time the Regiment's Commanding Officer landed, only one Centaur remained. Major Mabbott was wounded in the hand when a shell burst beside the landing craft, a jeep was drowned and a lot of the Regiment's stores and kit were lost in the landing.

Joe Minogue in his flail remembered: …*the tank commander hit me on the head with his microphone, which was his famous signal to do a 360-degree traverse in the gun turret to break the waterproofing round the turret ring. This gave me an absolutely fantastic view of the whole thing. There was absolutely nothing one could see on the beach in the way of opposition; I mean there weren't thousands of people waiting to fight us off, which is the kind of thing we vaguely expected.*

As I began a traverse to the left I saw an odd pillbox here and there, but I wasn't quite sure whether anything was coming from it or not.

The pillbox formed part of the strongpoint on the east of Jig Green which was the first objective of Major Tony Jones's A Company of the 1st Dorsets.

Many Sappers, including Major Elphinstone and Sergeant Scaife, were now ashore and had begun to clear the obstacles in their lane. The clearance teams from 73rd Field Company of the Royal Engineers were also hard at work, tackling the rows of various types of obstacle. Lieutenant Ian Wilson remembered: *Roughly speaking, the first rows consisted of wooden stakes, mostly with Teller mines or 75mm shells with push igniters attached. Higher up the beach were a variety of metal obstacles, some with mines attached. Each team spread out on a row of obstacles, fixed its charges and, on a signal, ignited them together, ran a short distance and lay flat for the explosions. It all added to the general noise and flying metal on the day. But the obstacles were not in neat lines and there were casualties in the teams and a watch had to be kept for other troops coming up the beach.*

Obstacles on Gold Beach

The Sappers' job was further complicated because *the metal of some obstacles was heavier than those practised on in training, and the obstacle was not destroyed by the three-pound made-up explosive charge. A quick solution was to double the charge, and was successful but halved the number of obstacles a man could deal with... The Royal Navy was to provide an underwater obstacle clearance team, but only one individual in frogman's gear was seen to be in action. There must have been more – no doubt they had problems too.*

As we have seen, the frogmen were indeed there. When, an hour or two later, Private Ernie Shepperd of the 1st Hampshires, whose landing craft was sunk during the run-in, landed on the beach, one of the first sights he encountered was a dead frogman. As only one frogman was killed on Gold Beach, we now know that this must have been the body of Leading Seaman Allisder Austin of Number 3 LCOCU. Twenty-three years old, he had married his fiancée, Lilian Fisher, in Southwark only a few months before D-Day.

Having successfully withdrawn from the beach, Jack Booker's LCT dropped anchor and spent several hours securing the door, which had been damaged. During that time, he recalled, ...*we had a grandstand view of the landings, waves of follow-up landing craft landing in the area cleared by the Royal Engineers. One of the sadder sights was that... of our AVRE tanks being hit and bursting into flames and their crews jumping out to save themselves.*

The surviving AVREs set to, trying to clear lanes up which the infantry could safely advance. The assault companies of the Hampshires and Dorsets were due to land any minute. Trooper Minogue remembered ...*as the turret came back towards the sea I could see the infantry just beginning to come ashore. I suppose there must have been a couple of machine guns raking across the beach. You could see infantry getting into the water from the small landing craft, some chest-deep, some waist-deep, and they would begin to run across the beach and suddenly you'd see the odd figure falling here and there.*

It wasn't a matter of a whole line of men going down; it seemed as though just one in five, or a small group, might go down. A chap would be lying doubled up on the beach and some people would run past him and then a couple of his mates might get hold of the epaulettes on his battledress and drag him forward to the shelter of the sand dunes.[7]

Enter the Hampshires

The infantry Joe Minogue saw landing were from Dick Baines's A Company of the 1st Hampshires, who were the first infantrymen ashore that morning. Leading one of the platoons was Lieutenant Jack Lauder, a Dorset officer from Herne Hill near Dulwich. He had joined the 1st Hampshires at the end of their campaign in Sicily and had taken part in what he described as the *farcical* landing in Italy. D-Day would be his second assault landing and his second day in battle. Small of stature and still only twenty-one, he was known by his Platoon as *the Nipper*.

Writing a year or two later, Lauder remembered how he and his men had made good use of the vomit bags, *made of first-class greaseproof paper; somebody remarked that they would be excellent for fish and chips.* As the landing craft neared the shore, *we began to strain our eyes to pick out the landmarks we expected to see by the beach, where we were scheduled to land.*

---

7. See Alan Norman's account on page 52.

'Look, there's the tower on the hospital,' someone remarked, pointing slightly to our right.

'That must be the breakwater with the big pillbox on it,' said someone else, indicating a spot to the left of the hospital.

And there, a little further to the left again, was the long stretch of open beach where we were to land, dotted with vicious looking obstacles, which could be covered by the sea when it came in. Each house, building, pillbox and obstacle, which had become so familiar in the photographs, began to stand out in detail as we approached. The tension in the boat increased.

Twenty-year-old Lieutenant Alan Norman, another platoon commander in A Company, had a disconcerting run in to Gold Beach. As they sighted the shore, his Platoon Sergeant, Arthur Sippetts, asked him if he had a hip flask. When asked why he wanted to know, Sippetts replied that it was always the first thing he looked for when his officer was killed or wounded. Norman, he explained discouragingly, was his third platoon commander in action.

In the same landing craft was Captain Tony Boyd, the Second-in-Command of A Company, who had won a Military Cross in Sicily. Looking through his binoculars, Norman said to Boyd. *'I can't identify anything.'*

Boyd then had a look and said *'Oh my God. It's not our area!'*

Norman had ordered his Bren-gunner, as soon as they were within range, to engage any shore targets he could see. *He said to me that he had not fired as many rounds for a long time, and even had to change the barrel and dangled it in the water to cool it! As we came in we were told to get under cover. I was looking through two slots in the ramps. We grounded and, with not a shot fired at us – remarkable! My sergeant said ours would be the first footsteps in the sand and we were of course. Out we come, everyone is supposed to run up the beach but we were so groggy. One man was so ill we had to carry his equipment. I carried his Bangalore torpedo and they dragged him up the beach by his epaulettes.*[8] *Jogging is the best we could manage.*

When *Nipper* Lauder's landing craft beached, he remembered: *The moment had come. The ramp was dropped and out went the leading section in water up to their waists. Rat-tat-a-tat, the enemy opened up. The leading Section Commander fell with a bullet in his head; we dragged him from the water, but could not stop to do any more. We pressed on as fast as we could with our heavy equipment. There were 300 yards of open beach before the sand dunes afforded us any cover. Our senses were numbed. Our every action was instinctive. Two more men fell wounded. God, our equipment was heavy! A Bangalore torpedo was dropped and lay forgotten.*

One platoon was lost. The Company Commander [Dick Baines] *hurried over to order us to take over that platoon's task. We altered our direction and*

---

8. This may have been the incident Joe Minogue described on page 51.

Lt Jack Lauder and Platoon of A Company, 1ˢᵗ Hampshires, May 1944

Left to Right Standing
L/Cpl H V Wannell – posted to 7ᵗʰ Hampshires before D-Day. Died of wounds 13 July 1944
Pte G Ansell – wounded
Pte Webber
Pte R A Butt – killed D-Day
Pte L Bampton – wounded
Pte D Freeman
Pte W H Bell – killed D-Day
Pte F W Clarke – killed D-Day
Sgt B R Sargent – wounded 11 August 1944
Pte Oz Bailey
Lt J E F Lauder – wounded D-Day
Pte T A Edwards – killed 11 July 1944
Pte R Prouten – captured 13 June 1944
Pte K Heath – still with Battalion October 1944
Cpl Johnson
Cpl D E Rose – died of wounds D-Day

Pte Dowling – wounded
Cpl L J Caines – wounded 15 June 1944

Left to Right Sitting
Pte A E Christopher – killed D-Day
L/Cpl L Dyer – killed D-Day
Pte J Stroulger – wounded D-Day
Pte Burchell
Cpl G Slade – awarded MM on D-Day, killed 4 October 1944
Private F Britton – killed D-Day
Pte Walker
Private A Farrar – killed D-Day
Private J Farrar – wounded 17 September 1944
Private Cooper
Private Jimmy Brett – still with Battalion October 1944
Private E Loader – killed D-Day
Private Allen

pressed on. Bullets were now beginning to spatter the sand like raindrops. Two more men fell. We must go on – can't stop to help the poor devils. This was more than we bargained for! Ten more yards to the sand dunes.

I felt a sudden, hot, sharp pain in my leg; I stumbled and fell; my leg felt damp and ached with dull pain. Blast! Some bastard has hit me! I crawled blindly forward. After what seemed an age I sank down behind a sand dune. My runner suddenly dropped like a stone a yard from me. The firing grew heavier: the rest of the platoon hurried on.

'Christ, they're in for a hot spot,' I thought. Then everything faded out. I was unconscious. My D-Day was finished.

Two of Lauder's men, Privates Jonah and Arthur Farrar from Batley in Yorkshire, were brothers. The older brother, Jonah, was first out of the landing craft with Arthur some way behind him. As they ran up the beach a bursting mortar bomb killed twenty-five-year-old Arthur.

A wireless-operator in A Company Headquarters, twenty-year-old Private Ivor Holley, had followed Tony Boyd out of the landing craft. *We were in the sea to the tops of our thighs, floundering ashore with the other assault platoons to left and right of us. Mortar bombs and shells were erupting in the sand and I could hear the burp of Spandau[9] light machine guns through the din. There were no shouts, only the occasional cry as men were hit and went down.*

The beach was filled with half-bent running figures and we knew from experience that the safest place was to get as near to Jerry as we could. A near one blasted sand over me and my radio went dead, riddled with shrapnel. A sweet, rancid smell, never forgotten, was everywhere; it was the smell of burned explosive, torn flesh and ruptured earth.

Boyd and Norman had landed some way east of their objective, Le Hamel. Instead, they were immediately opposite the strongpoint on the beach which was the 1st Dorsets' first objective. With the flexibility born of battle experience, Boyd adjusted the plan accordingly, leading Norman and his Platoon up the beach to take the strongpoint.

Norman recalled: *...Get up to the top, get down and almost straight in front of us is a pillbox. I immediately get one section to attack it on the run with a flanking attack while the other two sections lay down covering fire. Soon there was a great cheer and they all trooped back – it was empty!*

They then spotted a concreted-in slit-trench occupied by steel-helmeted figures, moving about. One of Norman's men fired a burst from

---

9. Known colloquially as the Spandau, the MG42 was a light machine gun, belt fed with ammunition and with a prodigious rate of fire of 1200 rounds per minute. Well hidden in defence, it could break up an infantry attack for so long as its ammunition held out. Its rasping bursts of fire became one of the most powerful memories of the British infantryman in Normandy.

his Sten gun over their heads and a rifle section of eight men dashed across and captured them.

A veteran of Malta, Sicily and Italy in Lieutenant Miller's Platoon, Private Stanley *Chalky* Chalk remembered *going up the beach, between the 'hedgehog' defences set in the sand, each with a mine on the seaward side. They would be covered once the tide came in. On my left as I ran was Corporal Bill Winter, already the holder of the Military Medal* [won in Sicily]. *He would be wounded within half an hour. On my right was Private Monty Bishop.*

Bullets were flying everywhere but strangely with the noise of the bombardment, the wind and the sea you didn't hear them! You didn't realise anyone had been hit until you reached the sand dunes. It was only then as I looked back that I saw our men lying wounded and dead on the beach. When we reached the sand dunes we went down into a kneeling position, grateful to get our breath back. Another platoon that had just landed was trying to sort out the pillbox to our front. I noticed that Monty was leaning heavily on my right shoulder and I thought that like me he was 'puffed' and pleased to have someone to lean on. But when we got orders to move forward and I got up he just fell forward on the sand. He was dead.

A bullet coming down the beach from the sanatorium on the seafront at Le Hamel, just to our right, must have hit Monty as he waited.

Meanwhile, with timely and effective help from an AVRE, Tony Boyd and Alan Norman's Platoon had captured the Dorsets' first objective. This particular AVRE may have been commanded by Major Harold Elphinstone, leading Y Squadron's breaching teams. His Squadron's war diary records his having attacked some pillboxes with his Besa machine gun very soon after landing. Sadly, it also records Elphinstone's death. Sergeant Bert Scaife remembered: *I had now got my head out of the turret in order to see around better but was soon to bring it inside again when a stray bullet or piece of shrapnel whisked through my battledress sleeve, just scratching my shoulder in passing. I soon realised how lucky I was when a radio message came over to say Major Elphinstone had been fatally wounded in the neck when he put his head out.*

When Trooper Edgar Lawrenson's flail was disabled by a mine and an armour-piercing shell and its wireless was destroyed, he was sent on foot to find his Squadron Leader. Lawrenson arrived to find that Elphinstone *had been killed and the beach was now under heavy fire from strongpoints in Le Hamel.* A Cambridge graduate, Harold Elphinstone was the son of a clergyman from Bickley in Kent. For his bravery on D-Day he was posthumously mentioned in Despatches. Command of his three breaching teams now devolved upon Captain Taylor of the Westminster Dragoons.

Having unsuccessfully tried to contact Dick Baines by wireless, Alan Norman sent his runner to find him. He returned with an order for the Platoon to turn west to attack Le Hamel. As they ran along a track behind the sand dunes, Norman suddenly found himself lying on his back in great pain. A bullet had gone through his arm and into his chest, smashing two ribs. He shouted to his men to press on to Le Hamel and Sergeant Sippetts, as he had so undiplomatically predicted a few minutes before, took over the Platoon. History does not record whether he first had time to hunt for his Platoon Commander's hip flask but, if he did, his efforts were wasted because Alan Norman did not carry one.

Lt Alan Norman, A Company, 1st Hampshires

Left alone on the beach, Norman saw an AVRE heading straight for him. Afraid that he would be run over, he raised his unwounded arm and waved, only to be shot again. Salvation came much later – at about 1630 – when a sergeant-major found him, removed his boots, administered a shot of morphine and marked him for evacuation. Someone stuck a lighted cigarette in his mouth: a kind gesture which, as a non-smoker, he did not appreciate.

Alan Norman's fears about being run over were not misplaced. Lance-Corporal Ron Hayles, who had landed with the Hampshires on Sicily and Italy, remembered: *We were always told never to dive under a tank, but I saw an officer who had sheltered behind one. It had then backed over him, pushing his stomach into the beach and his legs in the air.*

While Boyd and Norman had attacked the strongpoint, Dick Baines had led the rest of his Company across the sand dunes to the west, where they ran into the fierce defences at Le Hamel. Nineteen-year-old Private Jim Aldred, a recent recruit to Jack Lauder's Platoon, was among those rounded up by Baines, who was trying to get his men over the sea wall.

Up the beach I was lying beside these Teller mines, and my Corporal, Corporal Rose, was lying beside me. I was a young soldier and he was older. All of a sudden a bullet ricocheted across the water and hit him right in the head.[10] *I got up and 'pepperpotted' under heavy machine gun fire.*

I got to the sea wall of Gold Beach. The whistle went which meant we were to go over the wall. But the Germans opened up with Spandaus and whipped across. By luck, I fell down; I think I must have slipped as it was very damp. It knocked most of them out; I don't know how many were out. I lay with my back to the sea wall. Coming across the water's edge was my Major... and three other men. And he hollered out 'If there's no wounded, follow me.' I followed.

As I followed, it seemed to become quiet, then all of a sudden I felt I'd been hit. I keeled over and I lay in the water. I don't know how long I was in the water but I crawled. I couldn't walk as I was paralysed down one side. I dropped my rifle and crawled along and as I looked up there was a blast and the left eye of my glasses shattered. So I turned on my back, got into my ammunition pouch, found my spare pair of glasses I had. I took my old ones off and put them into my pouch and put the other ones on. So as I looked up I was able to read 'Achtung Minen', I was crawling into a mine field. I didn't know that until then, lucky I had learnt to read by then! I carried on crawling, and as I was crawling, I took my bayonet off, 9-inch bayonet, and I was prodding the ground all the way to the wall I could see in front of me. I was lying flat out, just creeping along. If I found something hard, I just moved around, taking another chance as you don't know what's on that side. I kept doing that until I got about half way, I'm not sure.

Jim Aldred then lost consciousness.

It was at about this time that his gallant Company Commander must have been killed. Dick Baines would never, as he had promised Tony Mott soon after sunrise, send up the success signal and empty his hip flask. Within a very short time of landing it had become horribly clear that success at Le Hamel, if achievable at all, would be hard-won and was going to take a great deal longer than planned.

A few minutes after A Company had landed, Major Mott's B Company, whose objective was Asnelles, beached some way to the east on the border of Jig Green and Jig Red. Mott later ascribed their landing in the wrong place to his having mistaken a fallen tree for a log which he had identified on a photograph to use as a marker. Given that almost every

---

10. Aged twenty-seven, Corporal Dennis Rose was from Eastleigh. He died of his wounds.

craft would land too far east that morning, this seems excessively self-critical. Nonetheless, B Company had arrived. Tony Mott remembered: *Down went the ramp and out I jumped, no doubt starting to shout 'Get up them beaches', as ordered. This ended in bubbles for the water was about seven feet deep. My Mae West saved me and brought me to the surface, with the LCA about to pass over me. I caught hold of a chain and was towed ashore. After a moment I saw an aerial, then a steel helmet, then the astounded eyes of Private [Cecil] Dossor, my batman, who was the only man to follow my example. For some reason I grabbed the aerials of his 38 set and kept them for most of the day.*

B Company landed from five landing craft. *Five columns of men began to make their way over some 300 yards of sand after wading the last eighty yards knee-deep. I was soaked to the skin. My GS watch had stopped at 0748. My map-case had floated away and for all I knew my Sten and ammunition were useless. My binoculars were misty.*

Flail tank with LCT and hedgehog obstacles (Tank Museum)

We could see tanks and a flail tank ahead of us and toiled on, walking rather than running. I found myself in the lead, going between the obstacles and up to a large, shallow pool which I waded through as I could not get any wetter and I was keen to get off the beach, which was starting to become less safe. At last we reached a thin belt of wire. We paused for a moment and I joined 11 Platoon and told a man with wire-cutters to get busy and a tape man to follow. The latter rather slowly and crookedly went forward, paying out the tape to mark a safe route through a field of reeds some five feet high. We stayed on the edge, waiting for something to open up at us. Eventually it did, mortars I think, with a little whistle and small explosion. I got my men away from the shingle, but some of Company Headquarters crouched down behind a tank and got a direct hit, as did another lot close to me. I saw a steel helmet lobbed into the air, and this may have been the luckless Private Dossor's, who died from his wounds next day.[11] *A section of 10 Platoon was also hit.*

From some way to Mott's right, Ivor Holley of A Company also saw the men of B Company's Headquarters hit by the shell. *They were gone in a blast of smoke out of which came cartwheeling through the air a torn, shrieking body of a stretcher-bearer with the Red Cross on his arm clearly discernible.*

Tony Mott and the survivors of B Company pressed on. *As soon as the tape was well out in front we followed in a long snake. Only a direct hit could have done much damage in the reeds. There were other snakes on either side and we got safely to the hedge which should have been La Gronde Rivière, some eighteen inches wide, flowing from Asnelles to the sea. But it wasn't. No doubt the tide had carried us to the left. This… must have made a tremendous difference to A Company and the defenders of Le Hamel.*

Three unexpected factors were knocking the carefully laid plans awry. The first was a phenomenon which sailors call *longshore* drift. On this stretch of beach there was a stronger tidal flow than had been allowed for and this, exacerbated both by recent storms and, as the day went on, by some vessels having to wait a few minutes before beaching, created an increasing drift to the east. The Hampshires' difficulties were compounded and their casualties increased because the DD tanks of the Sherwood Rangers had been unable to land. Finally, the 77mm gun and the other defences at Le Hamel, having miraculously survived bombs, shells and rockets, were inflicting much heavier casualties than expected on infantry, flails and AVREs alike.

Having landed in the wrong place, the Hampshires found themselves, unsupported by tanks, having to fight an infantry battle against well-entrenched German defenders armed with Spandaus, mortars and anti-tank guns. Decades afterwards, David Nelson Smith felt that his confident predictions at briefings before D-Day had given his Battalion the false impression that they would simply be stepping over rubble and wire to occupy their objectives. Because of the extreme weather, the reality was proving very different. As the Hampshire's young Colonel put it, *the planning went to hell.*

---

11. The Commonwealth War Graves Commission records that Cecil Dossor died on D-Day. Thirty-five years old, he was a married man who before the war had been a baker in Whitby, Yorkshire.

Enter the Dorsets

At about 0735 the first assault companies of the Dorsets arrived. If the Hampshires had landed where the Dorsets should have done, the Dorsets landed farther still to the east. Tony Jones's A Company, who should have taken the strongpoint on the beach, came in too far to the east of Les Roquettes. Meanwhile Pat Chilton's B Company, who should have landed opposite Les Roquettes and captured it, beached even further along the coast in the Jig Red Sector.

Everyone – especially the many veterans of the Brigade's previous assault landings – understood that the beach was the most dangerous place to stay and that their first task was to get off it, into the countryside beyond. One of the 1st Dorsets' stars was Bandsman Denis Bounsall, a stretcher-bearer in A Company who had won the DCM rescuing wounded under heavy fire in Sicily. Now ninety-eight years old, he remembers that, when he landed, *the water was about two feet deep and, as I stepped from the ramp, I caught my foot and went in head-first. I was already loaded with full pack, haversack and a large container of shell-dressings. The additional weight of water was the last straw and my imprecations were, to say the least, extremely salty.*

Bandsman Denis Bounsall DCM, A Company, 1st Dorsets

I lagged behind the others and passed the bodies of a few dead comrades as I crossed the open ground. There were also a few wounded, but we had to get to the top of the beach and divest ourselves of packs and other equipment before we could take the stretcher and attend to them. In later days it occurred to me that possibly fate was treating me kindly by putting me under water. Had I been standing erect, one of the bullets flying around might have come my way.

As they landed at 0737, B Company walked into fierce fire from a German position at the top of the beach. Among the first casualties were the Commander and the Sergeant of 12 Platoon. The combined loss of young John Whitebrook of the King's Shropshire Light Infantry and veteran Sergeant William Evans MM and Bar was an enormous blow to the Battalion. Company Sergeant-Major Balkwill was another early casualty, one of four Dorset CSMs wounded on D-Day.

Private Ted Vigour described how his platoon *jumped out under heavy fire and in great fear and tension. One of our lads fell face down in the water, but nobody stopped. I rushed up the sand and shingle with bullets whizzing past me and actually reached the top of the beach, and I heard yells and screams behind me on each side, which sounded bad. Our medics soon attended to the wounded. I lay head down in a state of funk with the remaining lads falling down around me in the same state, but we grinned in great relief to be alive. The noise was terrific and we heard some Jerry machine guns going not far away. A lieutenant and a sergeant came up and urged us on, so we crawled off that beach a little way and lost two more men. There was green grass and debris and a lot of mist and smoke. When I glanced back, I was amazed at the sight of the invasion fleet. It made me feel we couldn't lose.*

B Company landed where it was relatively easy to get off the beach, but beyond lay a marsh, which they would have to cross. And the Germans had mines, mortars and Spandaus positioned to exact a toll from any troops landing on their front. Their progress delayed, Chilton and his men would take ninety minutes to reach their first objective, Les Roquettes.

Making their way westwards along the beach, A Company were mortared and machine gunned, suffering several casualties. Denis Bounsall remembered that: *About fifteen minutes after starting to treat casualties, a shell or mortar-bomb exploded close to us and Slim Harrison* [Bounsall's friend and fellow stretcher-bearer in A Company], *in the act of dressing a soldier's wound, called out, 'I'm hit!' A fragment had caused an ugly gash between thigh and buttock. Snowy Burt and I stemmed the flow of blood and applied a shell-dressing, so he felt reasonably comfortable and insisted on continuing to dress wounds until he was evacuated to hospital in England with other casualties later in the day.*

Meanwhile, Major Jones, Lieutenant Ellis, and Company Sergeant-Major Howell had all been wounded when a shell landed beside them. Tony Jones's Second-in-Command, Captain Royle, assumed command. The Company was in good hands: John Royle was another veteran of the fierce battles in Sicily. Sergeant Terry took over Ellis's Platoon and led it with great skill and energy throughout D-Day.

The first of the Gunners were now beginning to arrive, including Lance-Corporal Bowstead of the 90th Field Regiment, who began setting up their wirelesses. Despite his earlier trepidation about landing at H+15, *Danny Bowstead would win the MM on D-Day for his bravery in the landing and the example he set maintaining good communications throughout the day, contributing in no small measure to the success of the 1st Dorsets.*

Capt John Royle, A Company, 1st Dorsets

Landing just behind his assault companies, Lieutenant-Colonel David Nelson Smith of the 1st Hampshires saw some of his Battalion's landing craft hit sandbars and drop their ramps, allowing their heavily laden soldiers to jump into deep water. Some of these men drowned and sometimes the landing craft, lightened of its load, was swept forward over the troops who had just disembarked.

Landing with Nelson Smith was Major Cecil Gosling, a battery commander in the Essex Yeomanry, who later recalled: *Regardless of our carefully synchronised watches and the fact that we were not due to land for another ten minutes, the Colonel urged our LCA on towards the beach through the obstacles and stakes...*

Having disembarked in deep water, *as we moved into shallow water... a swarm of angry bees buzzed just above our heads: our Hampshire comrades, war-experienced, recognised German heavy machine gun fire and ran forward. In front of us the sand furrowed and spurted from Spandaus firing down the beaches in enfilade on fixed lines from Le Hamel. The Colonel shouted to us to lie down, but the wet sand was unattractive, so we sprinted for the cover of the dunes fifty yards ahead.*

Some mortar bombs and 88mm shells were falling and one of the former landed just behind Lieutenant-Colonel Nelson Smith and me, smashing one of his arms and filling my left leg with small fragments. We managed to make it to the dunes and flung ourselves in a depression in the sand. Intermittent bombs and shells continued to fall and the bees swarmed through the reeds above our heads. We lay very flat and still.

The second wave

Four more companies – C and D Companies of the Hampshires and the Dorsets – landed ten or fifteen minutes after the first four. David Warren, commanding C of the Hampshires, reckoned he landed five minutes late. His objective, Le Hamel West, was partly obscured by dust and smoke but, when it cleared, he could see that his landing craft was heading for Les Roquettes, some way east of where he should have landed.

The obstacles gave no real trouble, however, and the LCA beached on a runnel about thirty yards from the waterline. Small bursts of small arms fire coming from the direction of Le Hamel and Les Roquettes were seen on the surface of the water, which at that point came well up to the thighs. There were some casualties.

Machine gun fire from Le Hamel East swept the beaches during disembarkation and mortar fire fell around the water's edge. On the beach itself there were tanks of all descriptions, including AVRE, Centaurs and flails. Some of them bogged owing to the peaty nature of the beach, one AVRE had turned over and several others were struggling to get up the beach. An LCT, beached and apparently unable to move, was being heavily fired on, whilst an LCT carrying a breaching team was being hit repeatedly by 75mm fire from the direction of Le Hamel.

About twenty British troops could be seen fighting near some pillboxes in the dunes. This was the left-hand platoon [Alan Norman's] *of A Company* [of the Hampshires] *dealing with two pillboxes at the edge of Les Roquettes. The enemy were not offering much opposition and, although some continued to fight on, many gave themselves up to the troops running up the beaches from their craft. With this platoon was the Second-in-Command of A Company* [Tony Boyd], *who said that... the two other platoons were last seen working toward Le Hamel against stiff opposition.*

Captain Beale, the Essex Yeomanry's Forward Observation Officer with David Warren's C Company, took over the wounded Major Gosling's Battery while Colonel David Nelson Smith, in great pain from a smashed elbow and peppered with mortar bomb splinters all down his right side, set out in search of his Battalion.

Arriving in this flight of landing craft were two of the Essex Yeomanry's forward observation officers, Captains Kenneth Munro and Derek Taylor. Both immediately established their observation positions on the fireswept beach. Once their guns had arrived and were in position, they would provide precious supporting fire for the Hampshires. Throughout the day these two young officers kept up with the leading elements of the Hampshire companies. During the assault stage of the landings, Major Christopher Sidgwick remained under fire and close to the shore, directing the Essex Yeomanry's run-in shoot. Immediately the assault companies were ashore, he landed and reconnoitred the beach to enable his Battery to lose no time getting into action having landed. As a result, 413th Battery would land and be engaging the enemy ahead of time. Sidgwick, Munro and Taylor were all later awarded the Military Cross. There was also a price to pay. During the action at Le Hamel one of Derek Taylor's signallers was killed while they were directing fire. Twenty-three-year-old Bombardier Norman Bottoms from Colchester had been one of the Yeomanry's leading boxers.

Meanwhile, when John Littlejohns's D Company of the Hampshires landed on David Warren's left, David Edkins, D Company's Second-in-Command, was run over by his own landing craft. He recalled later how this incident really helped his soldiers, who were laughing so much they forgot their fear.

Still further east down the beach, Willie Hayes's D Company of the Dorsets landed at 0750, accompanied by the Dorsets' Commanding Officer, Lieutenant-Colonel Evelyn Norie. Hayes remembered with humorous understatement:

Hitler's much vaunted and so-called impregnable sea defences of mines and bombs on stakes stuck in the seabed were, in the event, quite third form for the Navy to deal with. By careful judgement the tide was such that all these horrid things were showing above the sea. Thus by going at a steady pace we zig-zagged round all the hazards. Thus the entire battalion touched down on French soil without a single casualty – it was now up to us.

…Our well-liked and respected commanding officer, Lieutenant-Colonel Norie, was in my craft. Of course he leapt out too soon to lead the battalion onward. He was tall but his feet were nowhere near the bottom. Of course he couldn't swim, carrying all that extra kit. So I leant over the side and kept him up. This was simply super for me – all my secret and so important bumph was a sodden mess. I knew one couldn't fight the Germans eyeball to eyeball if all the time one was to stop and consult some code or essential report – what wasn't now in my brain was quite useless to me and my soldiers.

Much too far east, Hayes's Company suffered several casualties from mines and mortars as they quickly got off the beach. Following Pat Chilton's B Company, they paused before a minefield behind the beach. Hayes remembered that he and Chilton discussed the minefield and decided *just to walk in single file through… rather than wait on the beach as a super target for the Germans… So our two companies, 250 men, went off – due to experience every man knew this was far better than staying put to be killed for certain.*

We were through! Here was a German soldier with his horse and cart no doubt taking rations round – we left him completely alone. We were through – only one man in Pat's Company of our two companies was blown to bits. I believe one odd bullet hit the Thomkins anti-tank mine in his pack.

Once clear of the minefield, both companies turned westwards to make slow progress through the marsh towards Les Roquettes.

In command of the ten landing craft delivering Bobby Nicoll's C Company was Sub-Lieutenant Bernard Sullivan, a very young officer of the Royal Naval Volunteer Reserve.

...we arrived off the Normandy coast. It was rougher than we'd ever known for landing craft manoeuvring. Gold Beach had the worst weather of all five beaches but, after a few nightmares during the lowering process (one of my men had two fingers torn off), we formed up and started to follow the Motor Launch. This was it – and the more imaginative among us began to wonder if this was to be our last journey.

My craft carried the Senior Major [Bobby Nicoll] *in charge of the 330 very highly trained soldiers that we were taking in. We were very glad to have him aboard. He was everyone's idea of a hero: tall, broad, handsome and icy calm – just the sort of chap you need when you're beginning to get a bit excited yourself. He won the Military Cross about an hour later.*

We passed the tiny submarine and sped on, to applause from a lonely figure in its conning tower.[12] *Then the Motor Launch turned away. Half a mile to go...*

Soon we were near enough to discern the shapes of fortified houses and concrete pillboxes onshore. It was getting very exciting. Rockets were being fired, 400 a time, over our heads from the landing craft. Rockets, just astern of us, and heavy shells were whistling over like express trains.

Planes were zooming in from the East, the North and the West and, on our left in line with us, roaring in like a wave of surf, were the landing craft from the other ships in Force G.

At about this point, the soldiers in my boat asked my permission to smoke. What discipline! For all they knew, we were all within minutes of death...

'The old wreck should be out there on the left,' said the Major, pointing slightly to port. 'Can you see it?'

'No, I can't, sir,' I replied. 'But it might have been blown up.'

'I'd feel more comfortable if I could see some part of it,' he grunted.

We continued to scan the beach – he from his six-foot odd, me from about four-foot two. (I had less pluck than he, but perhaps more sense, and was crouching!) And then we both gasped 'It's over there', pointing to the right.

---

12. The midget submarine would have had no conning tower. It was almost certainly X-20 and the waving figure (standing beside the periscope on the hull) was probably its Captain, Lt Hudspeth of the Royal Australian Navy. His work on D-Day earned Ken Hudspeth, from Hobart, Tasmania, a Bar to his DSC. He later won a Second Bar.

The blasted wreck was well over to starboard! All the pinpointing by the midget submarine, all the state of the art radaring by the Motor Launch, and we were a quarter of a mile to the east of where we should have been! It was the weather of course.

I looked at the Major and he looked at me. He knew I had absolutely rigid instructions to go straight in after the Motor Launch peeled off and I now strongly suspected that, if we did so, we would land his men some 400 yards to the left of the strongpoint they were supposed to wipe out.

Strict naval training had reinforced my innate respect for authority and then, as now, I did not lightly disobey orders...

'Can we be sure, sir?' I asked him.

In reply he showed me his picture of the wreck, taken by the RAF a few days earlier. There was no doubt. That was our wreck, well over to starboard instead of slightly to port.

A few moments of absolute torment, with visions of very brave men being needlessly mined, sniped at or even set alight as they ran along the 400 yards of exposed mined beach, and then I shouted to my Signalman, 'Signal a ninety degree turn to starboard!'

'We can't do that, sir, we've...!'

'Do it!!' I roared at the poor nineteen-year-old.

He raised a green flag on a short stick and we waited impatiently for the coxswains of other nine craft to acknowledge that they understood the order by raising their right hands. Eventually, after a lot of shouting and cursing across the water, they did.

'Execute!' I screamed.

Down came the flag and all my ten boats turned to the right, crashing into waves that had been previously, and more comfortably, on our starboard quarter, and heading, it seemed, towards the Atlantic rather than France!

The Major grunted approval and he and I listened sardonically to shouts like 'What's the silly bastard doing now?' or, more kindly, 'Going home, chums?' coming faintly across the wind and water.

I said to him 'We'll keep our eye on that wreck, sir, and when we are level, I'll turn. That's if we can get level!'

'Thanks,' he replied – and I felt calmer and more prepared to explain to the court of enquiry which I was now sure I'd have to face.

After what felt like hours but was probably about five minutes, we seemed about level with the wreck. 'Say when,' I said, 'and I'll give the order.'

He waited another eternity (perhaps thirty seconds) and then said 'Now will do, I think, old boy.'

'Ninety degrees to port,' I roared to the Signalman.

Up went his hand with a red flag; up went the hands of the other nine coxswains.

'Execute!'

Down went the flag and we all turned for France, increasing to 1900 revs to try to arrive on the beach at the same time as the other groups, none of which had altered course. Shells and mortar bombs exploded in the water about ten yards directly ahead of us and again about ten yards astern, but that was all apart from some small arms fire and then we were through, straight to the beach.

The Major and his men, these strangers we'd never seen before and would probably never meet again, dashed (or if seasick were carried) ashore at exactly the place they needed to be, and we headed back to sea to pick up more soldiers.

Bernard Sullivan's moral and physical courage and his willingness to disobey strict orders ensured that Bobby Nicoll's was the first of only two companies of all three battalions to land exactly according to the plan[13], enabling them to race up the beach, past the strongpoint captured by Dick Baines's Company of Hampshires and on, up the sandy footpath, towards the farm at Les Roquettes. During the landing, however, Lieutenant Stratton's 14 Platoon somehow became separated from the rest and landed on the wrong sector of the beach. Nicoll therefore found himself at the top of the beach with only two of his three platoons, Colin Windebank's 13 and John Hamilton's 15.

Dorsets landing (Geoff Hebden)

---

13. The other was *Bubbles* Duke's C Company of the Devons, who would land about fifty minutes later.

Private David Bushell landed in deep water. His friend, George Davey, who was about five feet eight inches tall, jumped in and disappeared beneath the water. A Marine rescued him and Bushell followed. On tip toes, with his rifle held up above his head, he could just keep his nose above the waves. *We charged up to the top of the beach and laid down in rough grassy cover waiting for further orders. We were near the road at the back of the beach...*

Private Victor Jackson, a Portlander in the 1st Dorsets, was the last one off his landing craft. *I had got about fifty yards up the beach when the landing craft went up – hit by a shell.* As he made his way up the beach another shell landed a few yards away. *It didn't go off when it landed – I wouldn't be here today if it had done – but I didn't wait to see what happened. I got away from it as quick as I could.*

After being drilled that the only people in front would be the enemy, we discovered that the Royal Engineers were in front of us, making safe pathways through the beach defences. In the middle of it all one of them turned to me and said 'Good morning, mate.' Although what we were doing was deadly serious, there was still some comedy there. I will never forget the way that chap said it to me. It really helped relieve the tension.

All around them, the Sappers were still under fire and still busy with their task of clearing paths through and from the beach. They would continue heroically throughout the morning. Among the first to land, Corporal William Burns of the 295th Field Company had found himself separated from his platoon commander and sergeant. Gathering stray men on his part of the beach, which was under heavy, aimed mortar and machine gun fire, he set them to removing obstacles to clear one of the exits. When this first exit was opened he took his men to join a neighbouring working party and, still under severe fire, cleared a second exit so that hard-pressed infantrymen could get off the dangerous beach.

Lance-Sergeant Fred Bradshaw and Sapper Norman Wint were in Burns's Company but were responsible for making crossings over ditches to enable heavy weapons and mortars to leave the beach. Two of Bradshaw's five men were knocked out but Sapper Wint carried an assault bridge for a considerable distance under heavy fire and worked continuously in the face of heavy small arms fire. When the job was done, Sergeant Bradshaw returned to the beach and organised a gapping party under shell fire.

All three men – Burns, Bradshaw and Wint – later received Military Medals for their brave contribution to helping the infantry get off the beach.

One aspect of his experience that Lieutenant Ian Wilson of the 73rd Field Company omitted from his personal recollections of D-Day can be found in the citation for the Military Cross he won that day. *The enemy* brought intense fire from machine guns and 88mm guns to bear on the Section from strongpoints in Le Hamel, causing immediate casualties. Lieutenant Wilson, without cover on this open stretch of beach and showing total disregard for his personal safety, and by his coolness and his personal example, rallied his remaining men and at the most critical period of the assault led them on to destroy row after row of obstacles until a lane had been cleared. It was directly due to his inspiring leadership that assault battalions and build-up craft were able to reach the enemy shore in safety and thus guaranteed the success of the initial phase of the battle.

Working beside him was a team led by Lieutenant George Buckley, whose MC citation is almost identical. This was deadly work which gave no opportunity to take cover or to retaliate. It required cool courage and stoicism. Sapper John Fitzgerald was wounded in the landing but continued nonetheless to dismantle and destroy the obstacles, while Sapper Alec Close, separated from his team when they were machine-gunned, continued with his work alone and under fire. Both men were later awarded the Military Medal.

Major Leslie Wyatt, commanding 73rd Field Company, set a fine example under fire. At one point, his Second-in-Command, Captain Peter Smith, was killed by machine gun fire while reporting to him. Such was Wyatt's courage throughout D-Day that he was later recommended for the Victoria Cross. His citation described the *fierce fire from enemy small arms and 88mm guns. They were in addition subjected to heavy mortar fire. In the face of this opposition Major Wyatt, by his personal example of walking about the beaches unconcernedly and by his example of absolute indifference to danger, so inspired his men that, in spite of heavy casualties, they continued to demolish and tow away the obstacles on the beaches...* As the VC recommendation proceeded up the line of command for approval, it was first reduced to a DSO and finally to a Military Cross. But, fifty years after the event, Ian Wilson's respect for his Company Commander shone through the account he wrote of D-Day, in which he described how one *badly wounded Hampshire soldier was rescued by the OC 73 Field Company, who carried him away from the base of an obstacle which was being prepared for demolition.* In this deadly task under constant fire, 73rd Field Company excelled at a cost of eight killed and twelve wounded while 295th Field Company would lose five killed and ten wounded.

At about the same time as the second wave companies of the Hampshires and Dorsets landed, a reconnaissance party of the 2nd Battalion of the Cheshire Regiment beached. Drawn from 9 Platoon of C Company and led by Major Abel and Lieutenant Williams, they arrived –

like pretty much everyone else – about half a mile east of where planned. The rest of the Company, whose role was to provide Vickers machine gun and heavy mortar support for 231 Brigade, would follow soon after 0900. 9 Platoon would support the Devons, 10 the Hampshires and 11 the Dorsets.

Landing from a rough sea often in the wrong place, in deep water and under fire took its toll on the equipment carried by very heavily laden infantrymen.

Approaching the coast with the Assault Pioneer Platoon of the Hampshires' Support Company was Private Tim Dudley-Ward, veteran of Malta, Sicily and Italy. His Platoon Commander was *Topper* Brown, a twenty-eight-year-old married man from Lambeth, who had served in the ranks of the Hampshires before being commissioned six months before D-Day. In a letter to his wife, Eileen, Dudley-Ward described his officer as *very strict but a damn good bloke.* Their landing was eventful. The same letter describes how *they nearly drowned us by landing us too far out. We were wearing waders up to our armpits and as we dashed off the boat the water was that deep it just surged over us. As a result the damn things got full of water and with this, together with the equipment and a strong tide running along the shore, we had a rough time for a couple of minutes. I just cut everything loose and swam for it.*

A member of the Hampshires' Mortar Platoon, Frank Wiltshire *jumped from the LCA straight into about seven foot of deep water. I was the Number One of the mortar team of five men. There were six mortar teams. After landing in the water, I had to jettison the base of my mortar as it weighed over fifty pounds and it would have kept me under the water... I got the mortar in a firing position, but the barrel was full of sand and water, where somebody had dragged it along the sand. After seeing my friends killed and injured around me, I thought it would be my turn any moment.*

CHAPTER THREE

D-Day: 0800–0930 hours

The Hampshires attack Le Hamel

It was now past 0800. Major Baines was dead, his three platoon commanders wounded, and the survivors of A Company had gone to ground at the top of the beach, pinned down by heavy machine gun fire from Le Hamel. Here they had been joined by Major Warren's C Company. No armoured vehicle could get along the beach to help them without being knocked out by the 77mm gun in its concrete nest. It was a deadly place to be, in which any attempt at movement brought death and destruction.

David Warren was just considering how, with Le Hamel East still holding out, his Company could possibly reach their objective of Le Hamel West. *The fire from Le Hamel showed no signs of decreasing and, as C Company had to form up in the village to attack the locality at the western end, the situation did not look too agreeable, especially as fire was coming onto the beach from the southern end of Asnelles. At this stage the Commanding Officer* [David Nelson Smith] *appeared with his arm in a sling and ordered C Company to capture Le Hamel East.* Although in great pain from shrapnel wounds down his right side from shoulder to foot, Nelson Smith was trying to carry on.

Warren *realised that we should have to 'gap' our way ourselves, cut our way through the wire, and we started to do that. Meanwhile, the casualties were piling up because the fire was very strong and it was raking along the top of the beach where people were trying to get. This particular beach was enfiladed: that is, there was a German position at the end of it and they could rake the whole beach with fire. Also there was a gun, which appeared to be some sort of anti-tank gun, and that of course was in concrete.*

By this time, movement of any description was becoming well nigh impossible on the beach owing to the heavy machine gun and mortar fire.

One of Warren's platoon commanders, Lieutenant *Horace* Wright, had also landed too far east and crossed the beach, losing two of his men killed in the first few minutes. The survivors had then taken shelter in the dunes. A decorated veteran of Tebourba, Wright was weighing up whether to cross the minefield beyond the dunes or to try to skirt round it. A weight of machine gun fire was *coming down*, he recalled. *It was very unhealthy.*

Lt Horace Wright MC, C Company, 1st Hampshires

But we were very lucky. When I'd just made my mind up that we had to go through that minefield, a prospect I didn't like one little bit, a flail tank appeared on our left and began to flail through the minefield and got through to the far side. This was actually in the area of the 1st Dorsets to our left but I wasn't going to fuss about that and we went through the breach and we got through.

Corporal Bert Slade of A Company, a veteran of Palestine, Egypt, Malta, Sicily and Italy, ran forward under heavy fire to direct the tank commander. David Warren remembered: *A flail was standing about twenty yards down the beach, and by throwing pebbles at the turret the attention of the driver was attracted and he was asked to fire at the hospital in Le Hamel, from which most of the fire seemed to be coming. As he opened fire, movement down the beach towards Le Hamel was possible, although not without casualties, for the fire from the tank appeared to neutralise the enemy fire to some extent. The tank commander, however, decided to bring his flail further up the beach towards the enemy and was immediately hit by an 88mm firing from Le Hamel.*

The flail's commander, Sergeant Lindsay of the Westminster Dragoons, and all his crew were wounded, and later evacuated to England.

David Warren recalled: *The tank was soon burning fiercely and, as soon as the covering fire from the tank stopped, intense machine gun fire was resumed immediately. Casualties began to occur very rapidly and it was necessary to hold up the advance. Machine gun fire was now coming from several slit trench* positions as well as from the hospital and buildings in Le Hamel East, and if the enemy were to be reached in any strength it was clear that mortar fire as well as gunfire from tanks would have to be laid on.

Commanding the Hampshires' Mortar Platoon was twenty-three-year-old Lieutenant John Boys, who had been with the 1st Battalion since Palestine. To provide effective mortar support for the two rifle companies he had to control his mortars' fire from an exposed and highly dangerous position on the beach. But he stayed put until his mortars had fired all their bombs.

Horace Wright remembered ...*the further west you went the more unhealthy it was. The main trouble was coming from an enemy strongpoint at Le Hamel and those who landed closest to Le Hamel got the worst of it.* Having crossed the minefield following the flail's tracks, Wright's 16 Platoon turned towards Le Hamel. On their way west they encountered two enemy positions, both of which fired but quickly surrendered. Two or three Germans emerged from one with their hands up and were taken prisoner but, as Wright and his men reached their position, they found it was still occupied by several more Germans. When they threatened to throw in a grenade, the Germans rapidly appeared and surrendered. *It was very satisfying of course*, *Horace* Wright recalled.

Landing about now with the Hampshires' Anti-Tank Platoon was Private Ron White, a veteran of both of the Brigade's Mediterranean landings. As they reached the top of the beach one of their Bren gun carriers shed a track when a mine exploded. From then on, his Platoon made painfully slow progress through the dunes, prodding with their bayonets for more mines.

Sergeant Jim Bellows and his Signallers, nearing the beach with the Hampshires' Headquarters Company, suffered a particularly upsetting and troublesome landing. Their LCT, loaded with two Crocodiles and a bulldozer, stopped abruptly 300 yards from shore. It had hit a sandbank and its captain, a young naval officer, ordered the ramp to be lowered much too far out and in dangerously deep water. In despair, Bellows turned to the Adjutant, Captain Waters, who said: 'I cannot do anything about it. It is his ship and he's in command.'

Directly the first tank hit the water the bow came clear of the sand bar we had struck. The second tank was on its way but the bow had swung and the tank was facing away from the beach. The tank hit the water and was away. I found out many years later that one man swam off and was saved while the others drowned. The bulldozer followed the tank and just disappeared over the edge of the ramp dragging the trailer with it – the driver and his mate stood no chance. The boat was still swinging, one wheel of the trailer caught one of the lowering chains of the ramp, the bulldozer was still attached and dragged the trailer in the water, capsizing it and throwing some of its men into the water and trapping others underneath. The trailer broke free from the bulldozer, whose crew were already drowned, and floated away. Some men managed to climb back on.

At this moment as I was looking in horror at what had happened there was a terrific explosion – we had been hit. I rushed up and found the shell must have been an HE (high explosive), not an armour-piercing one. It had destroyed the winch but there were no casualties. The Captain was in a blue funk; he said 'I cannot get the kedge anchor in', which was a stern anchor.

I looked and said, 'Haven't you got a fire axe?'

He said, 'I don't know.' And a voice came from the engine room hatch and said, 'I've got one, Sarge.'

He came up with an axe in his hand; the kedge had a cable, not a chain, so I told the sailor to strike the cable where it went over the fall (a rounded piece of metal that ran over the stern). The cable was as tight as a bowstring. The sailor raised the axe and struck the wire cable – nothing. I told him to hit it again, which he did; the cable parted with a loud crack. The end had not hit the water before the Captain went to the ship's telegraph. I asked him where he was going and he said 'Back to Southampton for repairs.' I swore at him and told him he was going nowhere until he got us ashore. He did not look very happy as I had my hand on the butt of my revolver. The little sod could not have cared less about all the men who had just died; all he was concerned with was getting out of it. From the look of his crew they were on my side. Just then I saw a small empty landing assault craft returning from the beach. I told the Captain to order them on to the end of the ramp. They came alongside and two of the crew helped load the W/T trolley on; we then boarded and headed for shore. On the boat I left one man, who had cracked; he had run and tried to hide in a corner. He had pulled the cord of his gas cape and covered himself, shaking like a jelly. You have to feel pity when this happens to a man – he wasn't a coward but his mind could not take it. The Captain did not even wish me 'Bon voyage' but just slunk away.

We touched down on the beach. I jumped out but, before anyone else could follow, the boat started to go astern. I managed to jump back on and shouted at the coxswain and asked him what he was doing. All he could say was 'Mines.' Where we had landed was between two small obstacles with shells attached. There was no danger because we would have held the boat while we unloaded but again we had a brave sailor who refused to go in again. He was heading out to sea in a blind panic.

I then saw a small LCT coming in; it had a walkway running round it. I hailed the Skipper and asked him if he would take us in and he said 'Sure.' We pulled alongside and again had to transfer all our gear onto our new craft...

We eventually got everything down into the well of the landing craft, which was loaded with ammunition. The Skipper was a man of about forty. By now the tide was on the turn and several times we tried to get in but each time were thwarted by obstacles. The Skipper turned to me and said, 'Shit or bust, I'm going in.'

With that he headed straight for the beach. He dropped down the ramp and we landed in France without getting our feet wet. As I was going down the ramp the Skipper shouted, 'Sergeant!'

I turned and he took my photo. He was a real old sailor with all the guts in the world.

None of the three Crocodile flame-throwing tanks that were to support the Hampshires managed to land. All fell victim to the rough sea.

Enter the Sherwood Rangers

Delayed by forty minutes, the LCTs containing B and C Squadrons of the Sherwood Rangers closed to within 1,000 yards of Jig Red beach. Instead of landing just ahead of the assault troops, they were to land immediately before the first two companies of the reserve battalion, the 2nd Devons.

Aboard one of the LCTs was Lieutenant Stuart Hills, whose parents had been prisoners of the Japanese since the loss of Hong Kong two and a half years earlier. A freshman troop commander in C Squadron, Hills *gathered together what few personal possessions I had with me, and what I could not fit in my pockets I stowed in the tent-like container behind the turret – my shaving kit, a spare pair of socks and underpants, whisky flask and my wallet with a little money and a photograph of my girlfriend in the Wrens. We checked that everything carried on the outside of the tank was tightly lashed down and, when we were happy that all was done here, the crew climbed into their positions inside the Sherman.*

…I took up my position on the back of the tank, on my command bridge constructed behind the turret. With the extra height this gave me, I could see even more clearly the mêlée of ships as they approached their lowering and launching stations…

Our LCT and others began deploying into assault formation for the run-in to the beach. With action imminent, the knots in my stomach began to tighten. I tried to compose myself, to remember what I had to do, to keep a clear head as the excitement mounted. Around us could be heard the drumbeat of the shore bombardment as the cruisers and destroyers fired off their main guns and the aircraft roared in to their targets… Around us were other LCTs and assorted craft, breasting the considerable waves as the spray broke across their forward ramps. By now Geoff Storey had the tank's engine running and we could feel the throb of the 410-horsepower twin diesel. I gave the order for the canvas screen to be inflated to provide us with the flotation we would need in the water, and I checked communication through the headphones with my crew and the troop. Everything was now ready for the moment we would launch and swim to the beach.

Other LCTs, carrying Major Hanson-Lawson's B Squadron, were on Hills's right as the ramps dropped. Lance-Corporal Birchall in Squadron Sergeant-Major Robson's crew and Trooper Matkin in Sergeant Tagg's crew were wounded. Just as Hills was about to launch his own tank, his LCT was straddled by three shells, one of which hit the side of the ramp. Behind him in the LCT, the Second-in-Command of C Squadron, Bill Enderby, and Sergeant Sidaway were both wounded. Hills's Sherman had also been damaged and, when launched, it immediately began to let in water and to sink. Stuart Hills and his crew had no choice but to scramble out and take to their dinghy. They spent the rest of D-Day at sea.[14] Other DD tanks, even though launched much nearer shore than planned, also foundered and their crews had to swim for their lives.

Midshipman Stan Smith of the Royal Naval Volunteer Reserve was aboard LCT442 landing five of the Sherwood Rangers' Shermans. Years later, in an interview with Doctor Andrew Holborn, he described his experience. *My job was to supervise the lowering of the ramp, then to stand on the end of it, very mindful of the 'horns', and measure the depth of the water with a sounding pole. It was sufficiently shallow here to allow the first three tanks to swim a few yards before touching down on the sand. Then a mortar bomb exploded about thirty feet behind me on the tank deck. I was unhurt, but one of my sailors was wounded, and the flotation screens of the two remaining tanks were ripped. The Captain therefore had to drive the landing craft in closer so that these tanks could leave dry-shod. As they did so, another mortar bomb exploded alongside the last tank. Captain Eldridge was riding on the turret directing operations, and must have been mortally wounded.*[15] *He still managed to get his troop ashore, but we lost sight of them as they made their way up the beach. By then we were busy with our own problems.*

Our landing craft was badly damaged by the first mortar bomb and by Teller mines, which had blown a ten-foot hole in the port side, opened up the plating of the port bow and twisted the port rudder hard-a-starboard. Also, another LCT had broached to across our stern and severed the stern anchor wire. Having driven the ship so far up the beach, the Captain was having great difficulty getting her off without the stern anchor to heave on. I was busy raising the

---

14. Hills and his bedraggled crew landed without equipment in a dinghy on the morning of 7th June and were greeted by a Royal Navy Beachmaster, who said: *'This will swing the balance in Montgomery's favour; there'll be consternation in Berlin.'*
15. There is no record of a Captain Eldridge. This is therefore probably Captain Bill Enderby, who was indeed wounded, but happily not mortally.

ramp, and, with the aid of the Coxswain, Leading Seaman Armstrong, taking care of our casualty.

Eventually, our landing craft slid back into deeper water and floated off. As she moved astern, a stick of three mortar bombs exploded in the water immediately ahead of us – just about where I had been standing a few moments before. We made our way to a hospital ship lying off shore and transferred Able Seaman Laurence into their care. We then proceeded to a pre-arranged collecting area for damaged vessels and joined an 'old crocks convoy' for a night passage home.

On the beach, Lieutenant Jimmy McWilliam, a red-haired Scottish veteran of the desert campaign now commanding a troop in B Squadron of the Sherwood Rangers, calculated that his tank swam 1,000 yards to land. Other craft pressed even closer in, and one, landing C Squadron's commander Major Stephen Mitchell, beached because it had been damaged in a collision the night before. At last some DD tanks were ashore but several were rapidly knocked out and most of the others bogged down immobile in the clay patches on the beach. As the tide flowed in, the crowded beach was getting smaller and smaller, and the sudden arrival of two squadrons of tanks created a traffic jam. One vehicle that avoided these hazards was the Sherman of the Rangers' Colonel, which set off towards Le Hamel and quickly discovered that the west of the beach was a very dangerous place to be. Against sound advice from his Signals Sergeant, John Anderson stepped out of his tank on the beach to see where he was. Hit in the arm and thigh by small arms fire, he had to be evacuated. Command devolved upon the Second-in-Command, Major Mike Laycock – known in the Regiment as *Black Mike*. But Laycock was still at sea.

Corporal Digby's tank was launched successfully. Twenty-two-year-old Bill Digby, from Farndon, near Newark, was an experienced and respected tank commander from the Regiment's days in the desert. His gunner, Trooper Philip Foster, remembered the German shells pounding the sea as their tank swam ashore.

We had a nasty moment when one of the forward steel struts, holding firm the canvas structure, collapsed with the side caving inwards. Bill... managed to force the strut back into place.

...the Germans had the beach covered with their guns and there must have been a strongpoint up ahead enfilading the beach. Over the wireless tuned into the Regiment's frequency I heard our Troop Commander Lieutenant Horley say in an anxious voice that his tank was on fire... Then we heard no more...

As it landed, Monty Horley's tank was knocked out and he and his driver, Trooper Worboyes, were killed by a machine gun as they tried to scramble to safety. The son of the Rector of Bisley, Horley had lost his brother flying with Bomber Command in January 1942. Twenty-nine-year-old Jesse Worboyes left a young widow, Phoebe, at home in Forest Gate. They had been married nearly ten years.

Philip Foster remembered that: *We continued on and fired our first shell, but then things went wrong for us. Ahead the Germans had an anti-tank gun that started firing at us at fairly short range.*

The next moment we were hit by an armour-piercing shell, probably a 50mm, which penetrated the three-inch thick turret just in front of the gunner. The shell smashed through the knee of the gunner, took both legs off the commander above the knees and then hit my foot. Mercifully we did not catch fire as Shermans were prone to do... Bill asked me for morphine which we carried and I injected him... Meanwhile the driver started backing the tank but could not see where he was going through his limited vision. Very inconveniently, he drove into the sea where we got totally stuck, neither able to move forwards or backwards.

Bill Digby died of his wounds two days later. He is buried in Bayeux Cemetery.

All through this confusion, Major Stephen Mitchell could be heard on the wireless, swearing at someone crowding in on his frequency and obstructing him getting his Squadron into battle. The 77mm gun on the seafront at Le Hamel and guns firing from beyond the beach were making it almost impossible for tanks to operate on Jig Green. For the moment, those that were still functioning remained trapped further east on Jig Red sector with its strips of boggy clay. Meanwhile Captain Colin Thomson's troop advanced up the beach in search of an exit and the road to Le Hamel.

Enter the Devons

From 0810 the 2nd Devons' leading companies began to touch down. Once again, they landed too far east: instead of following the Hampshires, they came in behind the Dorsets. All four of the Devons' rifle companies were led by veterans of Malta, Sicily and Italy. Only one of the four would survive D-Day unscathed. The first to be injured was Major Howard, commanding B Company. After he had jumped from his landing craft with Company Sergeant-Major Benbow beside him, a large wave hit the craft, driving it straight over them, crushing ribs, smashing bones and very nearly drowning them both. They were lucky to survive, but both were seriously injured.

Landing with Franc Sadleir's A Company, Private David Powis of the Devons' Intelligence Section also nearly drowned in very deep water. On reaching the beach he saw one of the Sherwood Rangers' Shermans receive *a direct hit and burst into flames.* Powis may well have witnessed the end of Monty Horley's tank. In the landing the Company lost their wireless set, which was irreparably damaged by water.

Lieutenant David Holdsworth, leading a platoon in B Company, waded ashore between the dead bodies of Dorsets who had landed before them. *Their bodies were being gently washed by the water now but their deaths had been violent and bloody. And no one could help them.*

We stumbled on through the water and up to the beach, ducking and weaving as we went. And all the time, dinning through our ears and dogging our footsteps were the vicious sounds of machine gun fire and exploding shells and bombs.

I don't suppose that any of us cared to look back. Our orders were to land on the beach and to get into the countryside beyond. We were on the beach now. The noise was hideous. The sense of personal danger was felt in every step and breath we took. The wish to remain alive was paramount. But dead men lay at our feet mocking at us for our arrogance. They had been trained just as carefully as we had. And they were dead. What right had we to believe that we might escape their fate? But we did believe it. And we passed them by, claiming the right of the living to reject the evidence of the dead.

And there, now tantalisingly close, was that grassy bank inviting us to throw ourselves upon its green and peaceful slopes and there contemplate the new hazard presented by those cruelly simple signs advertising the presence of a minefield.

Panting with our exertions and our fright, we threw ourselves on the banks.

Meanwhile, *Bubbles* Duke's C Company and John Parlby's D Company had landed. Lance-Corporal Norman Travett remembered landing waist-deep in the sea and wading ashore through dozens of dead bodies. *We managed to get to the shore and we had a run up the beach. I think there was a wall at the top of the beach. It seemed to take a long, long time just to get from the boat to the wall. You could see bullets splashing into the water beside you and you could see bullets landing in the sand. We got what cover we could underneath the wall because there was still considerable enemy firepower from pillboxes. It was a low wall and I think it formed part of a road that ran along the top of the beach. There were lots of soldiers with me, everyone was trying to get as much cover as they could. We'd all landed not necessarily in exactly the same spot, but there were a lot of us, anyway, taking cover under that wall. There were officers and senior NCOs but I was only a lance-corporal then, so I was well down the list of seniority. I knew the people in charge, some of them were fearless, the only way I can put it. There was the average chap who took as much cover as he could, and then there was the other chap who'd say, 'Come on, come on. We can get from that wall to this wall, it's all right.' Though you thought twice about it sometimes.*

People were being killed because the shelling was still coming from inland onto the beach. In no way could you possibly advance until these pillboxes had been destroyed. So we lay there in our wet trousers, water oozing out of our boots, for what seemed ages...

C Company had landed remarkably close to where they should have done and, seeing the battle going on towards eastern Le Hamel, had turned to join in the fight being conducted by the survivors of A and C Companies of the 1st Hampshires.

Courage amid confusion

A Sexton of the Essex Yeomanry landing (Imperial War Museum B5262)

The self-propelled guns were now beginning to arrive. Battery Sergeant-Major Brown of the Essex Yeomanry remembered: *...from where I was, as we got nearer, I could see it was very rough. Some assault landing craft had overturned, some had hit the mines on the poles. One thing I will never forget is seeing these poor chaps struggling in the sea, these infantry blokes being kept afloat by their lifebelts. We had to get to the beach and there was no way we could avoid them; we just went through them, just passed them by. I don't know what happened. You couldn't help the poor souls.*

Gunner Percy Page from Woodford Green, serving in D Troop of 431 Battery of the Essex Yeomanry, remembered: *...wreckage was everywhere, ships were being hit. At this point we passed a sailor bobbing up and down in a* life belt yelling at us to give the bastards hell. We wonder if he lived. We saw the stern half of an assault craft with three or four men clinging, obviously sinking, but we had orders: hit the beach and give the infantry all the support we could. Reluctantly, we could only wish them good luck.

As Sergeant-Major Brown's landing craft reached the beach, it was hit. *Lieutenant Gregson, our GPO [Gun Position Officer], had gone forward with the navy to supervise the ramp going down when there was a violent explosion and the LCT shuddered. A shell had hit the ramp and wounded him and at least three of the navy people; one may have been killed. Everybody then struggled to try and get the ramp down, but it was jammed. We couldn't get it down, so we couldn't go in, so we hove to and started to drift with the tide, while they tried to fix the ramp.*

They brought Lieutenant Gregson back down right next to where I was and I could see he was badly hurt. We did what we could for him. Then another shell hit the little bridge just behind me but it was a dud. …there was so much noise you didn't know what was coming this way and what was going that way, honestly you didn't. Right next to us was this rocket ship – it was an LCT with all these rockets on. When they went off, you never heard anything like it. I heard them going off and glanced over and I thought, you lucky so and sos, that's your lot; now you're going to swing round and hop it. Just as I said it two or three shells hit them and they disappeared in smoke and flames.

Anyway, they managed to get the ramp partly down and the first SP [Self-Propelled Gun] went off and was hit the moment it got to the beach. The bloke who was wounded was a great friend of mine, poor old boy.

In their landing the Essex Yeomanry lost all their jeeps, medical and survey equipment. Four Bren gun carriers and four of their self-propelled guns fouled underwater obstacles and were lost in the rising tide. Nonetheless, their first flight of guns were in action by about 0830.

Soon after 0830 Tactical Headquarters of 8th Armoured Brigade landed, bringing with them Captain Leslie Skinner, the Sherwood Rangers' intrepid Yorkshire Padre. In rough notes in his diary, Skinner recorded: *Laurence Biddle Brigade Major asked for volunteers unroll coconut matting at prow [of] ship. I and three others volunteered, took places behind roll. See nothing but good front cover. As beached hit mine. Man either side me wounded – one lost leg. I was blown backwards on to Bren Carrier but OK.*

Landing doors jammed. Gave morphine injections and rough dressings to injured men and helped put them in chain hatches. Ship's Officer released doors and ramp. We rolled matting out. Water about six feet deep – sea rough, matting would not sink. Shellfire pretty hot. Infantry carriers/jeeps baling but left us to matting as tanks revved up. Washed aside but made it to beach though I had hell of pain in left side.

Capt The Rev Leslie Skinner, Sherwood Rangers

Despite the pain, Padre Skinner at once set to, tending wounded men on the beach.

Remembering that Monty had repeatedly told him during rehearsals that he was too far back to control the battle, Sir Alex Stanier decided it was time he and his own Tactical Headquarters went ashore. Their landing craft first hit a mine, was then hit by a mortar bomb and promptly began to sink. As a result they lost their wirelesses and were unable to communicate with anyone else until they could make use of Beach Signal Communications, which had already been established. The Brigadier leapt out into waist-deep water. He remembered: *As I waited for my jeep to come off, just as it was being pushed into the water, the landing craft lurched forward and crushed it...*

There was, in fact, only one other jeep with Brigade Headquarters, which Charles Hargrove [a French-speaking lieutenant in the Royal Fusiliers], *my interpreter, got ashore safely, so I used Charles as my driver for the day. Little did I realise that he had only just learned to drive. Being driven around by him proved rather more dangerous than the actual landing!*

Two members of 231 Brigade Headquarters received Military Medals for their bravery in the landings when both came under heavy fire from a pillbox. Sergeant David McKenzie of the Royal Electrical and Mechanical Engineers left his covered position behind a tank and ventured out on to the fire-swept beach to bring in wounded men from the shoreline. Despite this fire, he refused to leave the wounded and stayed on the open beach for three hours, attending to them. Meanwhile, Lance-Corporal Roy Kingswell, a Hampshire attached to the Defence Platoon in Brigade Headquarters, also brought in two wounded men despite being under fire from the same pillbox. Later on he managed to get his Bren gun into a good position to fire on the pillbox, enabling other infantrymen to close with the enemy.

With Stanier's Headquarters was the BBC war correspondent, Howard Marshall, who Stanier remembered *got his notebook very wet, helping to salvage equipment*. In the 1930s Marshall had become the BBC's first cricket commentator on the wireless. An Oxford rugby blue in his youth, although now nearly forty-four, he was still made of solid stuff. Despite being wounded in the hand, under fire on the Jig sector of Gold Beach he assembled material for a historic broadcast for the nine o'clock news that night.

We drove into the beach, rather broadside on in the wind and the waves, seeing the jets of smoke from bursting shells near us in the water and slightly further away on the beach itself. And suddenly, as we tried to get between two of those tri-part defence systems of the Germans, our craft swung, we touched a mine, there was a very loud explosion, a thundering shudder of the whole craft, and water began pouring in. ...we were some way out from the beach at that point. The ramp was lowered at once, and out... drove the Bren gun carrier into about five feet of water... we followed, wading shore...

That was one quite typical instance of how people got ashore... the troops out of that barge [landing craft] *immediately assembled and went to their appointed places, and there was no semblance of any kind of confusion. But the scene on the beach, until one had sorted it out, was at first rather depressing because we did see a great many barges in difficulties with the anti-tank screens, and we noticed that a number of them had struck mines, as ours had...*

Having spent several hours on the beach and talked briefly to many troops, Marshall left the beach to start his journey, via three different vessels, back to England. As he waded into the sea, he encountered Captain Peter Johnson of the Royal Army Medical Corps, whose landing had been severely delayed, wading to shore. Johnson greeted him and, years later, remembered: *he looked at me as if I was stark mad.*

Howard Marshall ended his broadcast that night with the assurance that *if one may judge from the individual spirits of the men on the beaches... there is every reason for the highest confidence.*

Landing (on his wedding anniversary) with Battalion Headquarters of the 2nd Devons, Sergeant *Ginger* Wills *could see assault troops running from their landing craft and a few Bren gun carriers leaving their LCMs* [Landing Craft Mechanised] *and moving along what was to be our landing beach. Then I noticed the tripod-type obstacles still partly covered by the sea and I saw one LCA thrown over by a large wave, or maybe a bursting shell, and it drifted upside down in the choppy sea.*

Dropped too far out, Wills swam for the shore. *All around me men were swimming and I saw our MO [Captain John Lloyd] helping his batman, Private Stone, who couldn't swim and almost sank like a stone from the weight of his battle order.*

After about twenty-five yards I could walk safely and was able to see more of what was going on. The CO, a fairly tall man, was on the beach and shouting for his signaller. The MO had set Private Stone safely on his feet and as he waded ashore he kept stopping to examine floating bodies, but as all were obviously beyond help he let them float away.

There were already one or two amphibious tanks moving up the beach from the sea and towards the sand dunes about thirty yards from the water. The LCTs were off-loading more tanks, and shells and mortar bombs were falling, but not in any concentrated manner, fortunately.

As I walked along the beach, trying to locate the track up which it had been intended the vehicles should drive to the de-waterproofing area, I heard a voice say, 'Hello, Wills. Get me a blanket if you can.' There was a bedraggled figure, half sitting, half lying against the sand dunes. He had a Devon Regiment shoulder badge and a major's crown. I looked hard at his badly smashed face and was eventually able to recognise Major Howard... of our Battalion.

Looking around the beach the only blankets to be seen were draped regimentally around the haversacks on the backs of military policemen who were sign-posting the various beach areas. As I walked by one he dropped suddenly and lay very still, except for twitching in his hands. A bullet, maybe from a sniper, had gone straight through his tin hat from front to back and taken some of his brains with it. There was nothing I could do for him, so I removed his neatly folded blanket and took it back to Major Howard. It was then that I learned he had been in the LCA which had capsized and that several of his Company had been drowned.

At about 0900 the doctors and medical orderlies of the 200th Field Ambulance disembarked with their Commanding Officer, Colonel Robinson. Their landing was mainly uneventful with only a few men missing, one officer believed drowned and one orderly, twenty-five-year-old Private William Armstrong from Workington, killed. The teams at once began to help the stretcher-bearers of the various battalions to collect casualties into nests. A medical orderly was left to tend each nest, from which the wounded would be collected and taken to the dressing station.

This stretch of beach, with constant traffic arriving and crossing it, and with no exit from it yet cleared, was a very crowded place, and in places it was becoming chaotic. A Royal Army Medical Corps sergeant encountered Colonel Cosmo Nevill and asked if he had seen his Field Ambulance. Nevill replied: *Field Ambulance be buggered. I can't even find my own bloody Battalion.* The Commanding Officer of the Devons had arrived on the beach much as everyone else had done. Landed in the wrong place, Nevill could find none of his rifle companies, which, dropped at different places on the beach, had made their separate ways forward. All around him the beach was jammed with vehicles, some of them burned out or ablaze, and crammed with troops, none of them Devons.

He was not happy. *We expected to see a nice clear beach with all the correct signs neatly arrayed pointing the way to our assembly area. A very different picture greeted us. The beach was covered with a swarm of troops lying flat on their faces, ostrich-like, trying to make as small a target of themselves as possible. All was not well.*

Writing his report in the third person, Nevill remembered: *The CO landed in the Dorsets' area. This shook him as of course he should have landed in the Hampshires' area. There were no signs of either of the leading companies, so he and his Intelligence Officer, Captain Bill Wood, turned right and walked along the beach towards Le Hamel. A number of tanks were knocked out on the beach, a flail had gone about twenty yards through a minefield, but its track had come off. There was a considerable noise of rifle fire from Le Hamel, and an occasional anti-tank gun opened up. He found the CO of the Hampshires, lying on the sand, trying to direct an attack on Le Hamel; but up to that time no way inland had been found through the minefield.*

The CO came across no Devons, so turned eastwards along the beach in the hope of finding a gap further along. Encountering Brigadier Stanier, he told him: *If I can find any of my chaps, I will bypass Asnelles and go straight for Ryes – anything to get away from this unhealthy beach.*

Soon after this, he met Major Franc Sadleir [A Company] *and Major John Parlby* [D Company]. *They told him that Major Mike Howard and CSM Benbow had been drowned. This fortunately proved to be untrue, although they were badly hurt and were sent straight home to hospital.*

At about the same time as the Devons landed, the leading members of Number 10 Beach Group arrived. Formed around the 6th Battalion of the Border Regiment, the Group included men from all sorts of units and all three services, whose job was to help organise the landings and to ensure that supplies were quickly unloaded and transported forward.

Among them were some Royal Naval Beach Commandos. Able Seamen Norman Harris's and *Taffy* Williams's first task was to deliver wireless equipment to a particular place on the beach. Harris recalled: *This was carried in a box with two handles back and front, just like a Sedan chair without the top. We jumped out of the craft up to our waists in water and ran for the back of the beach, passing a pair of legs without a body on the way.*

Our next job was to erect a great big beach sign about twenty feet high and eight feet wide. It consisted of two poles with a canvas sheet secured to them, painted bright green with a large letter 'J' on it denoting Jig Green Beach, and craft allocated to that beach could see it when out at sea, giving them a point to land on. Within minutes of erecting this sign the Germans started to concentrate their mortars and machine guns on it, and we started exchanging fire with them. While this was going on the Germans had an 88mm [actually a 77mm] gun dug in at Le Hamel, and this was knocking seven bells out of everything that beached... LCT D28 beached about thirty yards away and within minutes it had more holes in it than a sieve. We saw one man staggering about on the stern of the craft, so Geordie Farrow and I waded out and got him ashore. He was a young Sub-Lieutenant from Manchester and, although he was covered in blood, he was not seriously wounded, so we advised him to get down to the water's edge and jump on one of the landing craft which were disembarking, as we had no medical services with us.

Within Number 10 Beach Group was the 90th Field Company of the Royal Engineers, whose job was to clear mines on the beach. Among them was Corporal Douglas Oakley, a thirty-four-year-old piano-tuner from Croydon, who spent the rest of D-Day with his section detecting and removing mines and helping to clear an exit route off the beach. Landing at about 0800, Oakley spent most of the morning clearing mines under small arms and mortar fire and he was awarded a Military Medal for the cheerful and energetic example he set and for his prominent part in clearing an exit from the beach.

Landing from another LCA, having negotiated obstacles fifty yards from the shore, nIneteen-year-old Private John Prior and his friend Private Mohan, also of Number 10 Beach Group, were pulling a small trailer as they jumped into about two feet of water. *The Germans were firing from our right as we got near the beach, my friend was shot in his right arm. However, we managed to reach the beach and he was taken away to the casualty area. Eventually we reached the top of the beach, just below the sand dunes. We set about digging as the Germans still had some snipers. It was quite a sight to see: tanks (most of these were Bren carriers) moving, prisoners being escorted along the beach and frogmen removing these obstacles from posts in the water, battleships firing from some distance away.*

The beach, as Privates Mohan and Prior quickly discovered, remained a lethal place. Unlike his friend, John Prior would survive the day unscathed, but he was one of many unfortunates whose D-Day tasks required them to stay on the beach and endure the shelling, mortaring and machine gun fire. Another was Sergeant Albert Talbot, known throughout the 1st Dorsets as Alby, who was in charge of C Company's stretcher-bearers who scurried about, risking their own lives to bring in the many wounded lying in pain or unconscious on the sand or at the water's edge. Talbot himself moved up and down the fireswept beach, treating casualties and directing his stretcher-bearers to the wounded. He then nested the casualties and arranged for them to be moved forward to safer ground. Like the Sappers clearing the obstacles, he and his stretcher-bearers ignored the danger and got on with their work.

Capt 'Dick' Whittington, Unit Landing Officer, 1st Dorsets

So did two Unit Landing Officers, Captain *Dick* Whittington and Captain Eric Edwards. *Dick* Whittington, an officer of the Queen's Royal West Surreys, was acting as the Dorsets' Unit Landing Officer and it fell to him to direct traffic across the beach. To ensure he was immediately recognisable he had painted his steel helmet in Union Jack colours. Oblivious to the fact that what he called his *battle bowler* drew enemy fire, he went about his business. Wounded in one foot, he hopped and crawled about the beach, clambering onto tanks to give instructions to their commanders and directing other traffic as it crossed the increasingly packed beach. Meanwhile, Eric Edwards of the Essex Yeomanry had reconnoitred the beach under heavy fire and then, while being mortared and shelled, directed the landing of his guns. His thought and care helped to get the guns ashore practically unscathed and into action very soon after landing. Whittington and Edwards each later received a Military Cross.

Landing with the Essex Yeomanry was Gunner Charles Wilson. *I was one of the 'roly-poly' team, whose job it was to drag out to the shore a huge roll of matting and wire mesh, which was intended to prevent following vehicles getting bogged down in the sand. The 'roly-poly' was about eight feet in diameter, with an axle to which ropes were attached. Most of us stripped down to vest, pants and gym shoes.*

We hit two mines going in, but they didn't stop us, although our ramp was damaged and an officer standing on it was killed. We grounded on a sand bank. The first man off was a commando sergeant in full kit, who disappeared like a stone in six feet of water. We grasped the ropes of the 'roly-poly' and plunged down the ramp into the icy water. The 'roly-poly' was quite unmanageable in the rough water and dragged us away, towards some mines. We let go the ropes and swam and scrambled ashore. All I had on was my PT shorts as I had lost my shoes and vest in the struggle. Someone offered cigarettes all round, but they were soaking wet.

George Chapman in the Bren carrier was the first vehicle off the LCT. It floated a moment, drifted on to a mine and sank. George dived overboard and swam ashore. The Battery CP half-track got off along the beach, with me running behind. The beach was strewn with wreckage, a blazing tank, bundles of blankets and kit, bodies and bits of bodies. One bloke near me was blown in half by a shell and his lower part collapsed in a bloody heap in the sand. The half-track stopped and I managed to struggle into my clothes. Several shells burst overhead and shrapnel spattered the beach. Machine gun bullets were kicking up the sand.

A Bren Gun Carrier of the 1st Dorsets landing (Imperial War Museum B5244)

The situation at Le Hamel remained grim. The Hampshires could not get into the village, and the action had cost them heavy casualties. A Company had pretty much ceased to exist. The 77mm gun was keeping the British armour to the east of the beach, leaving C Company and the survivors of A facing an entrenched, determined enemy with machine guns and mortars. The Hampshires' Colonel, David Nelson Smith, wounded a second time, had this time been put squarely out of action. Private Reg Lawrence, one of Jim Bellows's Signallers, had dragged him off the beach and under cover. He would be evacuated after midnight aboard a huge American ship, but it would be five months before his wounds healed.

David Warren remembered: *A runner from Battalion Headquarters came forward to report that the Battalion Commander had become a casualty and that the Support Company Commander* [Jimmy Wicks] *had taken over command until such time as I could reach Battalion Headquarters. I handed over to the Company Second-in-Command* [Captain Ronald Kidd] *and went to Battalion Headquarters in the Les Roquettes position.*

Warren was to take over until Major Charles Martin, the Second-in-Command, could come ashore. Meanwhile, he found he had no wireless contact with Martin or with any of the Hampshire companies except John Littlejohns's D Company, who luckily had their Forward Observation Officer from the Essex Yeomanry with them, and his wireless set was functioning. Warren ordered Wicks to go and take command of any survivors he could find from A Company plus Warren's own C Company. Jimmy Wicks collected all the soldiers he could from the beach around him and organised them into a force two platoons strong. His new composite Hampshire Company and Duke's Company of Devons continued the fierce firefight beside Le Hamel.

A Squadron, Sherwood Rangers landing (Imperial War Museum B5258)

Meanwhile, Stanley Christopherson's A Squadron of the Sherwood Rangers had landed soon after 0900. The first person Christopherson saw was Bill Enderby, Second-in-Command of C Squadron, *wounded in the arm and in obvious pain, slowly making his way onto a tank landing craft, which was just about to reverse and return to England with other wounded on board*. Christopherson's own Second-in-Command was the poet, twenty-four-year-old Captain Keith Douglas, who carried in his heart the premonition that he would not survive the Normandy invasion. As his Sherman drove out of the sea Douglas spotted Padre Leslie Skinner standing at the water's edge and hauled him on to his tank for safer passage.

By now the tide was high and many of the beach obstacles that had not been demolished lurked menacingly below the breakers, where the successive flights of incoming landing craft could no longer see and avoid them. No exit had been found on Jig Green beach and, as we have seen, the Sappers' work clearing exits had been severely disrupted by their having been landed too far east and by the destruction wrought on the AVREs by mines, mortars and anti-tank guns. But, on Jig Red, beyond a massive bomb crater in the coastal road, the Sappers had cleared two exits. The exit further west was near Les Roquettes and the sandy footpath leading south towards Meauvaines.

Getting off the beach

Once, on hands and knees, the Sappers had painstakingly cleared a lane through and beyond the strongpoint captured by Tony Boyd and Alan Norman's platoon, Tony Mott's B Company were able to move forward. The smoke from some burning grass obscured the view but, when it cleared, Mott spotted Meauvaines Ridge and church and, over the top of a hedge, the spire of Asnelles church. Reaching some ruined and deserted buildings, he recognised them as the farm at Les Roquettes. This German strongpoint should have been the objective of B Company of the Dorsets, but Pat Chilton and his men were still making their way westwards through the marsh behind Jig Red Beach. Mott was joined here by Bobby Nicoll and most of C Company of the Dorsets.

Nicoll and Mott consulted. They had different objectives – Mott's to get through Asnelles and to attack Le Hamel from the south, Nicoll's to capture Point 54 a couple of miles down the road – but, given the fierce resistance the Hampshires were facing in Le Hamel, they agreed first to band together to quell the opposition in Asnelles. John Littlejohns's D Company of Hampshires had also appeared with the aim of skirting Asnelles and taking a wide sweep round before rejoining the coast beyond Le Hamel to capture the guns at Cabane.

There seemed a great many more minefields than their briefings had predicted. All around them were *Achtung Minen* signs. David Warren remembered: *…movement was considerably hampered as all fields in the area for at least one mile inland were wired off, with the well-known 'Achtung Minen' notice displayed. …it was assumed that our intelligence was faulty and that there were many more minefields than had been reported. It was noticed that some mine notices were painted yellow and others white, but it was not until much later that it was discovered that fields with white signs were quite safe and that the yellow signs coincided with known minefields.*

These ubiquitous signs understandably deterred movement beyond the farm, but by now large numbers of troops and vehicles had appeared on the beach. Pressure was mounting and precious time passing. Movement had to be made beyond Les Roquettes.

Lieutenant Frank Pearson, commanding the 2nd Devons' Assault Pioneer Platoon, had arrived on the beach an hour before to be greeted by the sight of two knocked out tanks and a headless British soldier. The Bangalore torpedoes they had employed to blast their way through the wire along the sea wall had all refused to fire. *Everything was soaking wet and all we could do was lay the pieces on the sand and hope they would dry out. Our rifle companies… were joining us by the sea wall and trying to figure out what to do. I suggested that, if we had any buckets, which we hadn't, we could make sand-castles.*

Pte George Laity, 2nd Devons

Private George Laity, a Barnstaple man and a PIAT gunner with the Devons, remembered: *…it was all confusion and bewilderment. German 88s started pounding the beach. My company was pinned down for some time and it seemed endless.*

Meanwhile, recalled Frank Pearson, *the tide was coming in as well as more and more troops, so the beach got smaller as the numbers on it grew. It seemed to me that the whole of 50th Division was pinned down on this beach and likely to remain so, and then the breakthrough came. A flail tank, one of the 'Funnies', climbed the sea wall and began to flail a path across the minefield. We peered over the wall, holding our breaths, and watched it flail across. Then, to the best of my knowledge and against all that the history books say, most of 231 Brigade and the forward elements of 50th Division followed in the wake of that one flail tank. Perhaps it wasn't like that, but that's how it seemed to me.*

Jig Gold Beach by Julia Pannett

A lane had been cleared through the minefield beyond Les Roquettes, and the Royal Engineers Field Companies were making brave progress in clearing more mines on foot and by hand. The citation for Lieutenant Neil Austin's Military Cross describes how, within 295th Field Company, he *was responsible for reconnoitring the Brigade's route inland for mines, booby traps and similar obstructions. He was the first person to walk along the road from Le Hamel to Asnelles carrying out his task under heavy fire in a manner which inspired all ranks in the vicinity*. Indeed, Colin Thomson of the Sherwood Rangers, trying later to get his troop of Shermans round the bomb crater[16] and through the traffic jam along the road to Le Hamel, provided covering fire for Austin. He never knew his name, but remembered him *as the bravest man I ever saw.*

---

16. The crater was finally filled by three fascines laid by the Sappers' funnies.

The arrival of Pat Chilton's B Company, whose job was to hold Les Roquettes, enabled the other Dorset and Hampshire companies to move on. Supported by a section of anti-tank guns and some three-inch mortars, Chilton established a defensive position to see off an armoured counter-attack.

At last – it was now after 0915 – they could move forward. Tony Mott *made a little plan to get into Asnelles, 10 Platoon giving cover from Les Roquettes while 12, followed by 11, went up a hedgerow, turning right up the slope and making for the wall, near which we knew the enemy post was – and indeed it started to fire at us. The loss of my Company HQ was a blow as it ruled out wireless communication and I had no runner, so I had to be pretty mobile myself.*

12 Platoon came up in savage mood, out for blood, as they had had some casualties. They went in single file up the hedgerow and turned right before anything happened. Then snipers and at least one Spandau opened up on them as they came into view about 150 yards from the wall. Lionel Bawden [commanding 12 Platoon] *was hit early on and killed instantly. Sergeant Smith, the Platoon Sergeant, a tough man, was also hit and wounded.*

This left them rather helpless, so I told Graham Elliott to get 11 Platoon on in any way he could, covering themselves as 10 Platoon's covering fire was by now ineffective. I went back to Charles Williamson [commanding 10 Platoon] *and at this point mortar bombs started pitching among us, though the troops thought they were mines...*

...I found Charles, who was doubtful about getting to Asnelles direct, owing to the minefield, but a flail came and set off a number of mines, which was fun to watch. I think 10 Platoon followed the flail track, but did not get to where I wanted them. Somewhere about then Charles was killed and Sergeant Bisson took over.

Tony Mott had lost two of his three platoon commanders in this tiny action. Only the baby of the Company, Graham Mason Elliott, three days short of his twenty-first birthday, survived. But 10 Platoon remained in good hands. Twenty-nine-year old Clement Bisson was a seasoned Regular soldier whose experience with the 1st Battalion dated back to their days in Palestine before the war.

Bobby Nicoll's C Company moved forward to join the Hampshires' fight in Asnelles. Private David Bushell recalled: *We were told to move off and went up this fairly gentle grassy slope. The guns were firing at us from the buildings further to the right. Walking forward, we came to a village and there were children playing! ...Then these French women started shouting at us because of the shelling.*

Meanwhile, Willie Hayes's D Company set off post haste for Buhot – or Boohoo as the Dorsets were wont to call it – the village just below the Dorsets' first objective, Point 54.

Sergeant Alby Talbot began moving his casualties off the beach. To do so, he and his stretcher-bearers had to cross the minefield and move up the lateral road, which was under heavy mortar fire. He led the way, established a dressing station in a less vulnerable place and began to organise the evacuation of his casualties. He was later awarded a Military Medal for his gallantry on, and in getting off, Gold Beach.

At about this time Major Martin, the Hampshires' Second-in-Command, landed and reported to Brigadier Stanier. Making his way along the beach towards Le Hamel to take command of his Battalion, Charles Martin was shot dead by a sniper. He was twenty-seven. His brother John, by now a Squadron Leader with a Distinguished Flying Cross[17], would miss him for the rest of his long life.

It was now 0930 and it had taken two hours' hard work under heavy fire and cost many casualties, but the Sappers – on foot or in armoured vehicles – had cleared two exits from the beach. As Frank Pearson observed at the time, more use would be made of the exit via Les Roquettes, which Tony Mott and Bobby Nicoll had been first to occupy and exploit. But having only two exits, instead of the planned six, would slow down the advance inland; it would be hours before the congestion, on the beach and on the road beyond, cleared.

The late arrival and losses of the Sherwood Rangers' DD tanks had been a major setback, leaving the assault waves of the infantry to fight their battle without armoured support. A handful of the AVREs and flails of the breaching teams had done their gallant best to help, but the enemy 77mm gun at Le Hamel continued to take a heavy toll of their vehicles and crews. The German guns had also sunk or damaged a number of landing craft.

Communication was another problem. Many of the wireless sets had been lost or damaged in the landing and, as David Warren had just realised, communication within the three battalions was unreliable. Jim Bellows, the Hampshires' Signals Sergeant, remembered: *Out of about twenty-two sets on my channel, we could get only two.* This problem extended to communication with other battalions, with Brigade Headquarters and with their supporting artillery and armour. The Gunner forward observation officers mitigated the damage by providing access to their wireless sets, but the infantry's problem communicating with tanks, once they had arrived, was acute. Co-operation relied upon what could be organised between individual tanks and companies or platoons of infantry engaged in the battle. It was piecemeal, haphazard and downright dangerous. If an infantry officer needed to attract the attention of a tank, he would almost certainly also attract the attention of the enemy and would be shot for his pains. Standing

---

17. The Distinguished Flying Cross (DFC) is the RAF's equivalent of the Military Cross.

on a tank in view of the enemy was suicidal. Standing beside one trying to communicate through a head set thrown out by the tank commander was nearly as dangerous and nigh on impossible amid the din of battle. Small wonder that, in the first few hours following the landings, the tanks and infantry were largely fighting separate battles.

Accidentally landing too far east had been a mixed blessing. In the main, those who, like A Company of the 1st Hampshires, had landed furthest west, had suffered the most casualties. But B Company of the Dorsets, who had landed farthest east, had hit a strongpoint, incurred casualties and then been severely delayed in reaching their objective at Les Roquettes.

In the 120 minutes since they had landed, the Hampshires had lost their Commanding Officer twice wounded and their Second-in-Command killed. A Company's commander had been killed and all three of his platoon commanders wounded. As they were located, any survivors from A Company were subsumed within C. B Company had lost two platoon commanders killed and was now fighting in Asnelles in a brave attempt to support the two remaining platoons of C Company who were embroiled in a protracted battle in Le Hamel. D Company had bypassed Le Hamel and Asnelles and were heading inland on their way to attack the gun positions between Asnelles and Arromanches.

A Company of the Dorsets had lost their commander, a platoon commander and their Company Sergeant-Major. B Company had lost a platoon commander and their Company Sergeant-Major, and had been delayed by ninety minutes by their doubly unlucky landing. C Company and Support Company had both lost their Company Sergeant-Majors on the beach and C, with one platoon missing, was now fighting in the south of Asnelles. D Company, so far with only a few casualties, was heading inland and A Company, now led by its Second-in-Command, was about to follow.

Knowing that his C Company had been drawn into the fight at Le Hamel and could not be withdrawn, the Devons' Commanding Officer was trying to assemble his other three rifle companies to lead them away from the beach to capture Ryes.

Although progress had been made and casualties overall had been lighter than expected, the execution of the plan was slipping behind schedule. For the operation to succeed, the surviving Hampshires would have to break through at Le Hamel and push on towards Arromanches while the Dorsets and Devons would have to extricate themselves from the beach area and press on at speed to their objectives inland. And the armour and guns would have to get off the beach, shake themselves back into order and set off rapidly behind the infantry to provide the support that was so desperately needed.

Who knew what the enemy had in store for them beyond the beaches? Would they succeed?

CHAPTER FOUR

D-Day: 0930–1200 hours

Enter the Commandos

With blackened faces the men of Lieutenant-Colonel Cecil Phillips's 47 (Royal Marine) Commando had been aboard their LCAs for four and a half hours, awaiting their time to land. As they began their run-in, one landing craft was hit by a German shell. The badly damaged LCA pressed on towards the shore with twelve dead and eleven wounded Marines aboard.

Scheduled to land at 0930 and to head for their objective, Port-en-Bessin, they had been delayed by twenty minutes, by which time the rising tide nearly covered the mines and obstacles. On the beach directly ahead of them, they saw a battle raging and realised that – exceptionally on this stretch of beach – they were landing too far west. They were approaching Le Hamel.

Seeing, as Bobby Nicoll had, that his men were about to be landed in the wrong place, Colonel Phillips ordered all his landing craft to turn as Sub-Lieutenant Bernard Sullivan had done two hours earlier. Sullivan had taken the risk and got away with it; Phillips was unlucky. The landing craft turned to port and began to run east along the coast towards Les Roquettes. In doing so, they turned broadside to the guns ashore and paid a heavy price. Lieutenant Peter Winter, one of his troop commanders, recalled: *the CO did something he shouldn't have and turned parallel to the coast to get to our correct landing beach and made a good target for the Germans.* Four more LCAs were holed. They sank with more men killed, drowned or wounded. Among those who died were Phillips's Second-in-Command, thirty-two-year-old Major James Feacey, a married man from near Bray in Berkshire, and nineteen-year-old Marine Robert Wilkinson from Slough. Two bodies – those of thirty-five-year-old Marine Charles Fewtrell and twenty-two-year-old Marine John Smith – were never recovered. They are remembered, respectively, on the Naval Memorials at Plymouth and Portsmouth.

The Commandos' Medical Officer, Captain John Forfar, remembered: *The orders were that incoming craft were not to stop to rescue men in the water as this would delay and disrupt the invasion landing schedules. As a consequence, wounded men would have had to struggle in the water and in their wounded state some drowned. Others were caught in a coastal current which swept them far from the landing beach.*

Corporal Arthur Pymm, 47 (RM) Commando

Nonetheless, some men, including Corporal Arthur Pymm from Melton Mowbray, ignored orders and helped to save some of those who were drowning. The citation for the MM he later received for several acts of gallantry begins: *During the landings on D-Day on the Normandy Beaches, Corporal Pymm's boat struck some underwater object, causing him and several others to be thrown into the sea; he saved one man who was wounded from drowning and, not content with this, he went back into the water and saved two more of his comrades.*

Dropped too far out, Sergeant Donald Gardner swam ashore *about fifty yards, under machine-gun fire and at one point I heard someone say, 'Perhaps we're intruding, this seems to be a private beach.'*

When Lieutenant Peter Winter's landing craft hit a mine, he *was knocked unconscious for a while. When I woke up, I found myself in the water. I had a broken leg and a broken arm and attempted to swim ashore but only ended up going round in circles. A sergeant saw me and, despite the awfulness of the situation, said, 'You won't get anywhere fast like that, Sir. You had better think of something better.' I eventually made it ashore, where my MOA* [Marine Officer's Assistant – batman], *Marine Woodgate, met me on the beach with the words, 'I thought you'd like a cup of tea, Sir?' I can tell you that no cup of* tea ever tasted better. The doctor could do little for us wounded, as he had few orderlies and they had lost all their medical equipment when their landing craft was sunk. It took me three days to reach hospital in England.

Landing with the Commandos was their Royal Artillery Forward Observation Officer (Bombardment), Major Marsh, whose job would be directing naval fire to support their operations. Marsh landed safely but half of his Gunner party were in another craft, which hit a mine. They swam ashore, losing their personal equipment but managing to save their precious wireless set.

Having lost most of their equipment, the Commandos were now scattered along the best part of a mile of crowded beach, which was still under machine gun, mortar and shell fire. The unit had embarked 420 strong. Landing cost them seventy-six (eighteen per cent) casualties, twenty-two of them (five per cent) fatal. Half of the survivors had lost their weapons and equipment. Such was the damage wrought by mines and shells that only two of their fourteen landing craft returned to their ships.

Marine John Wetjen of Q Troop remembered: *As far as it could be ascertained, A Troop had lost most of its weapons; Q and Y Troops had lost a complete craft. Heavy Weapons* [the Commandos' mortars and Vickers machine guns] *had lost one heavy machine gun and one 3-inch mortar and most of their mortar bombs and Bangalores, also the wireless sets were doubtful starters...*

This was a recurring problem throughout the morning's landings: damaged or lost equipment and weapons forced many units to fight their first battles ill-equipped, ill-armed or unable to communicate and therefore at a considerable disadvantage.

Brigadier Sir Alex Stanier later recalled the Commandos' *terribly rough landing* and how *none of their wirelesses would work. How their Commanding Officer collected them, I don't know. He must have had a megaphone and shouted; sent people hither and thither; perhaps even put a flag up. I don't know. I saw the Commanding Officer for five minutes while they were assembling just behind the sand dunes and him worrying about where his men had gone and getting his wirelesses and things and trying to get a move on. They were very independent, if I may say so. They knew what to do and they were quite happy to get on with it.*

The beginning of the citation for Major Patrick Donnell's Croix de Guerre suggests that he played a major part in assembling the scattered Marines. *When 47 (RM) Commando landed near Le Hamel in Normandy on the morning of 6th June 1944 the Commanding Officer became separated from his unit. Major Donnell the Second-in-Command collected the very disorganised unit.*

Colonel Phillips later recalled that the plan on landing had been for his Marines to move west along the small road and to rendezvous at the church in Le Hamel but, *when the leading elements reached a point just short of the road inland to Les Roquettes, it became obvious that Le Hamel was in enemy hands and that 231 Brigade were heavily involved in trying to clear it.* Sir Alex Stanier suggested that instead the Commandos took a detour via Les Roquettes before resuming their planned route west toward La Rosière and Port-en-Bessin.

The Devons leave the beach

By 1000, Pat Chilton's Company of Dorsets were firmly ensconced at Les Roquettes, together with their supporting anti-tank guns, ready to repel an armoured German counter-attack. But no such attack would materialise. D-Day had caught the Germans napping. Rommel was in Germany celebrating his wife's birthday. The elaborate pre-D-Day Allied deception plans had worked: he and his commanders had no inkling of when the invasion would come or where. Prompted by the British airborne landings on the east of the beach-head, the 21st Panzer Division had set off to counter-attack them. A brigade-sized battle-group, which Allied intelligence had not known about and which might otherwise have been employed to counter-attack 231 and 69 Brigades' landings on Gold Beach, had been sent to reinforce the defences behind Omaha. The Germans therefore had no immediately available force – and certainly no tanks – with which to repel the landings near Arromanches. If the leading units of 50th Division could successfully break through the existing defenders, they would face no immediate major counter-attacks from beyond. But the British troops could not know that, and some of the German defenders, especially at Le Hamel, still had plenty of fight in them.

Meanwhile, Lieutenant-Colonel Nevill of the 2nd Devons had found and collected three of his missing companies; the fourth – *Bubbles* Duke's C Company – were too heavily committed with the Hampshires in Le Hamel to be withdrawn. The others, Nevill recalled, *left the beaches in single file, along a narrow footpath the sides of which were supposed to be mined, in the following order: A Company followed by Advanced Battalion HQ, D Company and B Company. We suffered casualties from intermittent heavy mortar fire and snipers. As we got nearer to the hill on our left we expected any moment that the enemy would open fire.*

Frank Pearson, leading the Devons' Assault Pioneers, remembered: *On the other side of the minefield it was very quiet, with no sign of friend or foe. There were some of our tanks around and we hurried to catch up with our rifle companies, coming to a French hamlet, which I suppose was Asnelles.*

There was now fierce fighting in Asnelles, where Tony Mott's Hampshires and Bobby Nicoll's Dorsets were attacking north and south. Instead of following the original plan and assembling there, Nevill decided to skirt the village, going further south before turning west in open country to find La Gronde Ruisseau south of the town.

Suddenly the Devons were attacked head-on from the south by two companies of the 1st Battalion of the German 916th Grenadier Regiment. Private Powis remembered that: *Enemy machine guns were now firing along the road from our right-hand side when we reached it, so we quickly returned fire that way as well as to the front, where we could see the Germans running towards us. Our numerically decreased company entered the field to our front to take cover from us and get to grips with the Germans in hand-to-hand fighting... We were able to see that they were engaged in close combat with grenades, small arms and bayonets. I cannot be sure how far we went up the road inland before stopping for the* IO [Intelligence Officer – Captain Bill Wood] *to discuss the situation with the Battalion CO, who had moved up to the rear of B Company. This Company was diminishing in numbers and we had to be constantly ready for a German breakthrough. The CO explained that he knew A Company were engaging the enemy too far to the right, thus opening a gap between them and B Company.*

The IO told me to take the bicycle and go back to the Old Coast Road and turn left to where A Company was believed to be. I was to find the Company Commander and tell him to disengage and move back to the left.

Cosmo Nevill had realised that A Company was being drawn to the west, towards the fighting in Le Hamel, and he needed urgently to get them to disengage and head south. David Powis began his dangerous commission and survived a hazardous ride along the road, which was under fire. *I was forced to dismount and lift the bicycle over a large mound of lifeless German bodies, strewn across the road...*

It must have been about 200 yards along the road ... that I found myself among familiar Malta veterans of A Company. None of them could tell me where their Commanding Officer [Company Commander Franc Sadleir] *might be but they took me to their Platoon Officer... The officer carefully copied all my entries onto his own map, thanked me for the information and said that he was going forward and would pass on the details. ...he explained to me that one reason A Company had been forced to move to the right was because they had learned that 1st Hampshires had been badly cut up and lost a lot of men, including most of their senior ranks.*

Through the hedge on the way back, I spotted German infantry moving rapidly towards the coast road and had to get down to avoid being seen by them. There were men of my Battalion moving inland to the left. I informed those nearest to me about the advancing Germans but they were fully engaged with the Germans to the front of them.

Sustaining comparatively few casualties themselves, the 2nd Devons successfully repelled the counter-attack, killing and wounding a great many German Grenadiers.

The Commandos leave the beach and the Devons head for Ryes

It took the Commandos nearly two hours after their disastrous landing to assemble and sort themselves out. Acting on Sir Alex Stanier's advice, Colonel Phillips ordered them to leave the beach via Les Roquettes. Lance-Corporal Frank Wright of X Troop later described their arrival there.

We came to a halt at the top of the sloping beach where there was a low cliff, about five feet in height. On top of it was a field of lank grass. A well-worn path ran along the cliff edge and behind that a barbed wire fence with the signs that soon became familiar: ACHTUNG MINEN and the skull and crossbones. It took only a second to see this, then it was a case of heads well down.

The enemy fire continued, we scooped out hollows in the sandy cliff and pressed ourselves into them. Something told me we were to have a long wait. Le Hamel was to our right, hidden by a smoky haze. There was a strong smell of cordite mixed with, astonishingly, Gauloise cigarette smoke.

We waited, and waited, more landing craft arrived, men and tanks moved along the beach towards Le Hamel. The expression on the faces of the officers, who rounded up their charges before leading them away, spoke volumes. We waited, occasional shellfire, constant machine gunning – finally someone noticed signs of activity in the minefield. Sure enough, there were two Sappers patiently swinging their mine-detectors to and fro, to and fro – completely oblivious to everything that was going on around them.

The minefield was more than one hundred yards across. The whole operation took some time but finally we were moving – with, I may say, mixed feelings. We made our way onto the minefield, keeping carefully within the tapes. Then, half-way across, guess what? A traffic jam! We lay down alongside the tapes while a squadron of Sherman tanks edged their way past. Then on again.

Reduced to 340 men and without many of their weapons and much of their equipment, the Commandos began their twelve-mile march through enemy-held territory.

Further delayed by the German counter-attack, the 2nd Devons were pushing south towards Ryes when they encountered the Commandos heading for La Rosière. Private Powis remembered them as *drenched and dripping …they were almost completely unarmed and looked a very sad sight. Having armed themselves with what they could from dead soldiers, they welcomed anything we could spare in the way of armaments and ammunition. I gave them one of my two fifty-round bandoliers of ammunition, a grenade and two magazines for the Bren gun.* The Commandos went on their way, having furnished *themselves with small arms and ammunition from the German and British soldiers now lying dead there. They filtered through the leading Devon Company, engaging the Germans with their captured and borrowed weapons.*

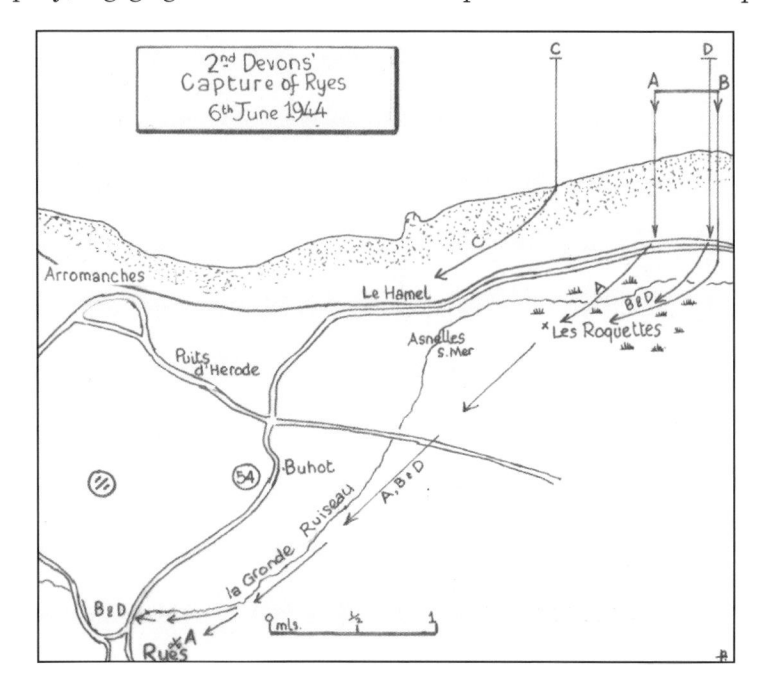

2nd Devons' Capture of Ryes 6th June 1944

Leading a platoon in B Company of the Devons was David Holdsworth, who *remembered that one of the physical features which would help me to find the correct way inland was La Grande Rivière* [sic]. *But there was no sign of anything that looked remotely like a Grande Rivière. However, in chivvying my lot to get on, serious contemplation of the whereabouts of what sounded like a fairly big river was not possible.*

We crossed some open countryside. Other units were doing the same thing, so I was satisfied that, at least, we were doing what was expected of us, and that we were going in the right direction. Things were now remarkably peaceful. The noise of the beach-head had been left behind. If this was war, then it wasn't too bad at all.

A whistle and an explosion reminded us that war was not a healthy game. As one man we disappeared flat on our faces into the long grass. Other shells followed and, when the bombardment was over, I got up. So did the rest of my platoon – all thirty of them.

'Yur yewmit!' shouted my batman. He, at least, was a Devonian.

I looked where he pointed.

He was only partly right. Bits of metal were certainly sticking out of the pouches on my shoulder straps and from the container which held my maps. Otherwise I was unhurt.

We went on.

In a ditch in a small copse ahead of me I saw my Commanding Officer bending over a Company Commander who had been hit rather badly. My CO waved me on with the news that my own Company Commander was a casualty as well.

This was the first David Holdsworth had heard of Mike Howard having been injured landing on the beach. Mike Holdsworth, David's brother, now replaced Howard in command of B Company. The other company commander (over whom Colonel Nevill was stooping) was John Parlby, who had been badly wounded in the leg by a mortar bomb. Company Sergeant-Major Reg Bollam, one of the 2nd Devons' stalwarts who had won an MBE on Malta and a DCM on Sicily, was stunned by one of the explosions but characteristically chose to press on. The advance continued.

CSM Reg Bollam MBE DCM, 2nd Devons

David Holdsworth suddenly realised where they were. *As he waved me on, my CO moved his right foot. Where it had been was now a puddle of dirty brown water. He was standing in the middle of La Grande Rivière.*

Many others, at the time and since, have made the same error. As we have seen, *La Grande Rivière* was in fact *La Gronde Ruisseau* – a small stream. Their Brigade Commander, Sir Alex Stanier, watched the Devons' progress through his binoculars. *I could see the Devons going up this brook... it was only a stream about as wide as a pocket handkerchief, toward Ryes. It had a certain number of willow trees along it and there was green corn, wheat, which of course gave quite a lot of cover again to the German snipers as they were withdrawing. It wasn't the number of bullets being fired, it was the odd* bullet that killed an odd man and it all adds up, particularly officers, because these blinking snipers could see the leaders moving about.

La Gronde Ruisseau (Simon Trew)

The Devons' objective, the village of Ryes, was now about two miles away and their CO, Cosmo Nevill, recalled that *we began to think that we were through the enemy crust and that we should have little difficulty in seizing Ryes.*

The Hampshires and Dorsets fight in Asnelles

At about this time Sir Alex Stanier decided he would take a look at Le Hamel himself. Accompanied by two Gunner officers and Captain Wheaton and Corporal Richards, both of the Royal Corps of Signals, he made his way westwards from Les Roquettes. Stanier described crawling *up a lane to the outskirts of Le Hamel*, where he found the Hampshires *badly held up by enemy pill boxes and 88mm guns further inland*. Corporal *Taffy* Richards, accompanying him, recalled passing *the enemy pillbox with a dead German sitting outside it on guard. The pillbox had* [received] *a near miss from a shell or rocket, but was not badly damaged. Many of our infantry had paid the extreme penalty along that road. They had all been covered by gas capes or ground sheets. A few wounded were being brought back on stretchers to the beaches. Our progress was not very rapid because we walked half crouched to be below the level of the banks on either side of the road. We did not know how thoroughly the adjoining fields had been cleared of snipers and we were not taking chances. Our progress was slow because of other transport, tanks and infantry on the road.*

Dead German by strongpoint on the beach (Geoff Hebden)

While the survivors of Tony Mott's B Company of the Hampshires were fighting a street battle in the north of Asnelles, Bobby Nicoll's C Company of the Dorsets were doing the same in the south of the village. Nicoll had still not found his missing 14 Platoon. Corporal Sam Thompson's section of 13 Platoon had led the Company's way off the beach and into the town. Corporal Vic Carter, a pre-war Territorial from Walworth, was leading a section in 15 Platoon. Although still only twenty-five, he probably had more battle experience than anyone else in the Brigade. He had fought with the Queen's in France in 1940 and in North Africa before joining the Dorsets and fighting with them in Sicily and Italy. Wounded in the advance from Les Roquettes, he had insisted on staying with his section as they approached Asnelles.

Asnelles was more strongly defended than they had been led to expect. The southern part of the village was held by a German platoon, who put up fierce resistance. Heavy machine gun fire came from some of the houses and 15 Platoon were held up. Private Joe Roland remembered: *our task was difficult because our mortars and guns were not yet ashore. We had what we called a firefight to cover other platoons into the village, further to the left. Once they were in, the enemy stopped firing at us and we were able to advance into the village.* Both the Platoon Commander, Lieutenant John Hamilton, and Vic Carter provided strong leadership in this action but, finally, it was Colin Windebank's 13 Platoon who won the day. Attacking from the south, they stormed the position, killing six Germans and capturing ten more. Joe Roland recalled: *When we were in the Jerries started to surrender as we came in behind them.*

Nicoll's Company spent sixty to ninety minutes clearing this part of Asnelles before finally disengaging and heading for Buhot and Point 54.

Sam Thompson's section was still leading and the wounded Vic Carter remained at the head of his own section as they left Asnelles behind them and headed into the hilly country beyond.

In the northern part of Asnelles, Mott's Company of Hampshires had already suffered heavy casualties. Two of the three platoon commanders had been killed. The redoubtable Sergeant Clement Bisson now led 10 Platoon, young Graham Elliott 11 Platoon and Lance-Sergeant Collins 12 Platoon.

By mid-morning, a handful of Sherwood Rangers' tanks, including Colin Thomson's troop from C Squadron, had got off the beach, made their dangerous way through the jammed traffic on the heavily shelled lateral road and found their way into Asnelles.

Mott *went up to 11 Platoon and found a Sherman near the wall and Graham talking to it and persuading it to have a go at the Boche, which it did not approve of as it knew of the anti-tank gun. But it stood and fired shells effectively into the wall and let off a stream of tracer bullets, so I told Graham to take his men into the orchard. We could see one of the Boche in a trench taking shots at us, but the troops were slow at answering. They were reluctant to follow Graham, who dashed forward into a crater and, as no one went with him, I did. We went to near a gap in the corner of the wall, with bullets very close to us from the tank, and crept into the gap, I with a 69 grenade in my hand. I saw two Boche in a trench so threw the grenade, but it did not go off. Back came a stick grenade, which did explode, and I was in great danger, as Graham bravely hurled his fifteen stone on top of me to save me. He did not get hurt. I lay by the wall, feeling very exposed, while Graham went back to the tank and called up some of his men, and Sergeant Bisson also came with some of 10 Platoon. I peered round the wall again and saw no enemy. There was an underground system of trenches and presumably the Boche thought that they would not last much longer near us.*

We went cautiously along the orchard wall, looking through gaps to try to locate our opponents, which was chiefly done by them shooting at us. Bisson was outstanding, shooting through gaps and rallying his men. He got a bullet through his helmet which nicked his skull, but carried on. At one time I saw two Boche turn through a gap, so fired single shots at them, and next day found two corpses with bullets through their heads – only twenty yards' range. At any rate my Sten was working. At this time we saw a woman coming out of a house, carrying a tray and disappearing into a shelter. The troops suspected she was supplying the enemy, but I was right in thinking that she lived in the house and was bringing in the mid-morning meal.

... I took my men along to where the wall ended and we came into the main street of Asnelles without seeing anyone. I was about to mount an attack on the position from there when I saw David Warren and some of Battalion HQ. He said that the CO had been wounded and Charles Martin killed, and that he

had been told to take over command. He wanted me to take a patrol down into Le Hamel and see if I could find A Company, of whom there was no news. I collected Graham and several men and we started down the road to Le Hamel, some quarter of a mile away. One of our tanks came down the road towards us. Suddenly I felt a blast and heard a loud crack and splinters came off the road into my face. I didn't know what it was, possibly another mine or stray shell, until I saw that a tank near me had been hit. Then came another blast and another, and it dawned on me that if nothing else there was an anti-tank gun in our way. We turned and began to look for another way to Le Hamel.

David Warren also remembered the Sherman, which was from B Squadron of the Sherwood Rangers, because it burst into flames outside his newly established headquarters. *One member of the crew managed to get out and reported that the gun was loaded and that the flames might fire the shell at any moment. This was most disconcerting as it pointed directly at Battalion Headquarters. So far as is known, however, the gun never went off, but the road into Le Hamel was completely blocked.*

The Sherman was almost certainly from John Hanson-Lawson's B Squadron. Standing beside it when it was knocked out, Lieutenant Graham Mason Elliott and Sergeant Rymer, his Platoon Sergeant, had both been wounded. Graham Elliott's wounds were horrific but, with most of his jaw blown off, he continued to lead his platoon until he collapsed. Private John Chalk, a stretcher-bearer in D Company, later walked with him to the church at Asnelles, where Lance-Corporal Roy Butt of B Company had established an aid post before the Hampshires' Medical Officer had arrived. Graham Elliott was unable to speak and Chalk, who had found him beside a knocked out tank, thought he was a tank officer. Here, Sergeant Jim Bellows also encountered him. *The MO couldn't do much for him, only pump him full of morphine and prop him up to stop the blood choking him.*

David Warren now ordered Mott and his patrol to go further west. Having lost all three of his platoon commanders and a great many men, Tony Mott realised *how small an army I had... I got round to the edge of Le Hamel and found King of C Company, who was mopping up some snipers and had some Devons with him but, as he seemed all right, I pushed on to Le Hamel West. It surprised me to see how much of Le Hamel was still standing after the bombardment.*

Lieutenant Alan King of C Company had picked up his Devons a little earlier. Approaching Le Hamel from the east, he had just ordered the nine survivors of his platoon to attack a German position when he spotted some Devons sheltering either side of the road. These were some of C Company, and they had just lost their much-loved young Company Commander *Bubbles* Duke.

Cpl Jock Russell MM, C Company, 2nd Devons

Corporal Jock Russell, who had won a Military Medal as a stretcher-bearer at Vizzini on Sicily in July 1943, was now leading a rifle section in 14 Platoon. He remembered: *We were held up by a strong point, which had us nailed down. Every move was stopped by machine gun fire. Two of my section had already gone down and, although we managed to get within twenty or thirty yards, there was little we could do with small arms. There was a sniper too. At that point Major Duke ran through the fire and into the ditch that held me and three or four others, and asked what was holding us up. I told him and, holding his binoculars, he immediately crawled out of the ditch to see for himself. I shouted, twice, to him to get down knowing the sniper would be watching, but it was too late. A bullet hit him in the head... he was killed instantly. C Company lost some good men at Le Hamel and the most tragic was Major Duke.*

Back in England someone would now face the horrific task of telling seventeen-year-old Jane Mawdesley that she had lost her fiancé.

Firing Sten guns and rifles from the hip, King's Hampshires and Devons drove the Germans from their position, killing and wounding fifteen of them. They then cleared a building of enemy snipers. Alan King later received a Military Cross for this exploit. It must have been after this that he encountered Tony Mott in Le Hamel.

Because the Hampshires were so close to their enemy and had no wireless contact with the ships, the Royal Navy were unable to provide gunnery support for fear of killing their own soldiers. But, despite the danger, Lieutenant-Colonel Robert Phayre of the Essex Yeomanry was on the spot, commanding his own guns together with some from the 90th Field Regiment. According to the citation for his DSO, he *repeatedly moved up among the leading infantry with total disregard of heavy enemy fire, to organise artillery support and to ensure that no opportunities for effective artillery action were lost.* It was indeed a dangerous place to be. Late that morning, twenty-two-year-old Lieutenant Nigel Calkin of the 90th Field Regiment had been killed by a sniper while fetching Colonel Hardie's tank from Le Hamel.

A veteran of Sicily and Italy, Private Dennis Hawes was a medical orderly with the 1st Hampshires. Years later, he would *vaguely remember dressing many ghastly wounds as I made my way along the beach, experiencing a terrible sense of helplessness.*

CHAPTER FIVE

D-Day: 1200–1500 hours

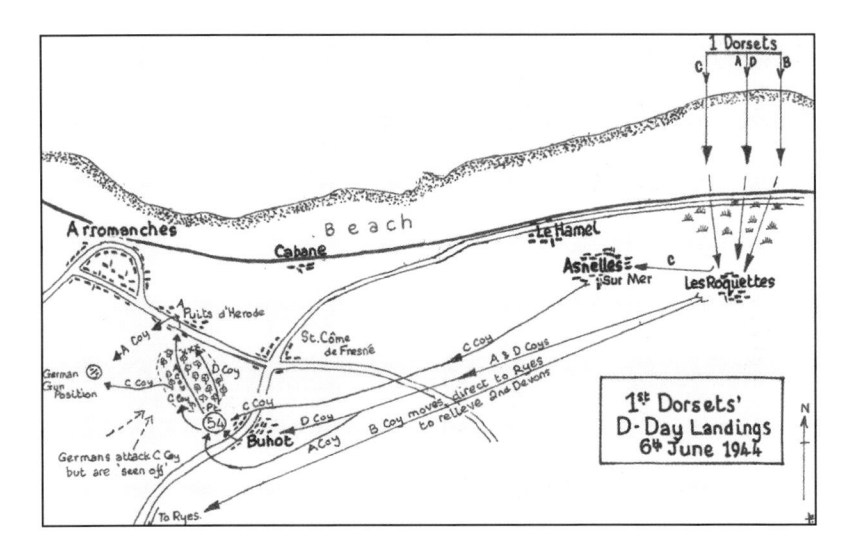

The Dorsets take Buhot and Point 54

At about 1000, as Willie Hayes's D Company of the 1st Dorsets had skirted Asnelles and begun their march for Buhot, they had been shelled and mortared from the high ground behind them to the east, near Meauvaines. Major Hayes was disappointed to hear that he would not be able to call on support from the guns of the Royal Navy. Instead, he would be accompanied by Captain Neville Bishop and his observation party from the 90th Field Regiment. Bishop's signallers, Lance-Bombardier Blanchard and Gunner Leopold, were killed by a shell. Both in their mid-twenties, Ken Blanchard was from Cleethorpes and Fred Leopold from Walthamstow. Bishop's wireless set was also put out of action but Colonel Ian Hardie, his Commanding Officer, lent him one of his signallers and another set. The Signaller was almost certainly twenty-five-year-old Lance-Corporal *Danny* Bowstead from Battersea, a pre-war Territorial and a veteran of Iraq, Tunisia and Sicily.

L/Cpl Denis Bowstead, Royal Corps of Signals

Willie Hayes's Second-in-Command, Lieutenant Thomas, was one of several Dorsets wounded as they pressed inland. Meanwhile, by word and courageous example, D Company's Sergeant-Major, Nick O'Connell, kept his men moving forward under considerable fire.

CSM Nick O'Connell, D Company, 1st Dorsets

An hour or so later, having finally broken free from Asnelles, Bobby Nicoll's C Company had taken the same route, and spent the late morning working their way west through the open country leading to the village of Buhot. Corporal Sam Thompson's section led the advance, throughout which the Germans maintained Spandau, mortar and 88mm fire on the Dorsets. West of the village the ground rose towards their next objective:

a German position near the top of Point 54, which was the first of several hills between here and the coast astride Arromanches.

On reaching Buhot, Hayes and his men went straight into the village itself, where they surprised an entire company of German pioneers and their transport, capturing the lot. In his lucid account of the landings on Gold Beach, Simon Trew suggests that D Company's prisoners may have been from the 59th Engineering Construction Battalion, who had a large number of troops in this area.

Nicoll and C Company arrived, skirted north of the village and headed for Point 54. Here, supported by Hayes's D Company, C attacked up the hill. As 15 Platoon ran up the open field towards the top of the hill, heavy fire opened from the small wood just below the summit. It was not Bobby Nicoll's lucky day. Just as the position he had attacked at Asnelles had been heavily reinforced, so had the German force defending Point 54. Lieutenant Hamilton and his Platoon Sergeant fell wounded, and Corporal Vic Carter, wounded even before the battle in Asnelles, took over the Platoon.

Seeing what had happened to 15 Platoon, Sam Thompson glanced to his left and spotted a tiny sunken lane running up the hill beside the open field. Ordering his section to follow, he raced up the lane, attacked the German positions from the rear and destroyed them one by one, killing, wounding or capturing their occupants. The citation for his Distinguished Conduct Medal reads: *His leadership in the face of heavy and accurate machine gun fire was an inspiration to all; he had no thought of danger and was the first into each successive enemy position.* The rest of 13 Platoon then cleared the positions on the top of the hill.

Sam Thompson's lane – the German positions were further up and to the right (Ken Chivers)

Private David Bushell remembered: *We went into this orchard and we were fired upon suddenly, and a nearby corporal fell shot across the head. We carried on through this orchard and cleared the Germans out. One of George Davey's friends[18] was killed by a booby trap in the orchard. When we returned fire each time, we moved forward, and the Germans sort of disappeared.*

Lieutenant Greenaway's troop of Shermans from the Sherwood Rangers supported this attack and, as the citation for Ian Greenaway's MC describes, *enabled the infantry to clear the position of enemy at the point of the bayonet.*

The top of Point 54 (Ken Chivers)

By 1400 hours Point 54 was secured. Seven Germans had been killed and two officers and fifteen other ranks captured. For his bravery and leadership from the beach, through Asnelles and to the capture of Point 54, Bobby Nicoll was awarded a Military Cross. Corporal Vic Carter, who had played a prominent part in two battles despite having been wounded leaving the beach, received a Military Medal.

---

18. George Davey was a long-serving pre-war Regular, who had befriended the young Private Bushell.

Cpl Victor Carter, C Company, 1st Dorsets

The battle was going the Dorsets' way and the weather echoed their mood. The morning's clouds had blown away and above them was a clear blue sky. Now C Company, who had led at Asnelles and on Point 54, prepared to support D Company's attack on Puits d'Herode.

The Hampshires capture the guns at Cabane

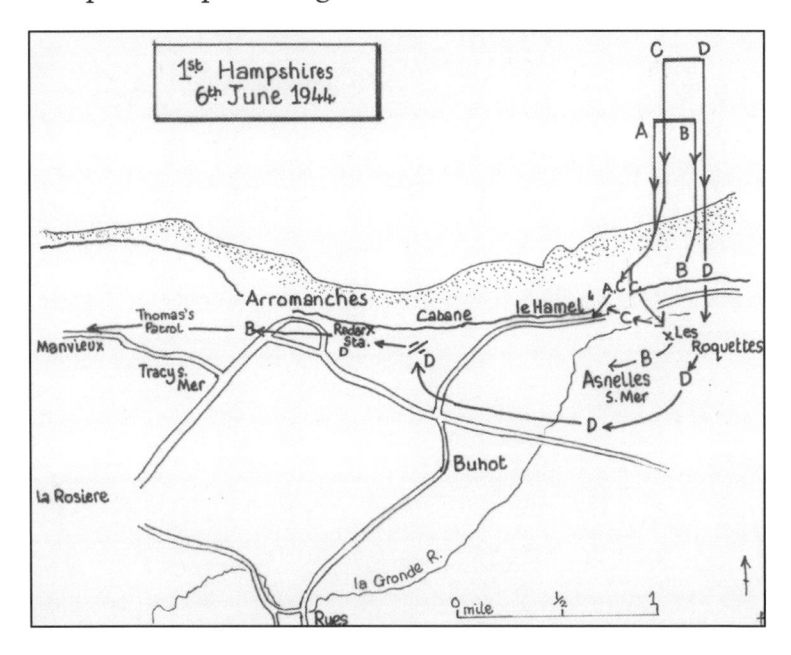

We last glimpsed John Littlejohns and D Company of the Hampshires at about 0930 as they got off the beach and headed inland. One of the Company's stretcher-bearers, Private John Chalk, had become separated from them before they left the beach. Setting out after them, he had found his friend Lance-Corporal Roy Butt establishing a Regimental Aid Post in the church at Asnelles. French nuns and local women were helping him tend the wounded. Chalk made two trips back to the beach to fetch drugs and dressings for them. Then, knowing that his Company were due to attack a position on high ground beyond Le Hamel, he set out at speed to catch them up, taking a lane east of Asnelles.

I was destined to be delayed again because going up this lane I heard two heavy explosions up ahead. Turning a corner I knew I had more work to do. The lane was littered with dead and wounded from a section of the Devons, about eight men, and one of our officers, who had been caught by what I reckon was heavy mortars. The corporal of the section was laying in the road with both legs blown off as close to the body as it was possible to get. As I stood wondering where to start, he asked for a fag. Although I was a non-smoker, I always carried cigarettes for this very purpose. One of the first things most wounded ask for is a fag. I put one in his mouth and lit it for him, and he was talking to me as if this was an everyday happening.

I did what I could for the wounded... and while kneeling among those poor fellows a section of Battalion HQ picked their way through, headed by the Adjutant, Captain Waters, who asked me if I knew where Battalion HQ was.

After they moved through I looked up to see a young girl with a bicycle, just standing there crying and sobbing. I realised she was afraid to move through what must have looked like hell to her, so I picked up her bicycle, took her by the hand and led her through. Goodness knows where she had come from or where she was heading for.

I knew I couldn't leave these poor fellows there without more help, so I decided to go back to the beach again. This time I was luckier, because just coming up from the beach was the Medical Officer of the Devons [Captain John Lloyd]*... I told him about his men and he said I should leave it to him.*

Once again, I set off inland, taking a short cut to where I thought the Company should be. By this time the weather had improved no end and the sun was shining when I came across a couple of Battalion signallers who had set up their radio in front of a cottage and one of them asked me if I would like a drop of char, as they had just brewed up. While enjoying this welcome drink I noticed the roses growing on the walls of the cottage and for some reason thought of the song, 'The Roses of Picardy'.

...someone thought there were some wounded in the cornfield which ran from the back of the cottage to a ridge of high ground. I found one dead sergeant at the top of the field and then made my way through the cornfield, searching. Suddenly I was fired on by a machine gun from the high ground. Fortunately

they missed and I went to ground with the bullets cracking through the corn. I then crawled to the edge of the field and, under cover of a hedge, made my way to the bottom end where I found a group of wounded from my own Company who had been caught by the machine gun while making their way across the field.

Capt David Edkins, D Company, 1st Hampshires

Among this group was the Company's Second-in-Command [Captain Edkins], *whose arm was shattered.* [A mortar bomb had almost severed David Edkins's left arm and damaged his back. Although his arm was saved and he recovered from both wounds, this was the end of his soldiering.] *Also in the group was a young chap wounded in the head, the bullet entering his mouth and lodging in the skull somewhere at the back of his eyes. His face was swelling badly and I really didn't have a lot of hope for him. (Months later I met him again in England and he was all right, apart from losing one eye.)*

After doing what I could for this group, I had to get a message back to Battalion HQ about them because, although fighting was going on all around, it was quiet in the corner of the field and it would be some time before they were found. So I trekked back to the cottage to get a message sent, then went back to the wounded to assure them that help was on its way. Then I continued on my way to catch up with the rest of the Company.

It was more than three hours since Littlejohns's Company had slipped away from Les Roquettes to capture the two German guns – an 88mm and a 75mm – on the cliffs at Cabane. Since then, they had skirted Asnelles to the south before turning west and climbing the ridge towards Arromanches.

Private Sam Curton remembered their difficult advance. *We had been under fire all the way from the beach but as we got close to the ridge we could see the battery behind the church. There was plenty of chalky white soil, so it wasn't difficult to spot. This was the first time, since the beach, that I felt I was the Jerry's personal target. Major Littlejohns led us on a route that avoided the fire from the guns, but the Spandaus were bad enough.*

As they approached Cabane, D Company were joined by five Shermans from John Hanson-Lawson's B Squadron of the Sherwood Rangers. Their arrival was particularly welcome because, as the Hampshires neared the German positions, they came under fire from the enemy guns at Puits d'Herode. They now reached their forming-up position inland of the two guns overlooking the sea. Sited high on a cliff, the guns had a commanding view north and east along the beach at Le Hamel, where, despite having been shelled earlier in the day, they had maintained fire on the beaches until now.

View of Gold Beach from gun position at Cabane (James Porter)

The Hampshires and the five tanks were in position. As D Company launched their attack, they came under heavy fire, which increased in intensity, making forward movement almost impossible. John Littlejohns personally led the Company forward and both gun positions were captured with thirty prisoners and relatively few casualties. Leading one of the forward rifle sections was twenty-seven-year-old Lance-Corporal Leslie Webb, who repeatedly exposed himself to heavy fire in order to move his men forward. He was seriously wounded braving the enemy fire once again to go and get orders from his Platoon Commander, but his Section rushed the German positions and captured their objective.

Sam Curton recalled: *The tanks moved ahead and around us, shooting up the battery. When we got in the wire, the Jerries were quick to surrender: most were pretty bomb-happy and a sorry sight.*

Captain Peter Johnson, a Royal Army Medical Corps officer whose job was to establish a dressing station on Jig Green Beach, had been severely delayed landing. He thus found himself just off the coast when John Littlejohns and his men attacked Cabane. *Borrowing the Skipper's glasses, I could see the battle going on. Then we saw a tank creep round the shoulder of the hill, and two quick rounds into each of the embrasures and all was over. The infantry swarmed over the hill, and in we went, watched more tanks skirting another hill, and dashing over the skyline.*

From the newly captured guns' observation position on the cliff, the Hampshires could see the field of fire the guns had enjoyed – eastwards along Gold Beach from Le Hamel to beyond where the Dorsets had landed in Jig Red sector. In his scholarly examination, *The D-Day Landing on Gold Beach*, Doctor Andrew Holborn describes these guns as *two of the most effective on D-Day, firing between them over 150 rounds*. Although heavily bombed from the air and bombarded from the sea, both had remained active throughout the morning.

John Littlejohns sent a message via the Essex Yeomanry's wireless to tell David Warren that the guns at Cabane had been silenced. Later, he and Lance-Corporal Webb would be decorated for their bravery in this action: Littlejohns with the MC and Webb with the MM. But sadly Leslie Webb's award came too late. Evacuated to hospital in England, he died of his wounds on 14th June and was buried near his parents' home in Portsmouth.

The Dorsets attack Puits d'Herode

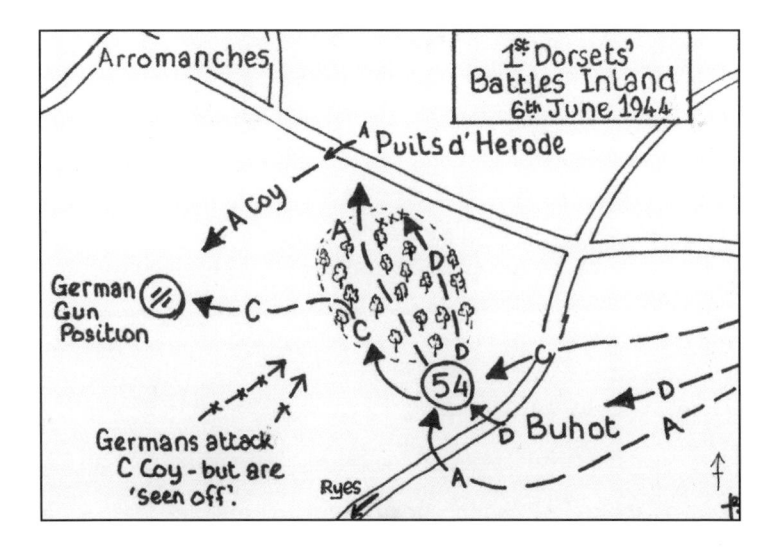

By now, eight tanks of Stephen Mitchell's C Squadron of the Sherwood Rangers had caught up with the Dorsets, who were preparing to attack the German position at Puits d'Herode. Colonel Norie had joined them and ordered Nicoll's C Company to provide supporting fire for an attack by Hayes's D Company. The Vickers guns of Lieutenant Leslie Kershaw's 11 Platoon of the 2nd Cheshires also lent their support, firing from the recently captured Point 54. Willie Hayes would also have support from Mitchell's Shermans and, directed by Captain Bishop who was up with D Company, the 25-pounders of his 90th Field Regiment firing from the ridge above Meauvaines. Held by a unit of *Ost Truppen*, the ridge had fallen easily to the 6th Green Howards, who were advancing inland from La Rivière. Bishop's Regiment were not, however, having an easy time near Meauvaines, which early that afternoon had been shelled by German 88s. Bombardier Stephen Prince, Lance-Bombardier Leonard Gates and Gunner Alfred Wyatt had been killed and three other experienced NCOs wounded.

Towards Puits d'Herode from Point 54, showing the wood D Company had to cross (Ken Chivers)

Willie Hayes remembered ...*my commanding officer said 'Willie, you see your objective. Here is your squadron of tanks rumbling along, so get on with it – I will watch and help if needed.'*

...*Our objective was a German position on high ground on the far side of a cornfield. So we set off in correct School of Infantry formation through the corn. Platoon of infantry with troop of tanks, platoon of infantry with troop of tanks, company headquarters and squadron headquarters, reserve platoon with troop of tanks. All fine and Aldershot to a tee! I was chatting away with the squadron-leader* [Stephen Mitchell], *who of course had his turret open. Suddenly the naughty Germans opened fire on us with 88mm anti-tank guns and machine guns. All turrets of the tanks closed at once and they were firing back and moving all over the place to present a difficult target. It was like having sixteen very cross and charging elephants in our midst. My soldiers were down in the corn, and I was afraid that they would get run over. Again we broke all the military school teaching. There was a lone tree on our left flank, obvious to see and a good target. However, I went round shouting to each soldier, the noise was terrific, to get to the lone tree. When about forty of my soldiers were there, I did not count them, off we went to take the German position from the right rear. Never did we attack again with tanks like that.*

Advancing across the open fields, Lieutenant Joe Bradbury, a Hampshire officer leading 16 Platoon, and Lieutenant *Bomber* Lancaster, commanding 18 Platoon, were killed together with Lancaster's Platoon Sergeant.[19] *Speedy* Bredin tells us that Private Harvey of 16 Platoon *sacrificed himself while carrying an important message to his platoon commander* but, as no Private Harvey appears in the list of Dorsets who died, we must assume that he was wounded and survived. Despite the fierce opposition, 18 Platoon had captured a mortar position, a Spandau position and an anti-tank gun. Now the gallant Corporal Bill Hawkins took over and led 18 Platoon on. Reaching the edge of the wood, he *went forward on a personal reconnaissance, located the enemy post and returned to his platoon. With great skill he then led his men round the enemy's flank, delivered a sharp attack and destroyed all enemy resistance.*

L/Cpl Joe Miller, D Company, 1st Dorsets

---

19. This was almost certainly 29-year-old Sergeant Arthur Horlick from Birmingham.

When Lieutenant Peter Robjohn of 17 Platoon was wounded, Lance-Corporal Joe Miller and his section of 17 Platoon led the way through the wood to the very edge, but there they were halted. Spandaus precluded anyone crossing the open field beyond.

The attack had failed despite the tank support, and not through any want of effort or courage on the part of the men of D Company or their Commander. At the end of this action Major Hayes was the only remaining officer in his Company: two had been killed, the other two wounded. Willie was later awarded a Military Cross for his courage and determined leadership in this battle, while Bill Hawkins and Joe Miller each received a Military Medal for theirs. That night Private Terry Parker of 18 Platoon would record in his illicit diary: *D-Day. What a day. Just Hell. Too much to write here. Heavy casualties. Taffy was slightly wounded, went back. 18 Pl*[atoon] *killed: 'Bomber'* [Lieutenant Lancaster], *'Spitter'* [Platoon Sergeant], *L/Sgt Abell, Cpl Percy* [Carter], *Ptes Canning, Wood, Bill Scrivens. Many others wounded as well. Only officer left is Company Commander.*

Led by Captain John Royle since Tony Jones had been wounded on the beach, A Company had meanwhile arrived to join C and D Companies. Denis Bounsall, the stretcher-bearer who had won the DCM on Sicily, was with them as they *passed a small wood that was believed clear of the enemy, but we came under fire and several casualties resulted. So we attended to them while A Company dealt with the enemy.*

A new plan was required and Colonel Norie provided one, ordering Royle's Company to attack from a different angle, with an impressive amount of supporting fire from C and D Companies, the guns of the Sherwood Rangers and the 90th Field Regiment, and the Vickers machine guns of the Cheshires.

Capt Bob Tucker MC, C Company, 1st Dorsets

During the attack, the Germans surprised C Company by counter-attacking from their left. Between them, Bobby Nicoll's Second-in-Command, Bob Tucker, and Corporal Sam Thompson ensured that the attack was repelled. They killed six Germans, wounded another two and captured two more. Their decisive action won the day, earning a mention in Despatches for Bob Tucker and contributing to the Distinguished Conduct Medal which Sam Thompson would receive for his bravery throughout D-Day. Both these stalwarts, Tucker and Thompson, had already been decorated for their bravery on Sicily: Tucker with the MC and Thompson with the MM.

Meanwhile A Company's attack went in across open ground from the south west, closely following a bombardment. The ground near the position was pock-marked with shell holes, helping the advancing Dorsets to avoid the mines and find some cover. When their Bangalore torpedoes blasted a way through the wire and minefields, the Dorsets clambered in and began clearing the various German bunkers and trenches. One position held out, fighting fiercely, but was captured thanks to the gallant Sergeant Terry, who had been leading his Platoon since Lieutenant Ellis had been wounded soon after landing. Stunned by the sudden onslaught, the German troops in the other positions surrendered. Royle's Company took forty prisoners. John Royle, who had fought on Sicily and Italy before leading A Company for most of D-Day, was later mentioned in Despatches.

The Dorsets' final objective

Supported by the guns of 90th Field Regiment, A and C Companies now advanced across the ridge to take the Dorsets' final objective for D-Day: the gun position eight hundred yards south west of Puits d'Herode. They had been briefed to expect a sizeable, well-defended position with eight weapon pits, a trench system and thick wire. Both C Company's previous objectives that day – in southern Asnelles and at Point 54 – had proved to be more heavily defended than expected. As he led his Company along the ridge, Bobby Nicoll must have wondered whether this last task might follow the same deadly pattern.

It didn't. In a welcome anti-climax, the leading platoon found the four 155mm guns deserted, a great deal of equipment littered around the gun pits and their crews gone. At considerable cost, the Dorsets' tasks were done. All three German gun positions which had been their D-Day objectives were now in their hands.

They had done very well indeed and some reaped rewards. Colonel Norie was awarded the DSO for his courage and leadership on the beach and his conduct of the battle at Puits d'Herode. They had also won three MCs (*Dick* Whittington, Bobby Nicoll and Willie Hayes), a DCM (Sam Thompson MM) and four MMs (Alby Talbot, Vic Carter, Bill Hawkins and Joe Miller). As we have seen, Lance-Corporal *Danny* Bowstead of the Royal Corps of Signals, attached to the 90th Field Regiment, also received an MM for his bravery that day. His officer, Captain Bishop, won the MC next day, supporting the 6th Durham Light Infantry south of Conde-sur-Seulles, but Neville Bishop would not survive the Normandy campaign. Killed on 12th August, he is buried in Cheux.

In casualties, the Dorsets were luckier than the Hampshires but less fortunate than the Devons. Forty-two of the Dorsets who had landed eight or nine hours before were now dead; ninety-four others were wounded. Fourteen of their forty-one officers were casualties; four of them were dead. A Company had lost three of their five officers, B Company one, C Company two and D Company four. Four out of five of the Battalion's company sergeant-majors had been wounded. But, exceptionally, the Dorsets had achieved every one of their objectives. The 1st Battalion were now firmly established back in France four years and one week after the 2nd Dorsets had embarked for Margate from the pier at Dunkirk after one of the worst British defeats in history.

Dorsets remember. Jig Green Beach, May 2014 (Johannes Koning)

CHAPTER SIX

D-Day: 1500–1630 hours

On the beach

Since early morning Padre Skinner had been tending the wounded. Having seen his fellow Sherwood Rangers set off inland, he had ordered his Sergeant to bring his half-track (a small lorry with front wheels but rear tracks) back to the beach. Positioning it hull down behind a sand dune, Skinner continued ministering to the wounded. In note form, his diary tells the story from the arrival of the half-track.

Start gathering wounded, mostly infantry. More as day went on from further down beach. No news yet of any Beach Dressing Station. Regiment clear now and moving well. By midday concerned to pass on wounded – to whom or what? Saw skipper of large LST waiting for evening tide to float him off. Persuaded him to take more seriously wounded when he left on rising tide. By 1430 hours got forty-three on board – all carried by hand up 'Jacob's Ladder' [a rope ladder] *and down near vertical companionways to crew's quarters. Terribly tiring. Sent radio message requesting our Doctor to examine these wounded if possible before leaving. He came about 1530. Saw them all. OK except one likely to die before reaching England.*

Got brief letter off to Etta [Skinner's wife]. *Skipper promised post it in England. Dr informed me CO wounded – gone Beach Dressing Station on next beach. Called and saw him off on DUKW* [amphibious vehicle] *en route UK. Comfortable. He told me Monty Horley had been killed. Set off after Regiment.*

While Leslie Skinner had been on the beach, 56 Infantry Brigade, delayed by two hours, had landed from about midday and set off towards their assembly area near Buhot. On their way there, the 2nd Essex and 2nd Glosters came under mortar fire.

At about the same time, 288 Battery of the 102nd (Northumbrian Hussars) Anti-Tank Regiment had arrived. Equipped with 6-pounder anti-tank guns and M10 tank destroyers (a 17-pounder gun mounted on a Sherman tank chassis), their role was to provide anti-tank defence for 231 Malta Brigade. But their landing had been severely disrupted. First the ship delivering their Tactical Headquarters hit a mine. Then in the landings they lost four 15-hundredweight lorries, a jeep and a self-propelled gun drowned. Finally one of their M10s had a track blown off by a mine. It was mid-afternoon before they were able to set off after the units they were supposed to be supporting.

The climax at Le Hamel East

Early afternoon found the Hampshires still trying to take Le Hamel. Dick Baines's A Company had ceased to exist and its survivors had been absorbed by C Company. The two remaining companies, B and C, depleted to half their strength and led by Tony Mott and Jimmy Wicks, were separately still engaged in the desperate battle for Le Hamel East. According to the plan, these two companies should by now have been taking the radar station above Arromanches. Instead they were still pinned down south and east of Le Hamel.

We left Tony Mott, after his encounter with Alan King of C Company, going north into Le Hamel in search of the survivors of A Company. He found no sign of them, although he did get closer to the strongpoint A Company had lost so many men attacking from the east. It was in a sanatorium, and Mott led the survivors of 12 Platoon to some higher ground overlooking it. He remembered: *There was a tank, cruising along the edge of an anti-tank ditch and another burning in a field nearby. There was the odd sniping shot, especially at the tank commander as I talked to him. I went back to Bisson* [the Sergeant now leading 10 Platoon] *and told him to make his way forward to the strongpoint, through back gardens and trees.*

Mott reported to David Warren by runner that the enemy strongpoint at Le Hamel East was still very active and that his Company were now holding a crossroads just south of it. Warren ordered him to hold firm and to provide covering fire while Jimmy Wicks's C Company moved inland from the beach, via the widely-used exit at Les Roquettes, to a position on the Asnelles-Le Hamel road. From here C Company would be able to provide fire to support an attack on the strongpoint by Mott's B Company. At this stage, Warren remembered, the *beach and Les Roquettes were being mortared heavily and there was frequent Nebelwerfer* [multi-barrelled mortar] *fire on the feature which I had given as the objective for the composite C Company.*

Down on the beach, Lieutenant Ian Wilson's 73rd Field Company had lost heavily. Two of their five officers – Captain Peter Smith and Lieutenant Donald Lofts – had been killed, together with six NCOs and Sappers. With twelve more wounded, the Company's casualty rate was just under fourteen per cent. Wilson remembered being disconcerted to see the infantry at the head of the beach get up and move *off to the left, away from Le Hamel where the main centre of opposition seemed to be. It left the demolition teams feeling exposed and unprotected on an open beach. It would have been nice to know at the time that the Hampshires were making use of a cleared beach exit on the Dorsets' front to put in a left flanking attack on Le Hamel.*

In fact, Duke's C Company of the Devons, now led by Lieutenant Frank Pease, were still on the beach east of Le Hamel and continued to engage the German positions from there.

According to David Warren, Wicks's Company's began their advance at 1345 hours. *Certain opposition was encountered and the lateral road was not gained until about an hour later. About twelve enemy were taken prisoner during this advance with others killed or wounded.* Although only 200 yards, it was painfully slow and hard-fought. Leading a composite group of Hampshires was Lieutenant John Boys, commander of the Mortar Platoon. Although severely wounded, he pressed the attack home, forcing the enemy to withdraw. He was later awarded the Military Cross.

Further west, Tony Mott recalled Sergeant Bisson returning with about fifteen prisoners from an attack towards the German strongpoint in the Sanatorium, which remained occupied with heavy fire still coming from it.

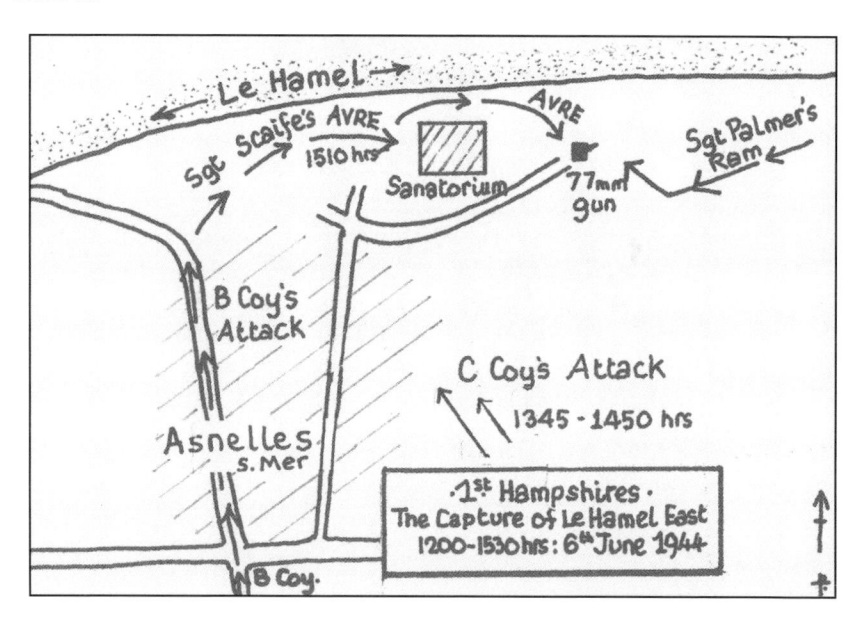

It was at this precarious moment that David Warren received news, via the still functioning wireless of the Essex Yeomanry's battery forward observation officer with John Littlejohns, of D Company's capture of the gun positions at Cabane. He badly needed good news just then. Having ordered Littlejohns to continue up the hill and capture the radar station and arranged some naval and Gunner support for D Company, he turned back to the firefight that was still raging in front of him. *Le Hamel East was still fighting grimly, with most of the opposition coming from the hospital buildings. B Company closed on to the objective, but were held up about fifty yards away from the hospital by a torrent of fire. Fortunately at this moment [about 1500 hours] an AVRE appeared, coming down the road from Asnelles to Le Hamel, and was contacted at the road junction.*

Sgt Bert Scaife RE (centre sitting) and his AVRE. (This crew is not the one he fought with on D-Day.)

The AVRE was called *Loch Leven*, and its commander was Sergeant Bert Scaife, whom we last met on the beach. Despite his brakes malfunctioning, he had moved west with four DD Shermans of the Sherwood Rangers. Their speed had outstripped Scaife's lumbering Churchill and, when they had gone off towards Cabane to support John Littlejohns in his attack on the gun positions, Scaife had returned to Asnelles, where he now encountered David Warren, who asked him to support Mott's attack on Le Hamel.

A Hampshire stretcher-bearer had worked his way up the road beside Scaife's AVRE. He remembered *many dead Hampshires along the road, so there was no doubting the direction I should take. Many of the casualties had been inflicted by enemy in a heavily fortified Sanatorium…*

To fire a Flying Dustbin bomb from its Petard mortar required Scaife's AVRE to get very close to its target. Fifty yards from the rear of the building, he fired. The stretcher-bearer recalled the AVRE *by which I was crouching opened up at the Sanatorium and nearly deafened me. As I cringed, someone waved at me from the wayside ditch; I stooped to speak just as a line of machine gun bullets hit the armour where I had been seconds before. In the ditch was one of our stretcher-bearers with a wounded man.*

Despite a great explosion and clouds of dust and smoke, David Warren recalled that Scaife's first round *did not stop the machine gun fire for more than a second or so; so a further round was ordered but it was not until five had been fired that B Company were able to close with the hospital and get into the building.* Sergeant Scaife remembered it differently: *...we used our Petard for the first time firing two Flying Dustbins which made the defenders surrender.*

The front at Le Hamel was a deadly place to be. The stretcher-bearer remembered: *Dragging, crawling and crouching, we carried the* [wounded] *man back to a large captured bunker being used as a dressing station. I was then too exhausted and scared to go back up the road.*

A number of Germans emerged from the Sanatorium with their hands up, and Mott's Company rushed in to capture any other survivors. Sergeant Bisson's Platoon brought out thirty stunned prisoners.

At last – after nearly eight hours' hard fighting – victory looked possible. With the capture of the strongpoint at the sanatorium, the gun emplacement on the seafront, whose 77mm throughout the long day had wrought such destruction on Jig Green beach, was now exposed to attack from two separate directions. As Sergeant Scaife's AVRE approached from the rear followed by men of Tony Mott's B Company, a Sexton self-propelled 25-pounder of the Essex Yeomanry was attacking it from the front.

A few minutes earlier, the 77mm had knocked out the tank of Captain Arthur Warburton, an Essex Yeomanry Forward Observation Officer with the Sherwood Rangers. Seeking retribution, Warburton told the commander of a passing Sexton from his own Regiment to *blow that damned thing up.*

The Sexton's commander, Sergeant Bob Palmer from Hertford, recalled the incident.

He yelled at me, 'Sergeant! Quick! See what's happening? You've got the best gun nearest to that! Put that out of action!' I climbed over the side of my self-propelled gun, got down on to the road, on to this unmade road, walked along till I got level with this line of trees. Then I looked across and with my field glasses I could ever so easily see what it was. There was this enormous monster of a place and it looked like a big, big mushroom. And as far as I could see, the only bit that was likely to be of any help to us, if we could get there, was their gun aperture point, where the gun barrel came out. The rest of it, if you hit it, you'd only be bruising the concrete, so we'd got to try and get one in that aperture.

Sgt Bob Palmer, Essex Yeomanry

I said to my crew, 'There's no good us going up there like all the others have done, we shall simply be number seven if we go up nice and steadily. We've got to do something different and take them by surprise.' So I said to the driver, 'When I say "Go", go.' Now those things weighed something like thirty-five tons but they would do about thirty-five miles an hour. And I said, 'When I tell you to stop' – a tap on the head, that's the signal to stop – 'I want you to immediately turn 45 degrees to your offside.'

...I hit him in the back, which was the signal to go, and off he went. We flew across as fast as we could and we got away with it, we caught them by surprise, they weren't able to pick us up. We did about eighty yards past the trees. I tapped the driver on the head; he stopped and immediately turned 45 degrees to his right. The gun layer, who was going to fire the gun, he could see quite clearly what the target was and I'd instructed him to travel with the gun already loaded and the safety catch off, which you shouldn't do normally, to save us seconds of time. And, as soon as the driver stopped and steered it to 45 degrees to his offside, the gun layer, with his wheels, was able to manoeuvre it on to the thing accurately and fire. And as soon as we had almost stopped bouncing, as a tank does when you stop suddenly, he fired immediately and the first shot actually hit.

From where I was, I could see we'd hit the target but it hadn't gone in the narrow bit that we wanted. It was a fraction high and a fraction to the left. So I ordered him to deflect one to the right and drop twenty-five yards and fire again. So he fired again and, would you believe, the next one was kind enough to go right in the actual aperture. Now, if we'd practised it all the morning we couldn't have got better than that, it was marvellous. That went in and of course exploded inside and put the gun out of action.

At about the same time Sergeant Scaife hit the rear door of the gun emplacement with another of his Flying Dustbins. *My Gunner (the one who had been so seasick) managed to put his first Dustbin straight through the back door and that was the end of them. He then (with machine gun fire) flushed out a sniper who was entrenched nearby and could not be got at by the infantry.*

At this time we found we had a small fire on the top deck of our AVRE, and my driver, Jim Baxter, and I had to nip smartly out to stamp it out; it seemed to be the remains of the waterproofing canvas but how it ignited we did not know.

The task of clearing the bunker fell to Company Sergeant-Major Harry Bowers MM of C Company. *The Germans immediately put out a white flag but did not come out. I thought, 'To hell with you, after all this trouble,' and I slipped in a 36 Mills grenade. After the explosion a few seconds passed and out they came shouting 'Russkis! Russkis!'*

Despite the untold carnage and damage the 77mm crew had caused on the beach since H-Hour, Sergeant Palmer felt a soldier's pity for his opponents, who had fought to the last with determination and courage. *About four people struggled out of the back of the emplacement with their hands over their ears. Poor devils, I felt sorry for them. Obviously they were badly knocked about.*

Between them, Bert Scaife and Bob Palmer clinched the Hampshires' hard-won victory at Le Hamel East. Until then, partly because of the rough sea and partly because of this gun, the Hampshires had had to fight almost entirely without armoured support. At Le Hamel, an AVRE and a Sexton, both engaged informally on the spot, had now swung a battle which had lasted eight hours and cost the lives of fifty infantrymen. But now the job was done and the gun that had knocked out so many armoured vehicles and landing craft, killed and wounded so many men and prolonged the battle into the mid-afternoon was finally destroyed. Bert Scaife was one of a handful of men to receive the DCM while Bob Palmer was awarded an MM. Sergeant Scaife had never fired a forty-pound Petard bomb in action before, but he seems to have mastered the art at once. He recalled: *I must say the effectiveness lived up to all expectations providing we could get near enough, as it had a very short range.*

Bert Scaife and his crew would stick with the 1st Hampshires for the rest of the day as they cleared the rest of Le Hamel and in their final capture of Arromanches. Before we leave him and his Squadron, it is worth considering their contribution to D-Day and the cost they had paid. With the 73rd Field Company, their twenty AVREs and the flail tanks of B Squadron of the Westminster Dragoons had been first on the beach. Four AVRES had been unable to disembark because their LCT had been hit on beaching. Four more landed but were bogged down on the beach. One had been hit three times by the 77mm gun, and another knocked out possibly by the same gun. One had been blown up by two mines and another, hit by a mortar bomb, had burst into flames. Another had overturned, its driver killed. Miraculously, in the course of D-Day they and the Westminster Dragoons' flails lost only four killed: the Leader of Y Squadron, Major Harold Elphinstone, Lance-Sergeant Eli George, Lance-Corporal Fred Johnson and Trooper Leslie Birch. Their five wounded included two officers.

Without the tank support they had expected and despite landing in the wrong places and suffering heavy losses, the flails and AVREs had first cleared exits from the beach, then provided precious armoured support for the Hampshires and finally clinched the capture of Le Hamel. No infantryman who landed on Jig Green on D-Day could doubt the debt they owed to the breaching teams from 82nd Assault Squadron and the Westminster Dragoons, and to the 73rd, 90th and 295th Field Companies of the Royal Engineers. They had got there first, and their collective efforts made a vital contribution to the success of the invasion.

Ian Wilson of the 73rd Field Company later recalled that, back on the beach: *Work resumed on obstacle clearance as the tide fell.* [Low tide was at 1746.] *It progressed with ever-increasing speed after Le Hamel was silenced. The clearance then made use of towing straps for the one remaining stores boat to work with the assault engineers' tracked vehicles to tow the obstacles into piles, having first removed the igniters from the mines. In this way, the end of D-Day saw over a mile of Jig Green clear of obstacles for unrestricted access by landing craft from D+1 onwards.*

The Hampshires clear Le Hamel West

Once the 77mm gun had been destroyed, the way from the beach into Le Hamel at last lay open. Lieutenant Jimmy McWilliam of B Squadron of the Sherwood Rangers remembered: *We cleared the beach up a fisherman's ramp near the gun emplacement which had knocked out Monty Horley. I had infantry on the back of my tank and took prisoners from a slit trench, at which point a gendarme appeared and asked what was going on.*

Even before Le Hamel East had been completely cleared, the surviving Hampshires of B and C Companies turned to attack Le Hamel West. Here they found themselves facing still more street fighting and house-clearing, but now they had some armoured support from Bert Scaife's AVRE and some of the Sherwood Rangers' Shermans. They were also able to call on support fire from LCTs (including variants with flak guns) to bombard the buildings they had to clear.

Although the Hampshires had at last broken the back of the defences, the defenders fought on fiercely. In *Gold Beach* Jig, his invaluable battlefield guide, Tim Saunders quotes Ron Eastman, a Hampshire who now faced the task of clearing Le Hamel West: *Bloody awful! After losing so many comrades, I just did what I was told. I didn't expect to survive.*

Major Saunders also cites Grenadier Agnussen, a German soldier who was in a strongpoint under attack.

The noise was tremendous when the enemy opened fire. I saw two of the strange tanks knocked out. We were firing through what had been large windows which we had boarded and sandbagged, firing our weapons through small holes. We had an excellent and wide field of fire and made a very strong impression on the British who were forced to go to ground and made no way forward against us. ...we began to feel that we would not survive as the bombardment continued. More tanks appeared and we began to suffer serious damage to our Wiederstandnest [strongpoint] and several men were killed or injured. It was terrible to hear them moaning and there was no chance of evacuating them. Our Hauptmann [Captain] was a very strong-willed man and came round continually, exhorting us to hold the enemy until help could reach us. He said the 21st Panzer would relieve us.

The battle seemed to go on and on and soon half our men were casualties and we were running out of ammunition and had nothing to eat at all. Then I received a splinter in my arm and had to lie down while Hans bandaged it up with a paper roll. Then I returned to my position in time to see two British tanks with heavy mortars opposite our position. The noise was indescribable as they fired great bombs at us. All hell broke loose as the building began to collapse around us. We were forced to retreat to new positions.

In this frustrating and hazardous operation several Hampshires excelled. Two of them had been among the first ashore that morning with A Company. Twenty-eight-year-old Lance-Sergeant Sippetts had taken over command of his Platoon when Alan Norman had been wounded in the first twenty minutes. He now led his section of seven men to a house in Le Hamel from which the enemy were firing machine guns. Although three men were killed or wounded in the assault, Arthur Sippetts and his four survivors cleared the house and took twelve prisoners. Meanwhile, Corporal Slade's section, survivors of Jack Lauder's Platoon, captured a position containing fifteen Germans.

Lance-Corporal Victor Waller, a young NCO from Skelmersdale, had already been wounded during the battle on the beach, but he had fought on in Asnelles and at Le Hamel. *In the afternoon, he led his section with such daring that he was able to deal with several snipers entirely on his own, largely due to his own determination and his display of courage.*

Meanwhile, Lance-Corporal Bull of B Company (who had helped establish the Regimental Aid Post in Asnelles Church) had joined Captain Ivor Joseph MC, the Hampshires' gallant Medical Officer, outside Le Hamel where he organised German prisoners into teams of stretcher-bearers. Roy Butt *then laid a tape* [to mark a route] *into the minefield and carried the casualties out under machine gun fire.*

Sergeant Sippetts and Corporals Slade, Waller and Butt were each awarded a Military Medal.

By this time the survivors of Tony Mott's B Company had pretty much given their all. They were also running out of all kinds of ammunition until their Bren gun carrier drew up, enabling them to fill their pouches and replenish their supply. Mott was able to reorganise, splitting the survivors of Graham Mason Elliott's platoon between the other two. He remembered: *...I had no officer platoon commanders, but Cecil Thomas remained. He spent his time coolly walking around, stick in hand, and I found him invaluable for he always knew what to do and displayed not the slightest concern when under fire. I put him in charge of 12* [Platoon] *for the time being and Bisson was still with 10... I suppose there were about fifty men left with B Company* [who had landed, less than nine hours earlier, 120-strong].

The three Hampshire rifle companies that attacked Asnelles and Le Hamel had begun the day with a total of fifteen officers. By 1630 only seven of these were still in action, and one of those seven was now commanding the Battalion as its third commanding officer that day. The 1st Hampshires were reduced to three rifle companies, two of which were down to two severely under-strength platoons.

The Sherwood Rangers' tanks involved in the final clearing of Le Hamel West included Captain Colin Thomson's troop from Stephen Mitchell's C Squadron. Pushing along a secondary beach exit towards Le Hamel, Sergeant Bracegirdle's tank came under fire and was hit repeatedly. The 50mm gun on the seafront there knocked out Thomson's leading Sherman – the Sherwood Rangers' twelfth tank to be lost. William Bracegirdle directed the fire of another tank onto the German 50mm gun while he moved forward, penetrating the enemy defences. Thomson's troop finally destroyed the gun position which had dominated this end of Le Hamel. Captain Thomson was later awarded a Military Cross and Sergeant Bracegirdle a Military Medal.

Three AVREs and a flail under the command of Lieutenant Ellis arrived to help just as the operation was almost completed. Bert Scaife and his crew, who had destroyed several machine gun nests that had been holding up the Hampshires, were delighted to see them. Scaife recalled: *...we had been on our own for a very long time and I was beginning to wonder if any more had got off the beach safely. We had by then about reached our objective for the day and shortly we parted from the infantry and the Squadron rallied to take stock and spend the night near Buhot.*

Fighting in Le Hamel would continue sporadically until early evening, when the tiny village was at last completely cleared.

The Devons take Ryes

Early in the afternoon Colonel Nevill's 2nd Devons approached the village of Ryes. Franc Sadleir's A Company were leading and, as Cosmo Nevill later remembered, when they reached a point about 1,000 yards north of the village they came under intense light machine gun and Spandau fire at close range from enemy hidden in thick hedges.

This became close fighting with a vengeance; we had no artillery or [three-inch] mortar support as they had not yet landed. The only fire support we had was from our destroyer, and it was not possible to fire naval guns within 1,000 yards of our own troops. However, our Forward Officer Bombardment, Captain Dupont, brought very accurate fire to bear on the outskirts of Ryes.

Nevill's men had run into other companies from the 1st Battalion of the 916th Grenadier Regiment, who were based on Ryes. It was the Devons' first experience of the deadly combination of the MG 42 Spandau and the dense Normandy countryside known as the *bocage*. Sergeant Bill Baker of 18 Platoon recalled: *After you got past the houses and that, you came into what they call 'close' country. It's all hedgerows. It's not open warfare like you trained quite a bit for; it wasn't like that at all. You had to stalk hedges. You daren't go out into the open fields because Jerry had these Spandau machine guns and had them perched in little corners.* Over the weeks to come, as they entered the Normandy *bocage*, Bill Baker's words would became the *cri de coeur* of every British infantryman in the campaign.

The citations for two awards earned in this action tell part of the story. Franc Sadleir's recommendation for the Military Cross describes how ... *towards Ryes Major Sadleir came up against a triple series of machine gun posts which had to be dealt with one by one. By skilful leadership and great determination these were successfully overrun one by one, each attack being led with the greatest gallantry by Major Sadleir.* In this attack A Company made good use of their two-inch mortars.

The citation for Private Aubrey Keenor's Military Medal tells how he *was manning a Bren gun in the leading platoon of 2nd Devons. When this platoon was held up by enemy light machine gun fire a patrol tried to work forward up a covered ditch. They came under fire from a Spandau which was trained on the ditch, and would undoubtedly have suffered heavy casualties had not Private Keenor leapt out of the ditch into the open and engaged the Spandau with his light machine gun. He remained in this position for several minutes while magazines were thrown to him across the ditch, and his prompt action and deadly fire allowed the remainder of the patrol to move to a flank and so destroy the enemy.*

While Sadleir's A Company bore the brunt of the battle in front of them, B and D Companies tried to work their way round the enemy's flanks. But the German Grenadiers had been reinforced by men from the 352nd Division's NCO Training School and, in the face of their fierce defence, the Devons' attack stalled.

Cosmo Nevill left A Company holding firm and sent the other two companies 500 yards to the right, skirting the enemy defences and pushing down the road into Ryes. This tactic worked and B and D Companies made rapid progress. A third of a mile north-west of Ryes they found some abandoned dug-outs and the German Battalion's deserted headquarters. Supported by Lieutenant May's troop of M10 tank destroyers from the Northumberland Hussars, B and D Companies met little resistance as they entered Ryes along the road. But David Holdsworth remembered his runner being shot in the head by a lone sniper who then withdrew. *This kept us on edge for a bit and we searched the village very carefully indeed before satisfying ourselves that there were no other Germans about. Indeed, there weren't any French people either. But plenty of dead cows.*

Bill Baker, Platoon Sergeant of 18 Platoon in D Company, remembered turning a corner while they were clearing Ryes and finding himself confronting a German soldier, who began to raise his rifle to shoot him. Baker was quicker with his Sten gun than the German was with his Mauser. He was the first man Sergeant Baker, thirty-two years old and an experienced soldier, had killed. It preyed on his mind. A while later he was violently sick and he found he was unable to eat for the rest of the day.

Meanwhile the Germans had launched a final counter-attack upon A Company's positions on the Gronde Ruisseau. Nineteen-year-old Private Cyril Oldridge was manning a Bren gun *in the right forward platoon of the leading company which had been held up by light machine gun and mortar fire. An enemy counter-attack developed on the right flank of the company, and Private Oldridge's platoon was ordered to re-adjust its position to deal with this attack. Private Oldridge remained with his gun in the original position and, although severely wounded in both legs and both arms by a grenade, successfully broke up the counter-attack.* Evacuated wounded, Cyril Oldridge died two days later. He never knew about the Military Medal he won that day.

By 1630 Ryes had been captured. The battle had cost A and D Companies most. A platoon commander attached from the Hampshires, twenty-four-year-old Lieutenant Edward Smith, was killed, and three Devon officers – Captain Crawley and Lieutenants Morris and Bull – were wounded. Captain Dupont, acting as Forward Observation Officer Bombardment for the naval ships bombarding shore targets, was also wounded. At the end of the battle, they realised that Lieutenant Foy, a Royal Sussex Regiment officer leading a Devon platoon, was missing together with some of his men. It was correctly assumed at the time that they had been captured by the Germans. Edward Foy spent the rest of his war as a prisoner near Brunswick.

Colonel Nevill now sent Mike Holdsworth and B Company, with help from both the Vickers guns of 9 Platoon of the Cheshires and the M10 tank-destroyers of Lieutenant Brameld's troop from the Northumberland Hussars, to establish that the high ground towards Puits d'Herode was clear of enemy. Once on the hill, which they found to be unoccupied, Mike Holdsworth sent his twin brother David and his Platoon on a fighting patrol through the scrub and foliage on the lower slopes.

David Holdsworth remembered: *I called up my own O Group* [an O or Orders Group was where a commander assembled his soldiers to outline his plans and issue orders] – *the first I had ever called in enemy territory. I had a fairly clear idea of what was wanted but not a very clear idea of where we were on the map. On the advice of my Sergeant we handed over our AB 64s* [pay books] *to the Corporal to whom I had given the responsibility of guarding our base until we returned. As we made off by sections, a Bren gun carrier appeared. The driver had been ordered to help me. He took one look at the scrub and the foliage and decided that he couldn't be of much use. I agreed with him.*

If there had been any enemy in the area which we patrolled they must have had plenty of warning of our approach. Men fell over, swore, barked their shins, swore, and had their faces and arms scratched and bruised by swinging limbs of trees and bushes. To our relief we met no one.

Two hours later, a sweating, scratching and bleeding platoon returned to its base and reported quite honestly that there was no sign of the enemy. Then we reclaimed our AB 64s. Nobody seemed to want us to do any more. So, with appropriate guards posted, my Platoon dug itself some slit trenches and went to sleep.

During the battle at Ryes the Devons' Colonel realised that his trousers, which had been soaking wet since landing, had at last dried out. Three uncomfortable weeks would pass before David Holdsworth and his men would have the chance to take off their boots and change the socks they had all donned in the early hours of D-Day.

Meanwhile, Cosmo Nevill had decided to hold fast in Ryes until his Battalion could be reorganised. C Company, under Lieutenant Frank Pease, had disengaged from Le Hamel and were on their way to rejoin the Battalion. But, by now, it was too late to set off to capture the battery at Longues. Colonel Nevill reluctantly postponed that task until the morning.

Overall, the 2nd Devons' casualties on D-Day had been relatively light: thirty-five killed, including Major *Bubbles* Duke and Lieutenant Edward Smith of the Hampshire Regiment; and sixty-six wounded, including Majors Mike Howard and John Parlby. As Sir Alex Stanier had remarked, casualties were heaviest among the Battalion's leaders. They had lost three of the commanders of their four rifle companies and a quarter of their officers. In the next few days Private Cyril Oldridge and others among the wounded would succumb to their wounds.

The Devons' Colonel, Cosmo Nevill, later received a DSO for his determined leadership on D-Day. He had collected his scattered companies, adjusted the plan and then taken his Battalion's fiercely defended first objective at a relatively low cost in casualties. Franc Sadleir won the Devons' only Military Cross that day but, during the attack on Ryes, the Intelligence Officer, Bill Wood, had seen some Devons in danger of being cut off. Seizing a Bren gun, he had successfully driven off the enemy. This incident was the first of several in a very long citation written in 1945 recommending Wood for a long overdue MC. MMs, as we have seen, were awarded to Aubrey Keenor and Cyril Oldridge.

Capt Bill Wood, Intelligence Officer, 2nd Devons

For the Devons, it had been a hard-fought day, encompassing confusion on the beaches, two German counter-attacks and finally, despite fierce defence, liberating Ryes. Tomorrow they would go for the big guns at Longues.

CHAPTER SEVEN

D-Day: 1630–2359 hours

The Hampshires capture the radar station and Arromanches

While B and C Companies of the Hampshires, with the help of Sergeant Scaife and a growing assortment of tanks and self-propelled guns, cleared Le Hamel West, John Littlejohns's D Company prepared to take the Battalion's next objective. The Luftwaffe radar station stood high on the cliffs beyond the gun positions at Cabane. Around the Wurzburg dish were three 20mm flak guns (deadly when used in an anti-personnel role), a field gun, a concreted machine gun position and various trenches housing an infantry platoon, whose job was to defend the entire set-up. The perimeter of the whole position was surrounded by a thick belt of mines and barbed wire.

The Radar Station above Cabane and Arromanches (Rob Fraser)

But things were looking up. The Hampshires were at last able to call on the sort of fire support that circumstances had denied them in Le Hamel. Through their Forward Observation Officer Bombardment, Captain Ian Beddows, David Warren arranged a bombardment by a destroyer. This would be followed by a ten-minute barrage from a battery of the Essex Yeomanry, their fire directed by the Forward Observation Officer who had accompanied Littlejohns all day. At about 1600 hours, as they closed on the radar station, D Company was accompanied by a troop of tanks from John Hanson-Lawson's Squadron of the Sherwood Rangers.

Second Lieutenant Gordon Layton, a nineteen-year-old platoon commander, remembered: *My Company was heading towards the radar station on the headland overlooking Arromanches and Major Littlejohns ordered me to advance with my Platoon towards it. There was much barbed wire and a sign saying 'Achtung Minen', so I queried the order as it was obviously very dangerous to go through a minefield. The OC, a real pre-war officer, stern and brooking no nonsense from his subalterns, told me in no uncertain terms to 'Get on with it!' And, encouraged by my Platoon Sergeant, who helped steady me, I 'got on with it'.* He later told his daughter Caroline that, because he was sure his Company Commander's orders would cause unnecessary casualties, he adapted them to save the lives of his men.

The naval and artillery stonks had done the trick and, with covering fire from B and C Companies behind them, the position was taken with few casualties. Gordon Layton recalled: *Shortly some Germans stood up, hands held high wishing to surrender. As I went forward to take them prisoner, they dived to the floor and a machine gun opened up and hit me... I was taken back down the hill to the church... where my wounds were treated.*

Layton, who had been severely wounded, was taken to the Regimental Aid Post in Asnelles church and finally to the beach. The ambulance crew found they could not open a gate on to the beach and instead took a detour. Later they discovered the gate had been booby-trapped: had they managed to open it, they would have been blown sky-high. Back in England, Gordon Layton's leg wound did not respond to treatment and the leg was amputated. His fighting war had lasted about nine hours. Years later, with admirable concision, he summed up his D-Day experience: *I was sea sick, deafened by the bombing and I lost my bloody leg.*[20]

Tony Mott, whose Company arrived at the radar station some time after D had taken the position, remembered a *good bag of prisoners* [forty], *including some sailors, and some more came up from Arromanches, just below, with a white flag.* Inside the position, *the canteen was undamaged, until the*

---

20. Attending the local commemorations fifty years later, in a bar in Le Hamel Gordon Layton met a woman who, as a sixteen year old girl, had helped treat the wounded in the church.

troops got there, and the rations store the same, as were the officers' quarters, which contained some useful kit. Many Hampshires made enthusiastic use of the German stores.

The survivors of B and the composite A/C Companies now assembled with D Company at the radar station. Jimmy Wicks, wounded earlier by a mortar bomb, was replaced in command of C Company, which he had led with great courage and determination since David Nelson Smith had been incapacitated. David Warren gathered his surviving platoon and company commanders and issued new orders. D Company were to move further west, over the hill and down and round the southern end of Arromanches, to take an enemy position there from the rear while B and C Companies would provide covering fire from the forward slopes. Once again there would be a preliminary barrage from a destroyer followed by another from the guns of the Essex Yeomanry.

D Company had already lost two of its officers – David Edkins and Gordon Layton. With his two remaining platoon commanders, Peter Paul of the Devons and Sicily veteran Malcolm Bradley, John Littlejohns took D Company over the crest of the hill to begin the liberation of Arromanches.

By now the German defenders were running out of steam, and the fierce preliminary barrage worked its magic. Littlejohns and his men took the position and, by 2100 hours, the town had been taken without a single Hampshire casualty. The Germans had gone but, as Tony Mott discovered, *Arromanches was full of French people. Flowers came out and Tricolors and Union Jacks. I had been told that all coastal inhabitants had been moved inland, but they were delighted to see us.*

Mott sent his indefatigable Second-in-Command, Cecil Thomas, *with a small patrol in the direction of Tracy, the Battalion's final task for the day. He got some way, but came under rifle and machine gun fire. The only casualty was a man's water bottle shot clean off him.*

At this moment there entered for the first time a character who was going to play a memorable part in the Hampshire Regiment's post-war history. He appeared in the company of three German soldiers who were bearing a white flag. Until now, he had served in the Wehrmacht, and he was highly disciplined and impressively athletic – he could clear a six-foot barbed-wire fence with ease. He was a black and white Pyrenean mountain dog, whose handlers were now prisoners of war. Taken to England, he would have been put to sleep had it not been for Leading Wren Elgar, who paid his quarantine fees of £18 (£775 in today's values). By this time Cecil Thomas had been wounded and heard of the dog's situation. From his hospital bed, Thomas raised the money from members of his Regiment to repay the kind-hearted Miss Elgar, and the dog – now renamed Fritz – became the Hampshires' Mascot until his death in 1949. On 17th May 1946, wearing a black velvet jacket bearing the Regiment's badge, he was presented to the King and Queen on their visit to Winchester, shortly before Fritz's new Regiment became the Royal Hampshires.

Fritz and the 1st Hampshires, Aldershot

Meanwhile, Tony Mott remembered: *We left Tracy for next day and were told to spend the night at the radar station. I organised B Company into two posts and we got into trenches whose previous occupants had no further use for them. Bisson* [the gallant Sergeant who had led 10 Platoon so bravely since their first entry to Asnelles and then carried on despite two wounds] *went to the RAP* [Regimental Aid Post] *about now. He got a well-deserved MM for his excellent day's work. Colour-Sergeant Eastburn came along and said the carrier was there, so we off-loaded ammunition and sent it back for blankets.*

Despite their exhaustion, the Hampshires had to be prepared for a German counter-attack. *Horace* Wright's 16 Platoon, who had miraculously lost only two men killed throughout the day, dug in at Arromanches in the gardens of some prosperous-looking villas. Hearing an argument in one of the gardens, Wright found an English woman in her early forties, who complained: 'Your men are digging up my flower beds. I demand they stop.' Wright remembered, *I was a bit put out.* If she didn't want to be shot, he told her, she should go home and stay down in the cellar until he told her she could come out.

Five decades later he recalled: *I forgot to tell her to come out. Perhaps she's still there.*

Tidying up

Now the day's fighting was over, there was reorganising and tidying up for everyone to do. Late in the afternoon the 200th Field Ambulance moved their Advanced Dressing Station to near Buhot. In the early evening Pat Chilton's B Company of the Dorsets, who had spent most of the day guarding Les Roquettes against a counter-attack that never came, moved to Ryes to relieve the Devons. Later that evening they were joined there by the rest of their Battalion, who had spent the early evening clearing the area between Puits d'Herode and Ryes.

Once A Company of the 1st Dorsets had completed their tasks, Bandsman Denis Bounsall DCM was sent back from Puits d'Herode to the Regimental Aid Post which had been established *on high ground overlooking about a mile of beach crowded with troops still arriving and every kind of vehicle and tanks. The sea for miles offshore was alive with ships discharging cargo or trying to find space to get out.*

...on arrival [I] was met by Sergeant A Talbot the Medical Sergeant (who later received the MM for his services this day). He pulled a couple of chevrons from his pocket and tossed them to me. 'You are promoted to Lance-Corporal so sew them on.' He kindly assisted me by providing a needle and cotton.

While I was talking to Sergeant Talbot I noticed the Medical Officer, Captain Lassman, listening intently to a French Catholic priest, clothed in black cassock and wearing a low-crowned black hat.

The MO came to Sergeant Talbot. 'The priest is asking for help for a badly wounded German soldier lying on a track beyond our forward position.'

Sergeant Talbot turned to me and said, 'Take some of the reserve bearers and bring him in.'

I signalled the priest to lead the way and with bearers and stretcher made way along a rough, narrow path that went about 400 metres to where a forward position with anti-tank guns was established. The track continued between steep banks in which I spotted the spines of mines showing about the rough grass, and after another 400 metres there lay the body of the wounded German.

He was one of the biggest men I've seen, several inches over six foot and I reckoned over sixteen stone. Splinters of bone fringed a wound on the left side of his head. He was still breathing but unconscious.

The return journey to the RAP was uphill and the track was uneven so it was with great relief that we were finally able to put him down. The MO was of the opinion that he would survive but probably be paralysed down one side.

During the long day my soaked clothes had dried on me but at last I was able to dig a slit-trench and sleep.

The South Wales Borderers, Glosters and Essex soldiers of 56 Infantry Brigade now took over the advance. They had landed at 1200, without casualties or incident, two hours later than scheduled, just east of where the Dorsets had landed on Jig Red. Late in the afternoon they had assembled near Buhot and tanks of the Sherwood Rangers were in action again, supporting their advance towards Bayeux.

Pockets of German troops, bypassed by the advance, were scattered throughout the beach-head. Some were still watchful and aggressive. Late in the day, Lieutenant Jack Holman, a troop commander in the Sherwood Rangers, found himself stranded near Buhot. His tank had been knocked out and his driver badly wounded when they had encountered an unexpected anti-tank gun position. Holman pulled the driver out and dragged him to a ditch, where the tank crew sheltered from persistent sniper fire. A while later another Sherwood Rangers tank arrived, commanded by Keith Douglas, Second-in-Command of A Squadron. Under fire, Douglas sprayed the area with his machine gun before climbing from his tank and running to the ditch.

Thirty years later, Jack Holman remembered: *This was the sort of work that Keith really enjoyed. He was so furious with the snipers and 20mm that were holding us up that he knocked the whole bloody lot out, otherwise we would never have got out unscathed.* Having helped Holman carry the driver and lift him on to the back of his own tank, Douglas then returned with them to the Regiment, which had assembled for the night close to Bayeux. Arriving late for leaguer[21], Keith Douglas was later mentioned in Despatches for his bravery in this incident.

Padre Leslie Skinner had meanwhile found his flock as they leaguered near Bayeux. Skinner wrote in his diary: *Bed on ground about 0130, dead beat. Fell asleep beside half-track indescribably filthy. Discover my patent waterproof pocket-bag full of sea water. Forty casualties to date, including missing.*

Happily, the Sherwood Rangers' casualties proved to be much lighter. Half the missing turned up, many of them having been rescued from the sea after their tanks had sunk. Despite the DD tanks lost at sea and the 77mm gun at Le Hamel having dominated Jig-Green sector of Gold Beach for so long, losses among the armoured regiments were lower than might have been expected – especially when counted in men's lives, rather than vehicles. The Sherwood Rangers' losses on D-Day amounted to sixteen tanks (eight sunk at sea and eight knocked out ashore), ten crew members killed and twenty wounded. B Company of the Westminster Dragoons lost four flails to enemy action and two bogged down and inundated by the tide; a handful of men were wounded and only two were killed. 82nd

---

21. At night armoured vehicles assemble in a defensive position known as a leaguer (pronounced lager).

Assault Squadron of the Royal Engineers lost three of their AVREs to enemy action and two killed and five wounded.

The field gunners' losses had been light: a total of seven killed (six from the 90th Field Regiment and one from the Essex Yeomanry) but the Sapper field companies, exposed for long dangerous hours tackling the obstacles on the beach, had been hit harder. Between them, the 73rd and 295th Field Companies of the Royal Engineers had lost thirteen killed and twenty wounded – a casualty rate of eleven per cent.

Among the surviving AVREs assembling near Buhot was Bert Scaife's *Loch Leven*. He remembered: *During training in England we had welded on to the side of the AVRE some spare ammo boxes and filled them with tinned fruit as extra rations, and when we stopped that night and started to prepare a meal my crew became very angry when they found it all ruined by machine gun bullets. After a meal and sorting the night guard out, I rolled in my blanket at the side of the AVRE and slept like a log until awakened for my turn.*

At about this time Major Tony Mott of the Hampshires *went to Battalion HQ for orders for the next day, and arrived as it was getting dark. Brigadier Stanier came along, very pleased, and gave us news of the rest of the assault, which appeared to be going well, at any rate on the British and Canadian Divisions' front. He also said that the Hampshires' name was right up at the top of the list for a magnificent show. I thought we would be getting a rocket for being so slow, as we hadn't done Tracy and had taken fourteen hours for a six-hour task.*

A German bomber or two came over very low as soon as it was dark to bomb shipping, but I don't think they did much damage – the only enemy aircraft I saw that day.

I went back with [Colour-Sergeant] *Eastburn and it was after midnight when my day's work was done. We got blankets issued and I had a bit of chocolate and a biscuit before lying down for an hour or two's sleep. I wonder what else I had had since breakfast on Crossbow. Very little, I am sure.*

Jim Bellows, the Hampshires' Signal Sergeant, remembered the end of D-Day at Battalion Headquarters. *We had to take up positions as a panzer attack was expected. I found myself in a ditch with RSM Jimmy Burgess,* [who wore the ribbon of the] *MM from the First World War. Jim had false teeth and he had scrounged two French sticks from the baker on the landing ship. They were sticking out of his small pack. I had started to brew up my first drink since first light. We were each issued with what was termed a Tommy cooker – two pieces of tin each with a slit in the middle which, when placed together, was shaped so that you could place a tablet of solid fuel under it which you lit to boil a mess tin of water. Jimmy had also made tea and then took one of his loaves; I looked at the RSM and asked him for a bit. He told me in no uncertain tones where to go. I said OK and then pulled out my spoils of war – the chunk of bacon and tin of mushrooms I had found in a German canteen. I cut some of* the bacon into the other half of my mess tin, opened the tin of mushrooms and put it with the bacon. Soon the air was filled with the lovely aroma of frying bacon. Jimmy could stand it no longer, he broke off a chunk of bread and said, 'Here you are, you bastard.'

We then shared our meal. We must have had the finest meal that anyone enjoyed on D-Day. After our meal I felt exhausted; it had been a hard day and I fell asleep. Jerry did not attack, shells were passing overhead but I slept.

But his most powerful D-Day memory – one which Jim would retain for the rest of his long life – came from earlier in the day. *Making my way along the shore road, I came up to two cottages, opposite which, on the grass verge, was a grave where one of our men had just been quickly buried. A Sherman tank was burning close by, shells were still whining overhead, and a very old lady came out of one of the cottages with a posy of flowers. She knelt by the grave, put the flowers on and said a prayer, then made her way slowly back to her cottage, oblivious to all that was going on around her.*

***

The 1st Hampshires' achievements on D-Day stand second to none. They had gained almost all their objectives despite having had to fight a protracted, bloody battle on and near the beach with almost no armoured support and, because of the closeness of their enemy, limited artillery support. They had lost sixty-five killed and another 118 wounded – twenty-three per cent of the Battalion had become casualties. Five of their officers had been killed and eleven wounded – forty-six per cent were casualties. Of their twelve rifle platoon commanders, only four remained alive and unwounded – a staggering loss rate of sixty-seven per cent.

Given the scale of their sacrifice and their achievement, the Battalion's rewards were sparing. Twenty-five-year-old David Warren was awarded an immediate DSO for his courage and leadership throughout D-Day, first as a company commander and then as Commanding Officer. His account of the day, told with professional restraint and accuracy (along with a large dash of modesty) remains a fascinating and important historical document. Among the company commanders, Jimmy Wicks and John Littlejohns each received a Military Cross for his enormous contribution to the victory and, reading the various accounts of the day, it is hard to see how the equally successful Tony Mott came to be omitted from the list of awards. As we have seen, John Boys of the Mortar Platoon received the Hampshires' third MC for his bravery both on the beach and in Asnelles, and Alan King the fourth for his gallant leadership at Le Hamel. A handful of brave NCOs and soldiers (Clement Bisson, Roy Butt, Arthur Sippetts, Bert Slade, Victor Waller and Leslie

Webb) received MMs. On a chaotic day of this kind in which so many men fought and so many died, who knows what other acts of bravery went unrecognised?

The final balance

The circumstances of 231 Brigade's landing – wading ashore in the wrong place to find that the German defences had survived the preliminary bombardments while the Sherwood Rangers' tanks were not there to support them – cost them dearly. Comparing their losses with those of 69 Brigade – who landed in the right place on King Sector, where the bombardment had hit its mark, and with their DD-tanks arriving on time and in support – is telling. While the two assault battalions of 231 Brigade lost seven per cent killed with total casualties of twenty per cent, 69 Brigade lost three per cent and eleven per cent. A combination of the effects of the weather and the coastal current, as well as simple bad luck, seems to have doubled the Malta Brigade's casualties on D-Day.

The disruption of wireless communication, especially during the morning, compounded their difficulties. The Brigadier and the three Commanding Officers were often prevented from influencing the battle, which was therefore fought as a series of company actions. There were nonetheless several instances of a commanding officer exerting effective control. Unable to contact any of his companies by wireless after the landings, Cosmo Nevill had agreed with Alex Stanier that his Devons should by-pass Asnelles and capture Ryes. Searching the beach, he had found three of his companies and led them all the way there before conducting a successful battalion action at Ryes. At Le Hamel, David Warren had abandoned the Hampshires' costly attack from the east, moved his composite A/C Company south to join B in Asnelles, and finally captured Le Hamel in the mid-afternoon. At the same time, by wireless Warren had directed D Company's successful operations up on the cliffs towards Arromanches. In the mid-afternoon, when the attack by D Company of his Dorsets had stalled before Puits d'Herode, Colonel Evelyn Norie had imposed a new plan and personally directed a successful battalion attack on the position.

In their third assault landing in eleven months the Malta Brigade had excelled. Nine months later, as the Allies prepared to cross the Rhine, *Speedy* Bredin met an officer of the Essex Yeomanry who had landed with 231 Brigade on D-Day who told him that the magnificent dash of the assault battalions had never, in his view, been equalled. Despite the shocks and setbacks which had caused delays, they had achieved most of their objectives and grabbed a sizeable chunk of Normandy as a beach-head that over the next few days would be secured and greatly expanded.

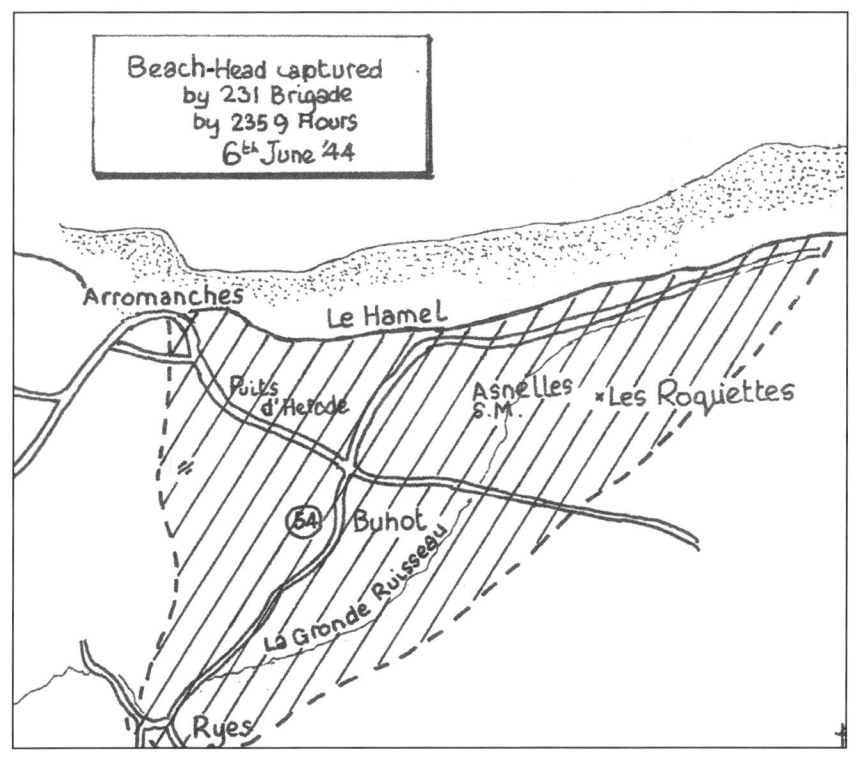

Beach-Head captured by 231 Brigade by 2359 Hours 6th June '44

Many old friends from Malta and Sicily – Lieutenant-Colonel David Nelson Smith MC, Major Charles Martin DSO, Major *Bubbles* Duke MC and Bar, Major John Parlby, Major Mike Howard MC, Captain David Edkins, Lieutenant Charles Williamson MC, Lieutenant John Boys, Company Sergeant-Major Benbow, Sergeant William Evans MM and Bar, Lance-Sergeant Len Bunning MM and many more – were dead or wounded. It was a first taste of what the Normandy campaign had in store for the survivors. The next three months would bring worse still, but the liberation of the European mainland had begun and 231 Malta Brigade had led it.

Ron White, a Portsmouth man and veteran of Sicily and Italy, landed on D-Day as a private soldier in the Anti-Tank Platoon of the 1st Hampshires. In November 1997, interviewed by the Imperial War Museum, he summed up the experience of D-Day for the whole Brigade of which he was a proud member:

We'd done it twice. We couldn't see us failing. We could have done, but we never did.

The temporary grave of Maj Hugh Duke MC and Bar at Le Hamel

CHAPTER EIGHT

Unfinished business: D+1–D+3

The Devons take the battery at Longues

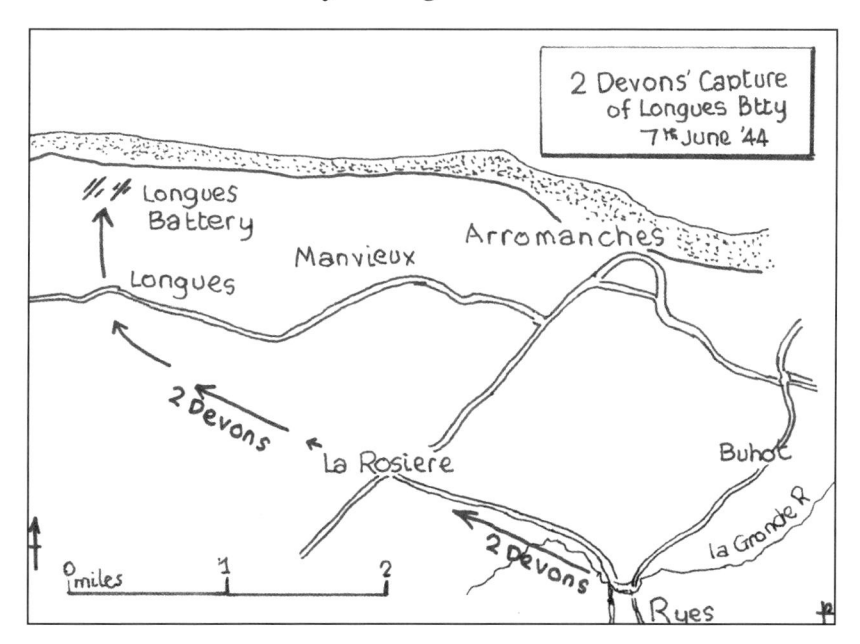

[Map: 2 Devons' Capture of Longues Btty, 7th June '44, showing Longues Battery, Longues, Manvieux, Arromanches, La Rosière, Buhot, la Gronde R, Rues, and 2 Devons' movement]

When C Company, led since *Bubbles* Duke's death by Frank Pease, rejoined the 2nd Devons on the evening of D-Day, they were sent straight on, westwards towards Longues. Their task was to capture some high ground, the Masse de Crodalle, but, when they encountered resistance at La Rosière about a mile short of their objective, this proved impossible. Finally, at 0530 the following morning, the whole Battalion moved forward, with B Company leading, and the Masse de Crodalle was occupied without opposition at 0700.

Colonel Nevill remembered: *The move towards Longues continued with C Company leading, supported by B Company. When we got to within 3,000 yards of the village we had our first view of the battery itself.* Examining the objective through their field glasses, Nevill and Pease were wondering if it was deserted when they spotted two Germans walking slowly across the area. *At this moment the Brigade Commander arrived to say that the guns of HMS Ajax and a squadron of fighter-bombers would be available to support the attack.*

Since the aerial photographs that Sir Alex Stanier had shown Cosmo Nevill as he boarded ship in England, the battery had taken still more of a pounding from the Royal Air Force on the nights of 3rd/4th and 5th/6th June. On the night before D-Day Air Chief Marshal Sir Arthur Harris had committed 1,180 of Bomber Command's aircraft, attacking the coastal batteries or flying diversionary or concealment operations in support of the invasion. Before H-Hour on D-Day, the Longues battery had been the target of three separate aerial attacks, the last of which had involved five squadrons of heavy bombers. The heavies had bombed through cloud, using Oboe wireless beams to pinpoint the invisible target. Thirteen aircraft were lost on 5th/6th June, but only one – a Pathfinder Lancaster from 582 Squadron based at Little Staughton – was from the force that attacked the Longues battery just before dawn on D-Day. Its captain, twenty-three-year-old Squadron-Leader Arthur Raybould DSO DFM[22], was a veteran of a remarkable total of seventy-eight bombing operations. He, the six very experienced members of his crew and their Lancaster, *D-Dog*, simply disappeared into the sea. They are remembered on the RAF Memorial to the Missing at Runnymede.

The cruiser HMS *Ajax* had bombarded the battery ninety minutes before H-Hour. Protected by 600 cubic metres of concrete, with four tons of steel reinforcement and walls two metres thick, the four 152mm guns long withstood the weight of high explosive visited upon them. They had continued to engage Allied warships until 0620, when *Ajax's* 6-inch guns had put all the guns out of action. Such was the accuracy of the cruiser's gunners that they even placed two shells through the embrasures of the casemates containing two of the 152mm guns. By the afternoon of D-Day, one gun had been repaired and opened fire on the ships off Omaha Beach. It continued to fire until it was finally silenced early in the evening by the combined fire of HMS *Ajax* and the Free French cruiser, *George Leygues*.

In his battlefield guide, *Gold Beach-Jig*, Tim Saunders helpfully calculated that, in the course of D-Day, the Longues battery fired some 150 shells and held a further 1,050 rounds in its magazines. This potential weight of fire on the Allied shipping would have been greatly damaging, especially on Omaha Beach, where the result hung so finely in the balance. HMS *Ajax's* outstanding gunnery, which suppressed the battery's fire, was therefore an important factor in D-Day's success.

---

22. The Distinguished Flying Medal (DFM) was the RAF's equivalent of the Military Medal.

The Longues Battery today

Despite this, Cosmo Nevill recalled, he and Stanier both knew that *the strength of the position was still formidable. It was decided that the guns of Ajax would fire until 0845 hours, at which hour the squadron of fighter-bombers would blast the place for five minutes. The MG* [Machine Gun] *Platoon of the Cheshires under Captain Bill Williams would give direct support to the infantry attack, timed to take place at 0900 hours.*

At 0852 Pease's C Company led the attack, supported by Captain Mike Holdsworth's B Company advancing through the tiny village and approaching the battery from the south. Bringing up the rear of the advance were Lieutenant David Holdsworth and his Platoon.

To my surprise, the leading platoons made their way beyond the place from which they were expected to carry out the final assault. My platoon was just about level with it. The Acting Company Commander [David's brother Mike] *realised this. Time was against a complete reorganisation to carry out the original assault plan by 0900 hours. There was only one thing to do. And he did it. He ordered an about turn. The effect was to make my platoon into the lead platoon and, therefore, commit it to immediate attack.*

Faced with barbed wire encircling the whole of the approach to the battery, and with those wretched 'Achtung Minen!' signs generously scattered around the area, we felt pitifully inadequate to the demands of the situation. The only pleasant feature about the whole affair was that no one was firing at us from the battery.

We advanced to the wire in a very open formation. Still there was no sound from the enemy. Gingerly we stepped over the wire and down one of the criss-cross paths. At that moment one of the massive iron doors of the battery swung open. Out came the enemy with white flags held out in front of them.

...Inside the chamber was a smell, which I can only describe as the smell of human fear. Having witnessed the bombardment to which they had been subjected, it wasn't really surprising that they had surrendered. I would have done the same.

Mike Holdsworth recalled: *My brother got some grenades and threw them through the embrasures. I was about fifty yards away and out came the Germans. It was all over and done with in about a quarter of an hour.*

The Devons' prisoners were mainly sailors, not soldiers, because the guns were naval guns crewed by officers and ratings of the German Kriegsmarine. David Holdsworth remembered: *Having disposed of the battery successfully and, to their relief, without much trouble, my Platoon displayed many of the usual symptoms of a victorious army. Inside the fortified central chamber were pictures of Hitler and other German leaders. Possibly because we hadn't had to shoot at anyone in anger yet, mixed feelings of relief and achievement found expression in the destruction of all the pictures hanging on the walls. ...It had been an exciting and, thank goodness, an entirely successful military operation for us, and we now indulged in noisy high spirits.*

The anti-climactic action at the Longues battery stands as a monumental example of inter-service co-operation. The Royal Air Force had photographed and bombed the battery. The Royal Navy, the Essex Yeomanry and the Cheshire Regiment had bombarded it. The Devons had taken the route through the village to avoid mines shown on the RAF's reconnaissance photographs and, when they reached the guns, they found that their destruction had been almost completed by the Royal Navy. *Ajax*'s gunnery had scored direct hits on two guns, killed their gun crews and shaken the fight out of 120 of their comrades, who put their hands up. The Devons' most difficult job was rounding up other Germans from the warren of tunnels below and among the huge concrete gun emplacements. In this task they received enthusiastic help from several visiting staff officers from 231 Brigade's and 50th Division's Headquarters, who were keen to join in the action.

No medals were won in this operation, but it must have been satisfying for the whole Battalion – and especially for the men of C Company, who had lost their heroic young commander only twenty-two hours earlier – to have captured such an important enemy position. Moreover, the capture had been achieved almost without loss. The Devon's Mortar Officer, Captain Clark, was their only fatal casualty. Mike Holdsworth remembered Clark telling *Lieutenant Pearson that he had seen seven Germans about 100 yards away who he thought were coming towards them to give themselves up. As Clark went to meet them they opened fire and killed him.*

Colonel Nevill remembered the loss of *Nobby* Clark, who had commanded the Mortar Platoon since Sicily, as *a severe blow and one that was keenly felt by all ranks.* Thirty-year-old Philip Clark left a young widow back in Plympton. He and *Bubbles* Duke are buried in the same block of graves in Bayeux War Cemetery. Corporal Jock Russell MM, who had helped Duke tend the wounded donkey at Vizzini on Sicily and had been beside him when he was killed, was himself wounded and evacuated.

After the battle, Sir Alex Stanier asked a German who had been in one of the concrete bunkers at Longues what it had been like being bombed by the Royal Air Force and shelled by the Royal Navy.

'It was like being in a cocktail shaker!' replied the German.

'And what do you know of cocktail shakers?' I enquired.

'I was a barman at the Savoy Hotel before the war,' he answered.

The Devons' unfinished business from D-Day had been completed. Yesterday they had taken Ryes; today they had taken the guns at Longues. But their Commanding Officer now heard that 47 (Royal Marine) Commando *were having a very stiff battle at Port-en-Bessin and were being hard pressed. Our Carrier Platoon therefore went to their immediate assistance...*

The Commandos capture Port-en-Bessin

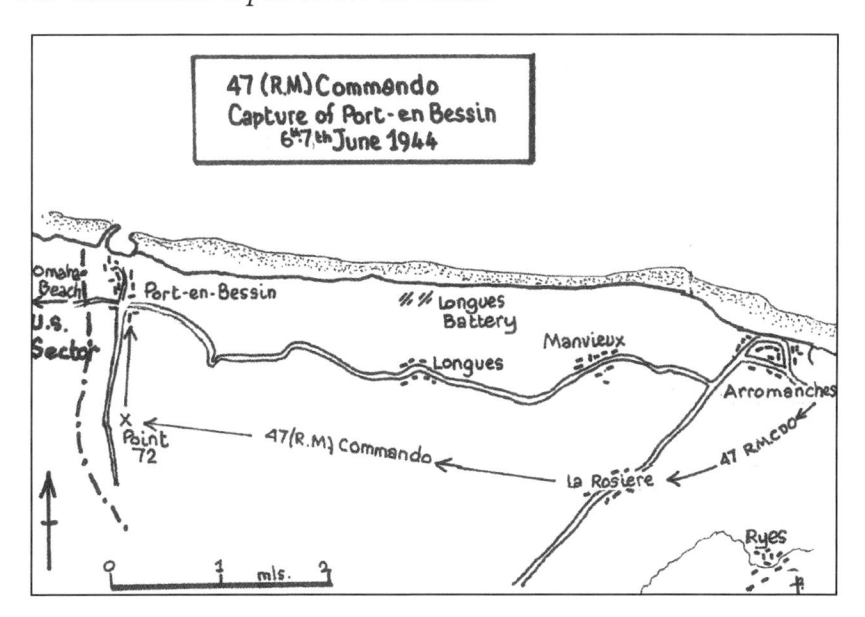

The picturesque fishing port of Port-en-Bessin, halfway between Gold and Omaha beaches, was framed on its east and west sides by steep 200-foot cliffs. To its front was an exploitable harbour and behind lay the road south to Bayeux. Its capture was important to the Allies for two reasons. It would provide a port, albeit a small one, through which they could begin to deliver supplies, and it would speed the link-up of the American and British armies.

Capturing the port and linking up with the American army had been 47 (Royal Marine) Commando's primary objective on D-Day, but their appalling landing, in which they lost many of their friends and weapons and most of their equipment, had rendered both impossible. In the afternoon of D-Day they had lost one man killed and eleven wounded in two skirmishes crossing the ridge south of Arromanches on their way to La Rosière. By early evening, despite stiff resistance from a company of German infantry, they had captured La Rosière and pushed on, continuing to collect German weapons as they went, to occupy Point 72. This highpoint – dangerously sandwiched between Port-en-Bessin to the north and the Headquarters of the 1st Battalion of the German 726th Grenadier Regiment at Chateau Maisons to the south – was where they had spent the night, sleeping when they could but planning and preparing for the next day's attack on the port.

At first light the Commandos' patrols returned, having failed to make contact with the Americans near Omaha. After the bloodiest and least successful landing of all five on D-Day, the American V Corps had not made the planned progress beyond the beach. For a while it had even seemed that their landing might fail, and Monty had consulted Dempsey about the feasibility of American landings having to be continued across Gold Beach. Thanks, however, to heroic American efforts, over the next three days they managed to achieve all their D-Day objectives. Nonetheless, early on 7th June when the Commando patrols were looking for them, the Americans were still confined to the beach and to two isolated pockets just above it.

The Commandos were still chronically short of ammunition, water and food. To have any chance of winning their next battle they needed supplies but, given their position, supplying them seemed nigh on impossible. In response, two heavily laden three-ton lorries were despatched, commanded by Captain Lindon with Sergeant Burt, both of the Royal Army Service Corps. As they passed through the 2nd Devons' positions, they were told that only Germans were ahead of them, and they were soon fired on by German troops from both sides of the road. Although their lorries were hit several times, they managed to find the Commandos at Point 72, deliver their much-needed supplies and return safely. Bryan Lindon from Malvern was awarded a Military Cross while Yorkshireman Tom Burt received a Military Medal.

For the first time since landing Colonel Phillips was at last equipped to carry out his orders. Considerable fire support had been arranged for the attack. A naval barrage began at 1400 hours with destroyers' guns augmented by the 6-inch guns of the cruiser HMS *Emerald*. A wing of RAF Typhoons rocketed the German positions ten minutes before the attack was launched. Then, because Captain Freeman and Lieutenant Irwin, two of their intrepid forward observation officers, had managed to reach Point 72, the Essex Yeomanry's 25-pounders were able to fire a barrage and put down smoke to cover the Commandos' advance. The Gunners' presence was doubly welcome because, having lost several wirelesses in their landing, the Commando Colonel had been able to contact 231 Malta Brigade via the Essex Yeomen's set.

Port-en-Bessin (Simon Trew)

The main German defences were on the two cliffs flanking the port, to the south on the Bayeux road and in the harbour. Phillips's plan for his Commandos was to bypass the German position on the Bayeux road and to work their way into the town. As they set off they suffered casualties from a Spandau firing from behind them, which had to be dealt with before they progressed. X Troop, under Captain Dennis Walton, led the attack. The citation for his Military Cross describes how, *quickly sizing up the situation, Captain Walton led his men straight into the assault and, by his personal leadership and example, so inspired his men that a very difficult problem was quickly solved.* Lance-Corporal *Shock* Kendrick of the Royal Army Medical Corps tended X Troop's wounded under heavy fire, although fresh casualties were being inflicted all around him.

When the Commandos neared the German position south of the town, they found it had been destroyed and that they were able to move into the town, where vicious street-fighting began. A Troop veered west and began to climb the hill towards the defences on the western cliff. As they moved up the slope they were fired on and grenades were thrown down on them. Lieutenant Isaac Goldstein, a South African officer attached to the Commando, went forward with a Bangalore torpedo to try to blast a gap in the wire. Although the explosion of his own torpedo blew him thirty yards back down the hill, Goldstein somehow recovered his composure and led the assault on the hill. Mines slowed their progress and then two German flak ships down in the harbour opened fire on them, killing or wounding half the Troop. Despite the heavy fire, Yorkshireman Lance-Corporal John Jesney of the Royal Army Medical Corps continued to tend and dress the wounded. Such was the ferocity of the flak ships' fire, however, that the survivors were forced to withdraw back down the hill. Of some sixty Commandos who attacked the hill, eleven were killed, seventeen wounded and Corporal Amos, who had stopped to tend the dying Sergeant Teddy Fletcher, was captured.

Captain Cousins led his Troop in two attacks on the German position on the cliff to the east of the port. Both brave attempts failed. Below in the harbour, the battle continued and B Troop was suffering heavy casualties in the house-to-house fighting. By 2100, the attack on the western cliff had failed, the attack in the town was proving slow and costly, and the eastern cliff remained in enemy hands. Colonel Phillips therefore ordered Q Troop forward from Escures and came forward himself to provide fresh impetus.

Colonel Nevill of the 2nd Devons had meanwhile sent Sergeant Sear and a section of the Devons' Carrier Platoon to support the Commandos' assault. When the Bren gun carriers were still three miles from Port-en-Bessin they were attacked by a German infantry company. In his carrier, James Sear stood his ground and covered the withdrawal of the other carriers. Throughout, his own Bren gun inflicted heavy casualties on the enemy. He then withdrew and led his section to the port, where they deployed their Brens and two-inch mortars to support the Commandos on the outskirts of the town. Sergeant Sear later received the Military Medal for his brave and skilful conduct of this dangerous little battle. Private Jim Wilson, one of Sear's carrier section, later remembered: *We were under fire on the edge of Bessin all night but we got some Jerries who were trying to get out of the town and up our side of the hill to join the Spandau boys* [on the hilltop].

During the course of the battle in and around the port, the 200th Field Ambulance of the Royal Army Medical Corps sent a convoy of ambulances to collect the many Commando wounded. Like Bryan Lindon's two three-tonners, the RAMC convoy passed through enemy-held territory and several times came under fire. Three men – Second Lieutenant Cooper, Corporal Dyer and Lance-Corporal Farrow – were later decorated for their bravery. Frank Cooper was repeatedly sniped while tending the wounded. At one point Graham Dyer and Cyril Farrow found themselves surrounded by Germans but, during the night, they made their way with their casualties into the port itself. Cooper received a Military Cross while Dyer and Farrow each received a Military Medal.

Meanwhile, B Troop's battle down in the harbour continued. Marine Roy Emsley and Sergeant Donald Gardner (whom we last met swimming ashore on D-Day) were among those wounded, but both pressed on, Emsley giving supporting fire from his Bren gun, to occupy the position which was their objective. Finally, Major Donnell led the survivors of B Troop through the houses by the quay and managed to capture both the flak ships. This incident later contributed to his award of the DSO.

In his history of the Royal Navy's part in D-Day (Operation *Neptune*), Commander Kenneth Edwards described the Commandos' final dusk assault on the German position on the eastern cliff. ...*Captain T F Cousins said that he found and reconnoitred a zig-zag path up the hill and thought that he could get up to the German position with twenty-five men by that route.*

Capt Terry Cousins, 47 (RM) Commando

Captain Cousins was given between forty and fifty men and set out. It was like a miniature replica of the storming of the Heights of Abraham at Quebec by General Wolfe. At dusk Captain Cousins and his men reached the skyline and they at once assaulted the German defences. These they penetrated, while at the same time another troop attacked from the extreme right. This troop penetrated the German defences and captured the German commander in his dugout. The German company commander was induced to lead the Marines forward through the mines and summon the remainder of the German garrison to surrender, and this they did.

It was found that the whole top of the hill was honeycombed with dugouts and trenches. Mopping up was therefore a slow business...

During these mopping up operations Terry Cousins ordered his men into some empty trenches while he attacked a concrete bunker. Taking with him his Bren gunner, Marine Delap, and Marines Howe, Tomlinson and Madden, he rushed the German position. Firing as they ran, they had several grenades thrown at them. Cousins was killed, Madden was wounded in the head and Delap concussed. The rest of the Troop, under Lieutenant Wilson, then ran forward and captured the blockhouse and all the surviving enemy.

Twenty-two years old, Cousins was the son of a Gurkha colonel. He and his wife, Bobbie, had married only a few months earlier. Recommended unsuccessfully for a Victoria Cross, he was instead mentioned in Despatches because, at that time, neither DSOs nor MCs could be awarded posthumously.

Cousins was not the only Commando to shine in this close-fought battle for the eastern cliff. Time and again, Marine William MacDonald, who was his Troop Commander's runner, crossed open, fire-swept ground carrying messages and orders. Marine McKenna made his solitary way across open ground swept by machine gun fire to hurl a smoke grenade into the enemy machine gun post. Under cover of the smoke, he then rushed the position and captured all five occupants. When Marine Ellis's section came under heavy fire from a German machine gun post, all the men except him went to ground. Ellis charged and captured the German position.

This was not, however, the end of the day. Another force of Germans, probably from the chateau to their south, attacked the Commandos' Main Headquarters at Point 72. Seeing troops advancing towards them, the Commandos at first thought they were Americans arriving from Omaha Beach. But then the attackers' machine guns and mortars opened up. Marine Derek Gadsden moved about, bringing fire to bear on the enemy from different positions, in an attempt to give the impression that the Headquarters was more strongly defended than it was. His attempts slowed down the Germans considerably but the feature was finally over-run and several Commandos taken prisoner. Capture was a matter of some anxiety because the Commandos knew of Hitler's order that Commandos were to be shot. Most, however, managed to escape during the confusion of the next day or two. Among those who escaped was one of their forward observation officers, Lieutenant Irwin of the Essex Yeomanry.

Corporal Amos, who had been captured during A Troop's abortive attack on the western cliff, had spent an uncomfortable evening there in a bunker with German soldiers and a Gestapo man. When Cousins's successful final attack went in on the eastern cliff, the Gestapo man disappeared. A German officer then offered Amos a cigar along with his troops' surrender. At dawn on 8th June Amos marched his captives in three ranks to the foot of the hill, where his Troop Commander greeted him.

'Amos, where have you been? You haven't had a shave.'

At 0400 that morning the Commandos took the surrender of the port. The action, frustrated horribly by their experience landing on D-Day, had been costly. In two days, the Commando, originally 420 strong, had suffered twenty-eight per cent casualties. Forty-six Commandos (eleven per cent) had been killed and seventy wounded. Their Colonel and their Second-in-Command had each won a DSO, two of their officers (Captain Walton and Lieutenant Goldstein) had won MCs, Sergeant Gardner, Marines Emsley, Gadsden, Griffin and MacDonald and two medical orderlies, Lance-Corporals Jesney and Kendrick, had between them won seven Military Medals, and Captain Cousins had been posthumously mentioned in Despatches.

Later on 8th June, as originally planned, the 2nd Devons would relieve their gallant survivors. But 47 Commando's battle was not quite over. That evening news reached them of two wounded Marines lying by the side of the road outside the port. Lance-Sergeant Ellis set out in a Bren gun carrier but, as he approached the men, he came under heavy fire from close range and two directions. Ellis leapt from the carrier and managed to bring both men to safety, earning an eighth Military Medal for his unit.

Other operations on D+1

The severely depleted 1st Hampshires spent 7th June licking their wounds. In the morning they sent out patrols to Manvieux and Tracy-sur-Mer, which, contrary to Cecil Thomas's experience the night before, they found deserted. Later in the day their new Commanding Officer arrived. Tony Mott had met him before, when he had been an instructor on a machine gun course at Ahmednagar near what was then Bombay. Lieutenant-Colonel Charles Howie, a thirty-six-year-old officer of the King's Liverpool Regiment, now assumed command of a Battalion that had done extraordinarily well but had temporarily shot its bolt. Once the Battalion's D-Day objectives were all secured, the survivors moved inland to Rubercy.

The 1st Dorsets were also licking their wounds and sorting themselves out. At about midday they were ordered to despatch B Company, under Major Pat Chilton, to engage a large pocket of German resistance. These Germans – part of a battle group – had been bypassed and cut off near Bazentin during the landings. At 1630 on D-Day they had ambushed,

After the Battle: Hampshire soldiers in Arromanches

Gold Beach on D+1 (Imperial War Museum B5140)

The 50mm gun position at Le Hamel after its capture
(Imperial War Museum B5252)

wounded and captured Brigadier Senior, commander of 151 Brigade in 50th Division. His driver and the Brigade Intelligence Officer had been killed in the ambush. Chilton now led his Company, with a mortar detachment and Captain Eric Hannah's Bren gun carriers, to the rescue. With assistance from the 1st Hampshires, 8th Durhams and some Shermans from the 24th Lancers, they found the Germans and assaulted their position, killing forty and capturing seventy more. Brigadier Senior managed to escape during the firefight. Pat Chilton lost only two killed. One was the Commander of 10 Platoon, Lieutenant Ernest Mayes, a married twenty-seven-year-old solicitor from London. The other was eighteen-year-old Private Leonard Hann from Bristol.

Pat Chilton's Company had done well, but even their performance was outstripped that day by the Dorsets' Padre, Captain Robert Watt, who with a few soldiers forming a burial party was engaged in the sad duty of finding and burying the dead. While digging some fresh graves, Captain Watt was horrified to see thirty or forty German soldiers approaching. He was unarmed; his men held shovels. There was only one thing to be done. He approached the German officer to offer his surrender. The German got in first, surrendering himself and his men to Watt. Having disarmed them, the Padre fell them in and marched them back to Battalion

Headquarters. Thus it was that, on 7th June 1944, the Dorsets' unarmed Padre captured more Germans than any other Dorset soldier throughout the entire Normandy campaign.

Private Terry Parker of D Company briefly noted in his diary the similar grim task facing the survivors of his sadly depleted Number 18 Platoon. *Consolidated in field, side of road. Bill Hawkins took out a burial party for Bomber* [Lieutenant Lancaster], *Spitter* [probably Sergeant Arthur Horlick] *and* [Lance-Sergeant Eric] *Abell. Met party of Jerries. Bill wounded in chest. Went back. Jerries* [taken] *prisoner.* That day Terry was promoted lance-corporal. He also acquired from a German prisoner a souvenir he would keep for the rest of his life: the pay book of a member of the *Ost Truppen*, recruited mainly from Red Army prisoners. This man came from Chechnya, which was then part of the Soviet Union. First captured fighting for one side, he had now been captured fighting for the other. The harsh reality for him and his Czech, Polish, Estonian, Lithuanian, Latvian, Ukrainian and Georgian comrades was that, whichever side won, their country's future would be ruthless domination by either Nazism or Russian Communism. At least Parker's Chechnyan had survived and, in the short term, would almost certainly be treated humanely as a prisoner of war.

The Devons capture the Chateau

On the morning of the 8th, Cosmo Nevill and the 2nd Devons advanced west along the coast from Longues to relieve the Commandos. After a short bombardment by their supporting Gunners and the Vickers guns of the Middlesex Regiment, they captured the German platoon post at Le Mesnil without loss to themselves, bagging another thirty-eight prisoners. As they pushed on and it became clear that opposition along this stretch of coast had melted away, Nevill decided to turn inland to retake the Commandos' Main Headquarters on Point 72. After capturing it the night before, the Germans had not had sufficient troops to hold on to the position. It therefore turned out to be a simple task for the Devons to reoccupy it.

Chateau Maisons (Simon Trew)

Below Point 72, however, around the Chateau Maisons remained the German battalion who had caused 47 Commando such trouble. Nevill decided to attack the Chateau and asked first Brigade and then Divisional permission to do so. Because the Chateau was in what should by now have been an American area, Stanier and Graham were reluctant to give such permission and twice sought Nevill's assurance that he was attacking Germans, not Americans. On the spot, it was clear to the Devons that the Americans from Omaha Beach had yet to reach that far and that the enemy in the Chateau remained a threat to Allied troops in the area.

Permission to attack was finally given at 1700 hours, but there was a catch: the guns of the Essex Yeomanry would be free to support any attack only until 1800 hours, after which their support was needed elsewhere. Nevill had less than an hour in which to plan and execute his assault. There would be no time for reconnaissance and the attack would have to go straight in.

Mike Holdsworth, who since D-Day had been commanding B Company, was sent for by Cosmo Nevill, who *told me we had to attack and take the place. 'You will be in command of D Company. You have got to get moving because you will lose the gunners at 6pm; they have another job to do.'*

I told Frank Sadleir of A Company that he would go to the right of the mansion and I would go to the rear. I did not know that there were two rivers in the way, in ditches about 100 yards apart from each other and about six to seven feet deep and ten feet wide. This was all on a completely open piece of ground about 400 yards wide plus, as I discovered later, there was a moat around it fed by a lake. The distance we had to go was about 700 yards.

An A Company runner arrived as we reached the first ditch to tell me they had found a bridge. We used that and then found a second one at the next ditch. So far we had no casualties and I told my soldiers to get a bloody move on.

The lake/pond was thigh deep and I found my Sten gun was not working properly and we then came under fire. My spare magazine didn't work and I knocked it on my knee and replaced it and fired on the windows up and downstairs in the chateau. We came out of the pond and I was walking round the moat and I told my men to go in the front door, which they did.

My Sergeant-Major [CSM Reg Bollam MBE DCM] was with me and suddenly from only twenty yards away a Spandau opened up on us but missed. The Sergeant-Major said to me, 'Excuse me, sir, I have a little job to do.' He fixed his bayonet and charged into the German trench and killed them both. At the same time my men came out of the chateau with some prisoners. That was really the end of the action; A Company had been equally successful.

By the time the two companies had reached the second river, the battery of Essex Yeomanry had had to pack up and move on, and the Sherwood Rangers' Shermans on the top of the hill were running out of ammunition. Cheers rang out from the hill as they saw the Devons go into the final attack across the open parkland.

In the Chateau the Devons found the remnants of their enemies' meal on the table, a great deal of kit scattered about and a sack of mail for Berlin. With only one man killed and remarkably few wounded, Sadleir's and Holdsworth's Companies had captured the headquarters and a hundred officers and men of the 1st Battalion of the 726th Grenadier Regiment.

Their saddest casualty occurred after the battle in an incident of gratuitous nastiness. Mike Holdsworth remembered: *I noticed two of my men talking to two German prisoners and one of my men pulled out a packet of fags from his pocket and offered a cigarette to the left-hand German prisoner. This prisoner I noticed put his hand in his pocket and I knew instantly he had a pistol. He had, and he used the bloody thing and killed him. The German threw the pistol into the moat and both of them ran into the middle of the German prisoners. There was nothing I could do about it as we had to move off in a hurry. I lost one man only in that attack … one man killed through lack of forethought.*

Sunset on 8th June saw a long awaited encounter when two officers of 47 (Royal Marine) Commando met some American soldiers at Huppain, just west of Port-en-Bessin. It was the beginning of the link-up between the British from Gold Beach and the Americans who had landed on Omaha. Later, Brigadier Sir Alex Stanier remembered his first meeting with an American battalion commander, who was wearing only a shirt because his trousers had still not dried out.

The Devons spent the night up on Point 72, watching the Luftwaffe trying to bomb the invasion fleet and marvelling at the colossal firepower of the Allied anti-aircraft barrage that successfully protected the ships and beaches against a determined attack that lasted most of the night. On the next day they moved to Bayeux and occupied part of the town while the Hampshires moved south west of Bayeux as XXX Corps pressed south to enlarge the Normandy beachhead.

He did not know what day it was but, at some point, probably on 8th June, Private Jim Aldred of the 1st Hampshires regained consciousness. We last met him early on D-Day as, wounded and with bayonet in hand, he had passed out while picking his way through the minefield behind the beach. Having landed with Jack Lauder's Platoon of A Company, he had been wounded in the first half hour at Le Hamel.

All of a sudden I heard voices and I looked up and I gave them my name, number and rank. This is what you do when you become a prisoner. A voice turned round and said 'Tommy, we are prisoners. We are here to pick up the wounded'. They were German. They tried to stand me up and I screamed out because my ribs went (cracked). So he took his overcoat and he laid it on the floor, they did something, I don't know what they did, but they laid me in it, and pulled me along, the two of them, to an overturned tank. In front of it was a big hole and they put me in the hole. The medic that was in there, a kind of trench it was, he saw blood coming out of my side and put a label on me saying 'No Water'. The blood coming out meant it was my lungs that had gone. There was an officer in there that said 'For God's sake, give the soldier some water.' So he gave me a sip of water.

They told me I was on the beach for two or three days before they picked me up. Then they hoisted me up, put me on a Bren gun carrier but this time it was carrying stretchers... This officer, who came with us, he turned round and said 'Lift these men up high, for these are your assault troops. Most of them died so you could come onto this beach' and I was lifted up high on their shoulders.

Pushing south towards Villers Bocage

It was a race against time. The British and Canadians were rapidly trying to secure and expand their bridgehead before the Germans could deploy too many tanks and fresh infantry to prevent them. That same day, the 1st Dorsets were assigned temporarily to the 8th Armoured Brigade to understudy for the 12th King's Royal Rifle Corps, who had yet to land. The 12th were one of a handful of motor battalions equipped with tracked armoured vehicles that allowed them rapidly to follow up an advance by tanks. Echoing the Devons' early experience in Sicily, the Dorsets were thus asked to act as a motor battalion, but without the motors. Packed into lorries provided by the Royal Army Service Corps, the Battalion moved forward and assembled at Rucqueville. At 1600 hours they moved south through the leading British units to St Leger, south-east of Bayeux. Their advance would take them – via Loucelles, the hamlets of Audrieu and Pavie, and the village of Tilly-sur-Seulles – to Villers Bocage. The first objective for the Dorsets, supported by the tanks of the 4/7th Dragoon Guards, was a feature called Point 103, between Le Haut d'Audrieu and St Pierre.

Despite having been wounded on D-Day, Tony Jones had rejoined the Battalion, and his A Company took Loucelles without incident. But, when Pat Chilton's B took over the lead towards Bas d'Audrieu, they were held up on the railway line by heavy Spandau fire. Despite determined attempts to cross the line, Lieutenant Morris's 11 Platoon were stalled. Private Brandon's section commander, Corporal George Pearce from Lyme Regis, was killed and half his section were killed or wounded. John Brandon took command and, firing his Bren gun from the hip, ran forward to kill two Germans and capture the position. Corporal Haines and Private Ward also played a brave part in the action. Brandon was later awarded a Military Medal.

A and B Companies were ordered to hold firm while Colonel Norie sent Bobby Nicoll's C Company and Willie Hayes's D round the flanks of the German positions. Because of the urgency to press on and take Villers Bocage, the Dorsets were ordered to continue their mopping up operations overnight. It was while leading a night fighting patrol into Audrieu that Nicoll's highly respected Second-in-Command, Captain Bob Tucker from Bridport, was killed. His was a particularly sad loss. A Cambridge graduate, Tucker was part of the furniture in 231 Brigade who had served on Malta and on the Brigade staff in Sicily, where he had won the Military Cross. On D-Day, as we have seen, he and Corporal Sam Thompson had helped repel the German counter-attack at Puits d'Herode. His loss was widely and deeply felt. The day had cost the Dorsets seven killed and many more wounded.

The Sherwood Rangers occupy Point 103

The Sherwood Rangers had also pressed south and gained some high ground (Point 103) above the village of St Pierre. En route, Major Stanley Christopherson of A Squadron recalled, they by-passed some anti-tank guns but Victor Verner, one of the troop commanders with his head out of the turret, was sniped. Evacuated with a head wound, he died next day.

On arrival at Point 103, the Squadron took up fire positions in the trees overlooking St Pierre, which appeared to be deserted by the civilians and Germans. As no infantry had arrived, John Bethell-Fox, one of my troop commanders, and Keith Douglas, my Second-in-Command, climbed down the hill into the village, but had the greatest difficulty in making contact with any of the civilians, who had all taken refuge in the cellars. They eventually persuaded an old Frenchman to come out of hiding; he told them that there were Germans in the village and tanks in the vicinity. ...they beat a retreat back to their tanks, but on turning a corner they came face to face with a German patrol under an officer. Such an unexpected meeting caused alarm and surprise on both sides and they turned about and made for their respective bases. Keith, however, managed to empty his revolver in the direction of the enemy, but did not wait to ascertain the damage.

Although that evening some anti-tank guns and some Vickers guns from the Middlesex Regiment arrived to help defend the feature, Stanley Christopherson recorded in his diary that: *On the morning of 9 June Point 103 became most uncomfortable and appeared to be the main target of German mortar and tank fire.* Three of the Rangers' tanks were knocked out and Peter Pepler, a troop commander in Hanson-Lawson's B Squadron, was killed by a piece of shrapnel as he climbed into his tank. John Bethell-Fox was sent to investigate whether some approaching tanks were British or German, and Keith Douglas offered to accompany him. The two Shermans set out down the hill.

Bethell-Fox later remembered: *We trundled down the slope, and smashed our way into this orchard, driving along the parallel line of trees. I pulled off another piece of aerial going through this orchard. Eventually we reached the end of the orchard and there, in front of us, was the river. Another fifty yards on was a small church, and a road with vehicles churning up and down. We both got out of our tanks, took a few grenades and a German sub-machine gun: Keith had collected that somewhere, and crawled out of the orchard to the river.*

Having waded across the river, they were crawling in fine drizzle towards the church when a machine gun opened up. They turned and ran back to the river bank, where Douglas, who had been winged by one of the bullets, crouched below the bank as if (utterly uncharacteristically) he was afraid to move. He then suggested that they should swim upstream a hundred yards to emerge at a spot where the Germans would not expect them. His ruse worked and they ran back to their tanks. Returning to Point 103, they dismounted to make their report when a heavy mortar stonk came down. Bethell-Fox's tank was hit and two of his crew wounded. Douglas was running along a ditch when a mortar bomb burst in the tree above his head. He was killed instantly by a splinter so small that it left no visible wound.

Colonel Laycock forbade the Padre to go forward to recover Douglas's body. It was much too dangerous because enemy were dug in there with tanks. In his diary Skinner records at 0300 next morning *sharp words with CO about not being allowed forward to recover bodies of Douglas and Pepler.* Later that day Leslie Skinner had his way. He buried Douglas in a corner of a field a couple of hundred yards from the lane from St Pierre to Audrieu, just below Point 103.

The loss of anyone aged just twenty-four is a tragedy. Other devoted mothers must have faced what Mrs Douglas described as *almost terror of the empty future and the knowledge that the last person to whom I mattered was gone for ever.* But Keith Douglas's death had another dimension: to post-war English poetry his was a unique and bitter loss.

In his last poem, composed while in England awaiting D-Day, he had written:

> *And all my endeavours are unlucky explorers*
> *come back, abandoning the expedition;*
> *the specimens, the lilies of ambition*
> *still spring in their climate, still unpicked:*
> *but time, time is all I lacked*
> *to find them, as the great collectors before me.*

At about this time the 1st Dorsets entered Audrieu and the various hamlets – from Le Haut d'Audrieu to Bas d'Audrieu – were cleared and secured. Captain John Royle, who had led A Company to capture Puits d'Herode in the afternoon of D-Day, was wounded. At the Chateau the Dorsets came upon the rows of dead bodies of twenty-four Canadian and two British soldiers. Recently captured prisoners or war, they had been gunned down, murdered by the thugs of the 12th SS Panzer Division. Like the murder of Mike Holdsworth's soldier, this was a reminder of the nature of some of those they were fighting.

Speedy Bredin, Second-in-Command of the 1st Dorsets, recalled that *our force was now operating in advance of the main bridgehead and both flanks were open... On our right the Sherwood Rangers with the 8th DLI [Durham Light Infantry]... from 151st Brigade, were trying to get into St Pierre on the outskirts of Tilly-sur-Seulles. Odd parties of enemy, including some Spandau groups, were hovering about on our flanks particularly on our left (east), and Audrieu seemed to be full of 'fifth column' rumours of German infiltration. 'Hundreds of Germans' approaching from all directions was the commonest story... There were one or two minor encounters and awkward moments. Corporal Redpath of C Company distinguished himself in one of these encounters...*

A pre-war Regular from Belfast, James Redpath commanded a section doing flank protection. For four hours they withstood heavy fire from Spandaus, snipers and a tank, which turned both its gun and its machine guns on them. His MM citation (with its ring of *Speedy* Bredin's vocabulary) describes how he steadied his section in a *very ticklish situation* and cheered them on *under very trying conditions*.

Evelyn Norie and his company commanders reached Point 103, which the Sherwood Rangers were still occupying unsupported by infantry. By the evening of the 9th, Point 103 had been secured and the 1st Dorsets had formed a protective box around the tanks and the self-propelled guns of the Essex Yeomanry, with A Company to the north-west, B to the north-east, C to the south-east and D to the south-west. Down in St Pierre, the 8th Durhams' fierce battle continued as they faced heavy German counter-attacks. But the Dorsets' defensive perimeter around Point 103 held firm all night and into the next day.

In the afternoon of 9th June Monty visited 231 Brigade's Headquarters. The Allies' five scattered, vulnerable beach-heads had now joined, forming a single, unassailable bridgehead in Northern France. Next day, with pride, satisfaction and relief, he wrote: *the lodgement area was 60 miles long and varied in depth from 8 to 12 miles; it was firmly held*. Operation *Overlord*, the largest assault landing in military history, had succeeded, and 231 Malta Brigade – the Hampshires, Dorsets, Devons and Commandos, together with their supporting arms and services – had played a star part in that success.

Lt Graham Mason Elliott, B Company, 1st Hampshires

Horrifically wounded in the face on D-Day, Lieutenant Graham Mason Elliott of the 1st Hampshires had been evacuated to the Royal Naval

Hospital Haslar, at Gosport, not far from his family home. On 9th June he died on the operating table. It was his twenty-first birthday.

His grieving parents received touching letters from his Commanding Officer, Company Commander and Company Second-in-Command. But, even among these, one letter stands out. It came from one of the crew of the ship which had delivered Graham to Gold Beach.

I would like you to know that most of us in this ship who had the honour of transporting your son and his gallant comrades to the beaches of Normandy on D-Day feel most deeply the news that he is no longer with us, and we would like you to know how well loved he was by us, just Merchant Seamen (and how much more he must have been loved by his own men).

We all feel deeply his loss and, at the risk of causing you pain, I felt I must write this letter in appreciation. He was known to us as the 'varmer's boy'. We have known him on and off for the past two months.

God bless him – it's hard to lose him, but he was everything a man should be.

POSTSCRIPT

What lay ahead: D+4 to VE-Day and beyond

The story you are reading really ends with that last chapter. This book is not a history of 231 Malta Brigade in the campaign in North West Europe. Instead, it tells the Brigade's story on D-Day and continues until 9th June only to complete business that remained unfinished on the 6th. But, having read this far, you may be interested to know what became of some of the people you have met. That is the purpose of this postscript, which will outline what the Brigade did for the rest of the war, and then briefly recount the post-war stories of some of the men who were lucky enough to survive to enjoy the peace.

Pushing south

By D+4 the Normandy campaign had become a desperate battle against an aggressive, resolute foe. German armour and infantry, massing in front of Dempsey's Second Army, would make the rest of the campaign a war of bloody attrition in which every tiny advance was bought with a huge butcher's bill.

We left the Dorsets under heavy shelling, each of their companies supported by a squadron of tanks, guarding Point 103 against repeated German attacks. At 1020 hours on 10th June D Company's position was badly hit and, Major Willie Hayes remembered: *...I took a small piece of shell in my right eye. I must have looked terrible because my soldiers were so concerned. That evening, after dark, the Medical Officer* [Captain Laurance Lassman] *arrived and told me that I would be blind in my right eye and that he thought I was bound to lose the sight in my left eye.* Hayes defied this dismal prognosis. Evacuated by air to hospital in Southampton, he was back with his Company within three weeks.

When Tiger tanks attacked Battalion Headquarters, Colonel Norie and Bobby Nicoll helped fight them off while *Speedy* Bredin ran from company to company, co-ordinating the defence. Major Peter Martin, commanding a Vickers machine gun company of the 2nd Cheshires, recalled: *For two days the battle for Point 103 raged on. I was hailed by the CO of 24th Lancers, sitting on the ground with his arm in a sling. He handed me a rifle, saying, 'Put a round in the breech; at least I'll take one of them with me.' I thought, 'Good God, it's as bad as that.' Shortly afterwards all firing ceased. It was the final attempt by the enemy before pulling out and leaving St Pierre.*

The Hampshires and Devons, meanwhile, had been pushing south from Bayeux. In the ups and downs of the *bocage* country, short views were framed by dense hedgerows, any one of which could hide a Spandau, a mortar or even a dug-in tank or 88mm gun. On the 10th the Hampshires put in a difficult attack on Bernieres Bocage, which was their first costly experience of this kind of fighting.

At 0600 on Sunday the 11th, the Devons advanced to take Trungy and an important crossroads at La Belle Epine. The position the Devons took was overlooked by nearby La Senaudière, which was on high ground occupied by the Germans. They were heavily mortared and German tanks approached, their commanders waving as if they were British, knocking out an anti-tank gun and killing its crew before a single defensive shot had been fired. Trying to form a defendable strongpoint, Colonel Nevill saw Corporal Ratnage, firing a Bren gun from the hip, knock out a Spandau. He remembered that later John Ratnage, a married man from Essex, *died most gallantly attacking another enemy post.*

In this shoot-out Mike Holdsworth rallied his Company under heavy fire and himself did good work with a well-placed grenade, earning a Military Cross. The Anti-Tank Platoon Sergeant, Sam Williams, won a Military Medal by moving his gun to a particularly dangerous place, from where he was able to repel the German attack. Finally at 2200, the day was saved by the arrival of the Sherwood Rangers, whose tanks helped the Devons recapture the village.

That evening also saw a German attack on the Dorsets. Among those killed was Lance-Corporal Joe Miller MM of D Company of the Dorsets. Twenty-five years old, he had won his MM just five days earlier at Puits d'Herode. Instead of returning to his young wife in Northamptonshire, he lies with many of his friends and comrades in the cemetery at Tilly sur Seulles.

On 12th June the Hampshires, supported by AVREs and flails, tried to advance beyond Bernieres Bocage. Their armour was quickly knocked out and, like the Devons, they found themselves exposed to heavy fire from the ridges above them. When the Germans launched a fierce counter-attack, the Hampshires drove it off. In the battle Private Robert Playford from Maidstone repulsed a German attack on his Company Headquarters. Firing his Sten gun and hurling a 36 grenade, he saved many lives and earned a Military Medal.

The battle cost the Hampshires many wounded. Three officers were killed, all of whom had done well on D-Day. The first was Major Jimmy Wicks MC, who had led the composite A/C Company to victory in Le Hamel; the second was Major Tony Boyd MC, the only officer of A Company to survive D-Day unscathed, and who now commanded the Company; and the third was Lieutenant Peter Paul, the Devon subaltern who had led a platoon in John Littlejohns's D Company at Cabane and Arromanches. This triple loss was the bitterest blow for the Battalion, who were losing not only good friends but also precious, rapidly dwindling, battle experience.

That day the 1st Dorsets rejoined the Brigade, which was warned for an advance first towards Les Landes and then, when this stalled, to clear the high ground at La Senaudière.

Private Dudley-Ward, who had nearly drowned landing with the Hampshires on D-Day, wrote on 23rd June from hospital in Nottingham to describe for his wife Eileen what had happened to his Assault Pioneer Platoon on the 13th. *A crowd of fellows and myself got pinned down between the two lines with both sides slinging everything they had at each other. I decided to get out so another fellow and myself made a dash for it and much to our surprise we made it. Then Topper asked me to go along with him, as I was the only one of his platoon he could find and we picked up three others on the way. We lined a bank to help give covering fire but this is as far as any of us got. Over came the bomb. I felt the shrapnel bang into my leg and when the dust cleared I saw that the others were dead. A padre and a stretcher-bearer helped me back to the ADS* [Advanced Dressing Station] *and that was the end of my fighting career for a while.* It was, in fact, the end of Tim Dudley-Ward's fighting war, which had begun on Malta, shortly after his marriage, and had encompassed all three assault landings. His officer, Lieutenant Edwin Brown, known as *Topper*, lies in Bayeux Cemetery; on his grave, chosen by his wife Hilda, is a quotation from Rupert Brooke's poem, *The Soldier*.

Captain David Hammond, a much respected officer in the Battalion who was attached from the Bedfordshire and Hertfordshire Regiment, was also killed that day. Fifty years later a number of Hampshire veterans gathered at David Hammond's grave. Asked why Hammond had been singled out in this way, *Horace* Wright described how, on 13th June at La Senaudière, the 1st Hampshires were being badly mortared. The new CO, Colonel Howie, ordered Hammond, who commanded the Carrier Platoon, to lead a foot patrol to destroy the mortars. David Hammond protested that this was suicidal: the patrol would all be killed as the mortars were some way behind the German front line. The CO was extremely angry and told Hammond that he was being cowardly, at which Hammond threw down his helmet and said he was certainly not a coward. He went off to do the patrol, on which he and four of his men were killed and his Platoon Sergeant, Robert Curley, won the DCM extricating the survivors.

David Hammond, *Topper* Brown and Tim Dudley-Ward all survived exactly a week in Normandy, but, unlike Hilda Brown and Phoebe Hammond, Eileen Dudley-Ward would be getting her young husband back.

Among the Hampshire wounded in two days of hard fighting was Captain Cecil Thomas DSO of B Company. Among their dead was Sergeant Arthur Sippetts from Farnham, who had won the MM leading Alan Norman's Platoon on D-Day. Lance-Corporal Henry Barnes of the 1st Dorsets won an MM for roaring about the battlefield on his motorbike, delivering messages to the scattered companies despite heavy fire. The Dorsets suffered fifty casualties in this battle, including the gallant Company Sergeant-Major Nick O'Connell of D Company, who had been the only rifle company sergeant-major in the Battalion to emerge from D-Day unscathed. He had already been wounded at Point 103. Now he was killed rallying men of his Company to beat off a counter-attack, for which he was posthumously mentioned in Despatches. His widow, Florence, lived for many years in one of the first houses built as a memorial to the dead of the Dorset Regiment in the Second World War.

More and more German Panzer Divisions were being drawn in on the British part of the bridgehead to block a break-out there. Over the next few weeks Monty would maintain pressure on the German defences in the east, finally making it possible for the Americans to break out in the west but rendering the fighting on the British and Canadian front costlier than ever. The rapid depletion of the surviving veterans of D-Day continued. On the 17th the Dorsets lost both their Adjutant and their Signals Officer, who were among a handful of men wounded by a few shells that fell near Battalion Headquarters. In his eleven days in Normandy the Adjutant, Graham Browne of the Royal Warwicks, had added a mention in Despatches to the Military Cross he had won with the 1st Dorsets at Pizzo in Italy. Eric Hannah, who had distinguished himself on Sicily and led the Carrier Platoon on D-Day, took over as Adjutant on top of his other duties.

The Battle at Hottot

After a brief respite, on 19th June the Brigade were ordered to capture the village of Hottot. Thus began a fierce and protracted struggle, during which, unsurprisingly, the village became known to the soldiers as *Hotspot*. The struggle would last for thirty days.

On the 19th, Lieutenant Frank Pease, who had taken over C Company of the Devons when *Bubbles* Duke had fallen to the sniper on D-Day, earned a Military Cross for his gallantry in facing repeated tank attacks. One of Pease's platoon commanders, Harry Heap of the King's Own Royal Lancaster Regiment, also won the MC in this action. The 2nd Devons lost three company commanders killed. One was a replacement who had arrived the day before; the others were Major Arthur Eteson MC and Major Franc Sadleir MBE MC, who had both been with the Battalion since Malta. Both had been married while stationed in Essex in the spring. Arthur Eteson left a twenty-one-year-old widow, Elizabeth, Franc Sadleir left a child he would never see. On 27th December 1944, in a nursing home in Exeter, Ruth Sadleir would have a son, who would be christened Franc.

In torrential rain that began just before lunch, the 1st Hampshires on the Devons' right advanced nearly a mile from La Senaudière. In the face of the usual Spandaus, mortars and Panther tanks, they lost one recently arrived reinforcement officer killed and four others wounded. Among those wounded were Bill Hand, now commanding the Anti-Tank Platoon, and their two most experienced company commanders, David Warren and Tony Mott. The Regimental history sings the praises of the MO, Captain Ivor Joseph MC, who throughout the long battle *worked day and night with the casualties regardless of his own safety.*

The 1st Dorsets suffered even more, losing nearly 100 casualties, including their Commanding Officer, who was mortally wounded by a mortar bomb. Evelyn Norie was not a Dorset and had commanded the 1st Battalion for only thirteen days in battle, but his loss was felt throughout the Battalion. He never knew about the DSO he had won on D-Day. *Speedy* Bredin assumed command while Sergeant Stevenson and others, armed with PIATs, bravely took on Panther tanks. Stevenson later received a French Croix de Guerre for his courage in this action.

Over the coming four weeks, the relentless fighting around Hottot claimed many more casualties. The Hampshires' long list of wounded in these battles included: John Littlejohns, Captain Malcolm Bradley, the last remaining officer from Littlejohns's D Company, and Alan King of C Company, who had won the MC on D-Day. William Mayne, Company Sergeant-Major of B Company, was captured on 20th June. The Hampshires had also lost many post-D-Day reinforcement officers, including their fiery new CO, Colonel Charles Howie, who was killed leading two of his companies in an assault. The Dorsets' list of fatal casualties included Major Tony Jones (who had been wounded on D-Day but had returned in double-quick time to resume command of A Company), Lieutenant Colin Windebank, who had led 13 Platoon so well on D-Day, and several reinforcement officers received since then. One especially tragic loss was Corporal Sam Thompson MM, who died of wounds on 24th June without knowing about the DCM he had earned on the 6th at Point 54.[23] The Devons' losses included their newly arrived Padre, killed in a mistaken attack by RAF Typhoons. Among the many wounded were their devoted Medical Officer, Captain John Lloyd, and their CO, Colonel Cosmo Nevill. Major Guy Browne, who was later mentioned in Despatches, temporarily took command of a saddened Battalion.

On 19th July – the last day of the Battle for Hottot – Lieutenant-Colonel Turner arrived to take command of the 1st Hampshires. He was the fifth officer to command the Battalion in six weeks. Of the twenty-six officers who had landed on 6th June in the Hampshires' five fighting companies, only two remained. Casualties among NCOs and soldiers were high, but thankfully not as devastating as those among the officers. Nonetheless, *Chalky* Chalk of A Company recalled that: *After five weeks of almost continuous action against the best the German army could put in the field, only myself and two other men remained of the ninety or more men of my Company who had landed* [on D-Day]. In the Dorsets, the picture was very similar, while by now the Devons had lost twenty-two officers and 350 NCOs and soldiers killed or wounded. The Brigade that would continue the campaign in Normandy was not the one that had hit the beach at 0730 on D-Day, but the survivors and successors of the D-Day men would fight on, adding new honours to the reputation won on that first day.

During the same period the 90th Field Regiment lost Captain Vine, one of their forward observation officers with the Dorsets, and Major Wells, a battery commander, both wounded. The Sherwood Rangers had already lost Sergeant Bracegirdle, wounded on D+1. They now lost their new Commanding Officer, Colonel Mike Laycock, who had taken command when John Anderson had been wounded on D-Day. Laycock was killed outright by a shell, together with his Adjutant and the Regiment's Intelligence Officer. Padre Skinner, Major John Hanson-Lawson and Lieutenant Ian Greenaway were all wounded in the battles around Hottot. Stanley Christopherson took command and would lead the Regiment with great distinction for the rest of the campaign.

After Hottot, the Malta Brigade were visited by General Montgomery, who presented ribbons to the tragically few who remained of the

---

23. On the morning of 4th July 2018 four of us involved in producing this book visited Tilly Cemetery and paid our respects at several graves. By the time we reached Sam's grave we had used our last poppy cross, but a family from the Midlands arrived. I told them Sam's story and that he was a Midlander, and their son, Eloi Roberts, kindly placed his own poppy cross on the grave. Sam Thompson's medals are displayed at the Keep Military Museum.

forty-two officers and men who had been decorated since D-Day. Among those decorated was the irrepressible Major Willie Hayes who, having regained his eyesight, had just returned to command D Company of the Dorsets. Bobby Nicoll was also there to receive his MC, but a second recurrence of malaria saw his disappearance soon afterwards. While they were out of the line, Major-General Douglas Graham visited the Brigade to congratulate them on their performance since D-Day. An old friend who had commanded 231 Brigade in Sicily and Italy, Major-General Roy Urquhart, also visited. Now commanding the 1st Airborne Division, he was about to play a leading role in an operation that would prove to be the Malta Brigade's last major action.

With most of the German army and almost all its armour facing the British and Canadian front, the Americans were able to begin their break-out on 25th July. Meanwhile, Monty ordered Miles Dempsey's Second Army to drive south towards Vire, Condé and Falaise. On 30th July, in an attack on the ridges above Villers Bocage, the 1st Dorsets lost their last remaining D-Day officer in a rifle company. Arthur Harris, now commanding B Company, and his batman were wounded by a mine.

On 6th August Captain *Horace* Wright, now commanding B Company of the 1st Hampshires, was wounded, and five days later the Battalion sustained another 100 casualties in an attack on St Pierre La Vieille. Next day the Dorsets repelled a fierce German counter-attack and occupied Les Forges, a few miles above Condé sur Noireau.

The Brigade's bloody campaign in Normandy was over. 43rd Wessex Division (in which the 7th Hampshires and 4th and 5th Dorsets together formed 130 Brigade) now led the British advance across the Seine. The Germans, finally routed after a savage and protracted campaign, were retreating in total disorder. The end of the war seemed in sight.

Into Belgium and the Netherlands

Although 231 Brigade played no part in the crossing of the Seine in late August, they did get drawn into the lightning advance into Belgium that followed. Transferred temporarily from the 50th Division to the Guards Armoured Division, the Brigade sped through towns with names thoroughly familiar to their fathers – Amiens and Arras – and on towards Brussels. After advancing ninety-seven miles in fourteen hours, bypassing or clearing opposition as they went, they reached Brussels at 1700 hours on 3rd September: the fifth anniversary of the outbreak of war. The 1st Hampshires, who had been the first infantry ashore on D-Day, became the first to cross the Belgian border and to enter the Belgian capital. A Company, so terribly depleted on 6th June, now took part in a Victory

Parade. Major-General Alan Adair, commanding Guards Armoured Division, published an order of the day: *The speed of the advance, the distance covered, the relentless way in which opposition was overcome, were admirable. I have no doubt that this operation will go down to history as one of the great feats of the war.*

Rejoining 50th Division two days later, the Brigade moved north to guard the south east corner of Antwerp along the eastern bank of the River Scheldt. From the 9th, again lent to Guards Armoured, they pressed on across the Escaut Canal towards Eindhoven. The question now was how best to exploit what had become a rout. Monty's answer, Operation *Market Garden*, was to try to force a crossing of the Neder Rijn at Arnhem and then to encircle and isolate Germany's industrial heart: the Ruhr. The *Market* part of the plan entailed dropping American and British airborne troops to secure several canal and river crossings in a line from Eindhoven, via Grave and Nijmegen, to Arnhem. The *Garden* part required Brian Horrocks's XXX Corps (including Guards Armoured, 50th and 43rd Wessex Divisions) to advance rapidly up a single road, with enemy often on both sides of it, to relieve each airborne pocket in turn.

In the initial advance the 1st Dorsets and 2nd Devons cleared either side of the road as Colonel Joe Vandeleur's Irish Guards Group motored as fast as they could up the road. During the advance the 2nd Devons became the first infantry battalion to cross the Dutch border. Despite their combined efforts, they made slower progress than had been hoped and, to everyone's frustration, delays multiplied, caused by opposition and simple traffic jams on the single road, which was frequently cut by enemy action. By the time 43rd Wessex crossed the Waal at Nijmegen, any chance of success had passed. After a gallant stand, Lieutenant-Colonel John Frost's 2nd Parachute Regiment, the only Airborne battalion to have reached Arnhem Bridge, had been forced to surrender.

The Operation had fallen at the last fence. With the bridge back in their hands, the Germans poured guns, tanks and troops south to create a fearsome defensive line across the flat *polderland* towards Nijmegen. The tanks of the Guards Armoured Division could not get forward without being knocked out by a screen of 88mm guns. The infantry of 43rd Wessex Division could not advance in the open country without being mown down by the screen of defending Spandaus. Despite this, the 4th and 5th Dorsets, moving rapidly in a column, managed to reach Driel, on the south bank of the Neder Rijn west of Arnhem. When the operation was finally called off, 300 men of the 4th gallantly crossed the river, where they found the remnants of British Airborne troops who had been holding a defensive pocket above the north bank. They had been pitchforked into chaos and many of the 4th were killed or captured helping Airborne survivors to withdraw. For the second time since the Battle of Hill 112 on

10th July, for all practical purposes the 4th Battalion had ceased to exist. Meanwhile, the 5th crewed small boats and bravely ferried the Airborne survivors and some of their comrades from the 4th back across the river.

The infantry of XXX Corps now faced the German defenders in a line that ran from Opheusden on the Neder Rijn south east to Elst, Aam and Bemmel. The German aim was to force the British back to the River Waal and to recapture Nijmegen. The British plan was to hold the line securely to retain the country gained in their recent advances. Since the 2nd Devons had crossed the Dutch border, large tracts of the Netherlands had been liberated. A successful defence of the flatlands between Arnhem and Nijmegen would prevent the area falling back into German hands and secure the river crossing at Nijmegen itself.

On 1st October the 1st Dorsets moved up near Bemmel to help 69 Brigade hold their part of the line. The Germans had just launched a fierce attack, which had overrun the positions held by one of the 69th's battalions. The 1st Dorsets' job was to help restore the situation and bolster the defence.

General Horrocks's response, founded on the solid principle that attack is the best form of defence, was to launch a two-brigade attack on the Germans above Bemmel at Heuvel and Aam. The Dorsets would attack on the left with the Hampshires on their right. On the Hampshires' right would be the 9th Durham Light Infantry of 151 Brigade. Sherman tanks of the 1st Coldstream Guards would be in support, together with some M10 tank destroyers (probably from the 21st Anti-Tank Regiment) and the Vickers guns of the Middlesex Regiment. The aim was to push the Germans back beyond the line of the Wetering Canal.

The Hampshires led with A Company and the Dorsets with A and B Companies. It was a bloody, hard-fought battle, in which the Brigade took more than 100 prisoners and killed at least seventy of the enemy. The Dorsets suffered nearly ninety casualties, including both company commanders killed. Among the Hampshires, Major *Horace* Wright was wounded and badly shaken by a shell bursting beside his slit trench, but continued the battle, winning a Bar to the MC he had earned at Tebourba in 1942. Once again, he was rescuing wounded under fire. One Hampshire subaltern was killed and five wounded. Sicily veteran Sergeant Medway of A Company won the MM but, sadly, Sergeant Bert Slade, who had won the MM at Le Hamel, was among those killed.

As the battle developed and more companies were drawn into the battle, other veterans of D-Day were luckier. Willie Hayes, still commanding D Company of the Dorsets, won a Bar to the MC he had won on 6th June. Like *Horace* Wright, he had been buried by a shellburst but quickly recovered to reorganise his Company under heavy fire. Sergeant Richard Mattock, who had been the Dorsets' Signal Sergeant since D-Day, and Company Sergeant-Major Norman Elgie of A Company, each received a Military

Medal for their bravery that day. *Speedy* Bredin was awarded the DSO for his brave and skilful handling of the Dorsets' share of the battle. When the Germans attacked the 2nd Devons' position, Sergeant Tom Woodcock went out into dangerous ground, under mortar and machine gun fire, to bring in wounded men. He too received a Military Medal. But the action cost the Devons the life of their Anti-Tank Platoon Sergeant, who had won the MM early in Normandy. A Devonport man, Sam Williams was twenty-five.

Thus ended the Brigade's final battle in their long campaign from Malta, via Sicily, Italy, Normandy, Belgium and the Netherlands. It was a high note to end on. A few days earlier, a three-man patrol of the 1st Dorsets (Lieutenant Walsh, Sergeant Pinfold and Lance-Corporal Davis) had been the first infantry to enter Germany.

Major Wells, commanding 465th Battery of the 90th Field Regiment who had been wounded during the Hottot battle, was again wounded in the battle at Aam but remained hard at work providing the fire support his infantry needed. He was later evacuated to the Casualty Clearing Station; later still he received a Military Cross and a Croix de Guerre. This incident reminds us how many of the gunners and tank-crews who had supported the Brigade since D-Day had been killed or wounded.

A glance at the history of the Sherwood Rangers reveals that, of their officers and men mentioned here because of the part they played on D-Day, very few survived the campaign unscathed. On three successive days from 25th June, Jimmy McWilliam was wounded by splinters from a high explosive shell, Ian Greenaway received multiple shrapnel wounds to his body and leg, and John Hanson-Lawson was evacuated with burns to his legs, hands and face. Stuart Hills had a lucky escape in mid-August crossing the River Noireau when his Sherman was hit by a Panzerfaust. At Gheel on 10th and 11th September Colin Thomson was wounded and Jimmy McWilliam, who had returned to the Regiment six weeks earlier, was sent back to the UK with burns and a head wound. The nature of their wounds, carefully recorded by Padre Skinner in his notebook, point to the peculiar horrors of tank warfare.

The casualties incurred by the infantry of 231 Brigade itself are powerfully illustrated by a letter from Lance-Sergeant Jonah Farrar, who had landed on D-Day in Lieutenant Jack Lauder's platoon in A Company of the 1st Hampshires. On 13th October he wrote from hospital to Lauder, who was still recovering from his own wound. Sergeant Farrar had been wounded on 18th September during the second day of XXX Corps' advance up the road from Eindhoven to Nijmegen. For his bravery in the campaign he was later mentioned in Despatches.

L/Sgt Farrar 4756658
1st Hamps
Ward
Cumberland Infirmary
Carlisle
13-10-44

Dear Sir

Just a few lines in answer to your letter. I am improving and I hope you are the same. If you are getting fed up of sick leave you will have to let me have your share.

I think I can give you some news as regards some of the boys you mention in your letter. To start with, Britton, I am sorry to say, is buried near my brother and Major Baines, also Clarke. Dyer, the only news we got about him was missing. There was a lot of unknown graves there so whether he was one of them or not I could not say. Stroulger was wounded and definitely got back to England. Prouton was missing in the same attack as Major Boyd got killed on the 13-6-44. We never saw him again after that and, if he was killed, we never found his body. We came to the conclusion he was taken prisoner. Of course that is not official, it is our view.

Me and Sgt Medway had a bit of trouble seeking Cpl Rose... he was reported wounded yet his people never heard from him. At the same time someone told his people they had seen his grave, and his people were in a sorry state and did not know what to believe. So they sent a letter to Sgt Medway asking him to find out for them. We got a pass down to the beach and we had a good look round at the graves. We found his in a little churchyard but he had Pte Rose marked on his cross. We checked his number and it turned out to be Cpl Rose's grave. He died in the CCS [Casualty Clearing Station] so we solved that one for his people.

I will close now hoping to hear from you again.

All the best, Sir, from your old friend Sgt Farrar.

PS Did you see the Daily Mirror today? It mentions our D-Day landings and gives us High Praise.

The two Farrar brothers from Batley in Yorkshire, Jonah and Arthur, had landed with Jack Lauder on D-Day. Arthur, aged twenty-five, had been killed in the first few minutes at Le Hamel. Corporal Denis Rose, as we have seen, was mortally wounded beside Jim Aldred. Twenty-five-year-old Frederick Britton, twenty-four-year-old Frederick Clarke and twenty-one-year-old Leonard Dyer were also killed. Private Dyer's body was never found, but all the others, including Major Dick Baines, are buried in Bayeux War Cemetery. Sergeant Farrar's deduction about Private Prouten was correct: he spent the rest of the war as a prisoner in Poland. In another letter, along with other news, Jonah Farrar told Lauder that, by 3rd October 1944, of the thirty-six men who had landed in his Platoon on 6th June, only two – Corporal Heath and Private Jimmy Brett – remained.

The end

After occupying the area south of Arnhem on and off until the end of November, the Brigade heard that the 50th Division was to be stood down and returned to England to train other troops. The 2nd Devons, who had not lost quite as heavily as the other two battalions in the Brigade, were to remain and join the 7th Armoured Division. Long-serving soldiers and officers would return with their much reduced battalion; the rest would be dispersed mainly among other battalions of their regiments. Most Hampshires would join their 7th Battalion while most Dorsets joined either their 4th or 5th Battalions. As the 7th Hampshires and 4th and 5th Dorsets together made up 130 Brigade of the legendary 43rd Wessex Division, most of the Malta Brigade's survivors would at least stay together within XXX Corps in another good brigade in another fine division.

As we have seen, few veterans of 6th June remained – especially among the battalions' officers. At the top, *Sammy* Stanier was still there. *Speedy* Bredin brought his skeleton Battalion home with Willie Hayes and 130 men. In the Hampshires, Frank Waters, who had been Adjutant on D-Day, now commanded a company. Captain Tom Wilmer, who had commanded HQ Company, and Freddie Stone, the Quartermaster, also remained.

Having suffered casualties on this scale, the British were running out of infantry, and soldiers were being combed out from other arms and services to supply the deficiency. The skeleton 1st Dorsets and 1st Hampshires were sent to Yorkshire to instruct Gunners being converted into infantrymen. The Brigade was nominally kept in being and the 2nd Devons' place in it was filled by the very experienced soldiers of the 1/6th Battalion of the Queen's Royal Regiment, veterans of North Africa, Italy and North West Europe.

When 231 Malta Brigade was formally disbanded shortly after the end of the war neither Sir Alex Stanier nor Speedy Bredin was there to see it happen. Stanier had moved to command 69 Brigade while Bredin had returned to North West Europe and taken command of the 5th Dorsets, whom he led across the Rhine and to beyond Bremen. Shortly before the Rhine crossing Bredin had returned to London to lead some of his 1st Dorsets to an investiture at Buckingham Palace. Here, in a rare honour, the Dorsets received their awards together before all other recipients. Joining them on the day was Mike Holdsworth of the 2nd Devons, receiving the MC he had earned at La Belle Epine.

The Brigade's history – enduring the blitzes on besieged Malta, making three successful assault landings and fighting countless fierce battles in Sicily, Italy, France, Belgium and the Netherlands – was a proud one. But, among their many achievements, none exceeded their brilliance on D-Day. In his final communication to his Brigade before the landings, Sir Alex Stanier had urged everyone to conduct the operation with *dash and determination*. The 1st Hampshires, 1st Dorsets and 2nd Devons had exceeded his hopes and excelled. In doing so, they had earned themselves a proud place in history.

Though much is taken, much abides

In 1945 the surviving officers and men of 231 Malta Brigade dispersed. Some stayed in the post-war Regular Army. Many, often through their regimental associations, maintained contact with some of their comrades. Others were scattered to the four winds. Most were profoundly grateful to have been granted an opportunity that so many of their friends had been denied: to return to their homes and families, to hot food, warm houses and clean sheets. This final section briefly tells what happened in peace to some of the men we have encountered in war.

The Brigadier

For his part in the final battle south of Arnhem Sir Alex Stanier DSO MC was awarded a Bar to his DSO. He also received two Belgian decorations and a French Legion d'Honneur. Having commanded 69 Brigade and then reverted to Lieutenant-Colonel to command the 1st Battalion of the Welsh Guards, he left the army in 1948. He returned to Shropshire, where he farmed and took an active part in local life and politics. He became High Sheriff of Shropshire, a Deputy Lieutenant for the County and County President for St John's Ambulance. *Sammy* died in 1995, aged ninety-six. He is proudly remembered at Arromanches and Asnelles as the man who led their liberation.

The Stanier Memorial at Arromanches (Rob Fraser)

The Hampshires

David Nelson Smith MC returned from convalescence to command the 1/5th Battalion of the Welch Regiment in Holland and the Ardennes. Wounded a third time in 1945, he ended the war on the staff at XXX Corps Headquarters in Germany. In 1947 the Belgians appointed him a Chevalier of the Order of Leopold II (the Croix de Guerre). Such were the effects of the post-war army reductions that it was 1947 before the man who had commanded the 1st Battalion of his Regiment on Gold Beach on D-Day was promoted major, and it was 1956 before he regained the rank of lieutenant-colonel. He commanded the 14th Battalion of the Parachute Regiment (which was the 5th Territorial Army Battalion of the Royal Hampshire Regiment). After three years on the staff at Sandhurst and a posting at the War Office, he was promoted Brigadier and commanded two Territorial Army Brigades (131 and 133). He retired in 1964 and became Secretary of the County of Surrey TA Association. When this job disappeared under the savage cuts of the Territorial Army in the mid-1960s, he spent ten years as Administrator of St Godric's Secretarial College in London. He always attended the 1st Hampshires' Annual D-Day Lunch and, on 6th June 1994, he led the huge parade of Normandy veterans as they marched past Her Majesty The Queen at Arromanches.

When David Warren DSO MC recovered from his wounds, he married before taking up a staff posting in the Sudan and Eritrea. He commanded the 1st Royal Hampshires in the West Indies in the early 1960s and served in South Arabia, Germany and Libya before retiring with the honorary rank of Brigadier. He was Colonel of the Royal Hampshire Regiment for ten years from 1971 and was appointed Deputy Lieutenant for Hampshire. Another distinguished Royal Hampshire, Captain Roger Coleman, who served from 1954 until 1981, remembers Warren visiting the Sergeants' Mess when he was Regimental Sergeant-Major of the 1st Battalion. On the wall hung the oil painting which appears on the dust jacket of this book, and Roger remembers asking him. *Where are you in the painting?* Brigadier Warren hesitated, and then replied with a wee smile, *'I was dug in!' 'What were your thoughts after a very long day?'* He replied, *'I rather thought we had a long way to go (to Berlin).'* A keen yachtsman, David Warren lived in Lymington. He died, aged eighty-two, in 2001.

Tony Mott – known in his own Regiment as *Maggie* – was born in Lichfield but followed his father and grandfather into the Queen's Royal Regiment. Commissioned from Sandhurst in 1933, he joined the 1st Battalion in Quetta in 1935. He served in Waziristan and Peshawar, was mentioned in Despatches and became Second-in-Command of his Battalion before being returned to England in 1943, where he was attached to the 1st Hampshires. He was severely wounded at Hottot on 19th June. After the war he instructed at the School of Infantry and served on the staff before returning to the 1st Queen's and serving with them in Siam, Malaya and Singapore. In 1950 he was seconded to the King's African Rifles. He left the army in 1956 and joined the Overseas Civil Service in Nyasaland. He retired to Devon in 1965 and died, aged eighty-nine, in 2002.

John Littlejohns MC was born in Devonport in July 1916 and was commissioned into the Hampshire Regiment, serving with them in India and Palestine before the war. Severely wounded in Normandy, he transferred to the Royal Artillery in 1947 and served with them for eleven years before retiring with the honorary rank of lieutenant-colonel in June 1958. He died in Fleet, Hampshire, in 1993 at the age of seventy-seven.

Born in 1918, Edward George Wright MC – known as *Horace* – was commissioned into the Hampshire Regiment in October 1940. He fought with them in Tunisia in late 1942, winning a Military Cross for rescuing wounded under fire and being captured at Tebourba. In September 1943 he and five other officers hid in a tunnel for two and a half days before escaping from their prison camp and making their way down Italy to reach the Allies. He was mentioned in Despatches for his courage and endurance. Having been wounded in Normandy, he returned and commanded a company in the fierce battle of Bemmel. Wounded again, he won a Bar to his MC again for rescuing wounded under heavy fire. He was later mentioned in Despatches for a second time. After the war he was promoted Captain and became a Regular officer, serving in Libya and Palestine with the 1st Hampshires. Fighting in Malaya in 1951, he was again mentioned in Despatches. He was promoted Major in 1953 and appointed MBE for his dedicated work as a staff officer in the British Army of the Rhine. A quiet, gentle, almost pedantic man, he had enormous reserves of courage and determination. On leaving the army he lived quietly, running an electrical shop in Bournemouth and devoting a great deal of his bachelor life to charitable work. Asked years later what was the most dangerous thing in Normandy, *Horace* – a professional to his fingertips – replied: *Any form of patrol, especially at night and coming back into your own lines. Sentries were extremely quick to fire. Yes, patrolling.*

Awarded a Military Cross for his bravery with the 1st Hampshires on D-Day, Alan King of the Sherwood Foresters was wounded near Hottot and evacuated to the UK. The son of a doctor in Brigg in Lincolnshire, he had already lost his older brother, who was killed in November 1943 flying as a bomb-aimer with the Pathfinders. By the time Alan's wounds had healed, 231 Brigade had returned to England. He was therefore sent to join a battalion of the Wiltshire Regiment in 129 Brigade of the 43rd Wessex Division. He was killed on 15th February 1945, during the fighting to clear the west bank of the Rhine. He was twenty-two.

Despite being told that he would spend the rest of his life in a wheelchair, twenty-one-year-old Jack Lauder recovered from the wound he received at 0735 on D-Day. After he was demobilised, he returned to Exeter University to resume his studies in classics and education. There he met Mary Vines. They married in 1949 and, following Jack's appointment as a classics teacher at the Royal Grammar School, they moved to the Guildford area. Jack spent his entire career at the RGS, becoming head of the Classics department, and eventually retiring in 1984 as Deputy Headmaster. For many years he also ran the School Scout troop while serving on his local church's PCC. Jack and Mary raised four children and, in retirement, moved to North Wales to be close to their eldest son and his family. There, they enjoyed more than twenty years of retirement, their house becoming both a base for overseas travel to visit family and friends in Greece, America, and New Zealand, and a focal point for the family to gather. Jack died peacefully, aged eighty-six, in 2009.

Alan Norman was evacuated from Normandy on D+1 and that night was admitted to a hospital near Slough. Recovered from his wounds, in early 1946 he married Lilian Taylor, who had nursed him at the Derby Royal Infirmary. Back with the army, he helped train the Ethiopian Army and met Haile Selassie. After university and training as an engineer, he spent most of his life in Nottinghamshire. As an officer in the Territorial Army, he reached the rank of lieutenant-colonel, commanding a Territorial battalion of the Sherwood Foresters. In 1967 he received the second clasp to his Territorial Decoration and the following year was appointed OBE. In 2014 Alan's son, Adrian, remembered: *Some years ago we undertook a family expedition to Normandy – my parents, my brother, myself and my partner, and my sons (teenagers at the time) – and retraced my fathers' D-Day actions. We saw where he landed – slightly off course! We saw the pillbox he assaulted, the dunes where he took some prisoners, and the likely location of the machine gunner who shot him! We also found the graves of his men who survived D-Day – many of them were killed in the following two weeks and are in the cemetery in Bayeux.* Alan took part in the D-Day 50th Anniversary celebrations in Normandy and was very keen to attend the 70th anniversary commemorations in 2014, but he died before they took place, shortly after his ninetieth birthday.

D-Day left young Gordon Layton in a very bad way. The bullet in his leg had severed the sciatic nerve while the one in his chest had punctured a lung. It was two years before the bullet in his chest was removed. The loss of his leg must have been a bitter blow to a keen and gifted cricketer. He had enjoyed soldiering and would have relished a peacetime army career but that, too, was not to be. Fitted with an artificial leg, he constructed a new life. He met Colleen, a very young nurse from Portsmouth, whom he pursued with great determination and success. They married in 1954 and together had a son and two daughters. With similar determination he built his career as a building society manager and, in his spare time, returned to cricket, batting with the aid of a runner. Many of those who knew him never guessed he had lost a leg. Few knew about his dramatic part in D-Day, but he maintained his friendships within the Royal Hampshire Regiment until his death in 2001.

2/Lt Gordon Layton, D Company, 1st Hampshires, in later life

Company Sergeant-Major William Mayne DCM, who as a young soldier had scored the Hampshire hat trick (earning three campaign medals in four years), had enlisted in 1931 and then survived a spectacular career in the war. Having served on Malta, he won the DCM in Sicily, was wounded landing in Italy and survived D-Day as Tony Mott's CSM in B Company before being captured near Hottot. He was held in two prisoner of war camps for nearly a year before being released and repatriated at the end of the war. Sadly, his health had suffered acutely and he died, aged only thirty-seven, on his way to hospital in May 1946. His medals, donated by his sister Marjorie, are on display at the Royal Hampshire Regiment Museum.

Channel Islander Sergeant Clement Bisson MM, who led 10 Platoon of the 1st Hampshires so courageously in Asnelles and Le Hamel, married in Yorkshire in 1945. Soon after, he returned to St Helier where he became a postman. He died, aged eighty-six, on Jersey in 2001.

Sergeant Jim Bellows was born in Southampton in 1917 and enlisted in the Hampshire Regiment in 1934. He served with them in India, Palestine, Egypt, Malta, Sicily and Italy and throughout the campaign in North West Europe. Having been Signals Sergeant, he joined the Post Office as an engineer. Married with three children, he later worked as a stevedore at Southampton docks. In his eighties he wrote two books: *When In Doubt, Brew Up* (about his army career) and *My Southampton* (about his home town in the 1920s and 1930s). He died, aged ninety-one, in 2008.

The loss of his brother Arthur as they both came ashore on D-Day remained a profound and constant sadness through the rest of Sergeant Jonah Farrar's life. Recovered from his wounds, he worked for some years for an international carpet company and returned to playing rugby league. Before the war he had captained an under-19s team who had won three cups in a record-breaking single season. He emigrated with his family to Australia where, a few years after his first marriage ended, he found happiness in his second. A devoted family man, he took deep pride in his children's and grandchildren's achievements. His grandchildren remember playing backyard cricket with him when he was in his seventies, by which time his principal sport was bowls. Jonah died, a few days after his eighty-second birthday, in 1997.

Private Jim Aldred, who had joined Jack Lauder's Platoon just before D-Day and had been wounded soon after landing, lost a lung but recovered from his wounds and completed his service in the Parachute Regiment. He lived latterly in Hastings, became a devout Christian and returned to Normandy for the sixtieth anniversary of D-Day.

The Dorsets

Alexander *Speedy* Bredin DSO MC was born in 1911, the son of an Indian Army officer. Commissioned in the Dorset Regiment, he served in

Palestine and Waziristan before the war and briefly in Malta at the start of the siege. He returned to the Regiment as Second-in-Command in time for D-Day. A remarkable and fearless commanding officer, he astonishingly emerged from the Second World War unscathed. One of his predecessors died of wounds, the other was taken ill, but he survived to command the 1st Dorsets from Normandy to Arnhem and the 5th Dorsets across the Rhine, winning first the MC and then the DSO. A proud Dorset, within a year of the end of the war, he had personally written the history of the 1st Battalion and had seen to it that a history of the 5th was also produced. His own history of the 1st Dorsets is clear, human and eminently readable, exuding a good commanding officer's abiding interest in, and affection for, his soldiers. He later became Colonel of the Devonshire and Dorset Regiment. He died in Honiton, aged 80, in 1991.

Maj Speedy Bredin, Second in Command, 1st Dorsets, later in his career.

Pat Chilton MC was commissioned into the Dorset Regiment in 1937 and joined the 1st Battalion as they were about to leave India. He served throughout the siege of Malta, won the MC commanding B Company at Agira on Sicily and landed in Italy in September 1943. Wounded in Normandy, he was evacuated to England and, on recovery, was sent on a lecture tour to the United States of America. After the war he was an instructor at the Royal Military Academy Sandhurst but left the army in 1950. He died, aged seventy-seven, in 1994.

Born near Bideford in 1914, Bobby Nicoll MC was commissioned into the Dorset Regiment in 1934 and served with the 1st Battalion on the North West Frontier, on Malta and on Sicily. In the invasion of Italy in September 1943, the landing schedules were thrown out by appalling weather. Instead of the Commandos, followed by the assault companies, first ashore was the Dorsets' Second-in-Command, Bobby Nicoll, carrying a sack of mail for the troops. After a dazzling performance commanding C Company on D-Day, his campaign in Normandy was disrupted by recurrent bouts of malaria. Later he served as a staff officer at XXX Corps Headquarters before attending the Army Staff College. Having been Brigade Major of the British Brigade in Japan, he served on the staff in Korea during the Korean War. He was the last Commanding Officer of the 1st Dorsets in Minden when the Regiment amalgamated with the Devonshire Regiment in 1958. He retired from the army in 1960 and died near Honiton in 1996. His medals are displayed at the Keep Military Museum.

Willie Hayes MC was born in Bournemouth and joined the Dorset Regiment because he had played them at cricket and liked them. Educated at King's School, Canterbury, and Sandhurst, he was commissioned just in time to join the 1st Dorsets on Malta in September 1939. He served throughout the siege, commanded the Bren gun Carrier Platoon on Sicily, landed in Italy and commanded D Company through most of the campaign in North West Europe. He served after the war in Kenya and Germany and with the Dorset Territorials. After leaving the army, he headed the cadets for many years and lived in Osmington, near Weymouth. He was appointed a Deputy Lieutenant for the county he had adopted. His medals, donated by his son, are displayed with Bobby Nicoll's and Sam Thompson's at the Keep Museum.

Born in Reigate in 1908, *Dick* Whittington MC first served in the Territorial Army from the late 1920s. Although a Queen's officer, Whittington maintained his close links with his adopted Regiment, attending post-war dinners and social gatherings. He also attended the Dorset investiture in March 1945, when he received the MC he had earned on D-Day. After the war he remained an officer in the Queen's TA until 1958 while he worked as a stockbroker. He died, aged eighty-four, in Hereford.

Alby Talbot MM also attended the special Dorsets' investiture in 1945. Like *Dick* Whittington, with whom he shared a long day on Jig-Green beach, he was older than most of the fighting soldiers. Born in 1911 in Marylebone, he had enlisted as a Boy Bandsman in the Dorset Regiment in 1926. He continued to serve until 1950, becoming first Band Sergeant and then Colour Sergeant. He retired to Torbay and died, aged seventy, in 1981.

In an extraordinary army career, Victor Carter MM fought with the Queen's Royal Regiment in France in 1940 and in North Africa before transferring to the 1st Dorsets, with whom he fought in Sicily, Italy and North West Europe. Awarded the Military Medal for his bravery on D-Day, he was wounded twice and returned to England in February 1945. The following month he attended the Dorsets' investiture at Buckingham Palace. Promoted sergeant, he was awarded the Territorial Efficiency Medal. After the war he worked for thirty years in the coal mines in Derbyshire and he and his wife raised five children. He died, aged 70, in 1989.

Denis Bounsall DCM was another who attended the Dorsets' investiture in March 1945 but, as a Regular soldier, he still had three years left to serve. A gifted artist, on leaving the army he worked as a painter for a leading stained glass studio but soon got involved in designing, cutting and leading. After his wartime marriage ended, in 1952 he emigrated to New Zealand, where he has spent the rest of his life. He married again in 1955 and settled in Auckland, where he worked in insurance, played in dance bands, painted and indulged his lifelong passion for dogs and the beautiful country around his home. In 2004 Denis attended the commemorations of the 60th anniversary of D-Day. Two stained glass regimental panels, designed and made by him, are displayed in the Mairie at Asnelles and at the Keep Military Museum in Dorchester. He and his wife were happily married for fifty years until her death, aged ninety-five. A proud and distinguished Dorset, active and sociable, Denis still drives his car and lives independently in a comfortable flat, surrounded by his own paintings of his much-loved dogs.

In his diary before D-Day young Private Terry Parker had written *God watch over me* and *I wish everything was alright with Jess*. He did and it was. As we have seen, Terry survived D-Day. He was wounded in the face on 25th June and brought back to England, where he was reunited with his girlfriend, Jess. They married in 1946 and had two sons, Andrew and Tim. Terry spent most of his career as a sales representative in the confectionery business and, in his spare time, he enjoyed watching boxing and following the fortunes of Cardiff Rugby Football Club. Sadly, he died of a sudden heart attack, aged only fifty-three, in 1978.

Terry and Jess Parker on their wedding day, May 1946

The Devons

Cosmo Nevill DSO recovered from his wounds and served after the war with the United Nations Military Staff Committee before commanding 6th Infantry Brigade in the British Army of the Rhine. A high-flier, he was appointed CB and promoted to Major-General, commanding the 2nd Infantry Division in Germany before a heart attack prematurely ended his career. He retired to Suffolk in 1960, served on West Suffolk County Council and became an Honorary Lay Canon of St Edmundsbury Cathedral. The Royal Fusiliers appointed him their Colonel in 1963. He died, aged eighty-five, in 2002.

Having recovered from his D-Day injuries, Mike Howard MC rejoined the 2nd Devons later in the campaign. For his bravery commanding C Company near Schilburg in mid-January 1945, he won a Bar to his MC. He had been wounded three times during the war and, having attended Staff College and held a staff posting in Athens, he was invalided out of the army in 1950. In retirement he became Joint Master of the Dartmoor Foxhounds and a steward at Newton Abbot race course.

The twin brothers Mike and David Holdsworth were born in Torcross, Devon in May 1918, two of nine children of a soldier. After the war Mike remained in the army, serving with the Parachute Regiment in India, Germany and Cyprus before rejoining the Devons to fight the Mau Mau in Kenya. After a secondment to the Gold Coast Regiment, he left the army in 1957 and tried his hand as a salesman before training as a teacher. He taught for sixteen years at Rushmoor School in Bedford, where he became acting Headmaster. David, meanwhile, was mentioned in Despatches and, thirty years later, the town of Bayeux awarded him La Medaille de Bayeux. After the war he left the army and continued a very successful career in the Police. Awarded the Queen's Police Medal in 1968, he was appointed Chief Constable of Thames Valley Police in 1971 and appointed CBE in 1976. He died, still serving and aged only sixty, in 1978. Diana, David's wife, published posthumously his candid, touching and amusing memories of the campaign, *One Day I'll Tell You*. Mike Holdsworth MC retired from teaching in 1984 and returned to Devon, settling in Ashprington, near Totnes. In later life he gave a very helpful interview to Doctor Andrew Holborn, and it is extensively quoted here. Mike died, aged ninety-four, in November 2013.

Brought up in Surrey as an orphan, Jock Russell MM originally enlisted as a Bandboy in the Devonshire Regiment in 1935. Recovered from the wounds he received on 7th June 1944, he returned to North-West Europe and fought with the King's Liverpool Regiment before rejoining the Devons in Berlin after the war. When he attended the investiture at Buckingham Palace to receive his MM, because he had no family he took with him two lady volunteers from a nearby pub. When he left the army he emigrated to New Zealand, where he died in 2010.

The Sappers

John Stone MC, who led the three-man reconnaissance patrol on the Normandy beach on 15th May 1944, served in Normandy, Belgium and the Netherlands and was demobilised in 1946. Married to Nora Collins in 1946, they had three daughters. After working in local government for a spell, he joined a firm of consulting engineers, where he became a partner. Retiring in 1987, he settled in Weymouth and belonged to the Rotary Club and the local branch of the Royal Engineers' Association. He died in November 2011, aged eighty-nine.

On 5th June 1994, Ian Wilson MC wrote from his cottage in King's Somborne to the Museum of the Royal Hampshire Regiment. His letter began: *The history of the Royal Hampshire Regiment comments on the problems of 1st Battalion, The Hampshire Regiment with the beach obstacles and exits from Gold Beach in Normandy on 6th June 1944. I was serving with 73 Field Company RE, whose task was to make lanes through the beach obstacles for the use of landing craft. Hence an account of that task, which I thought might be a useful addition to your archives.* And so it has proved. I have drawn heavily on a very brave man's modest recollections written twenty-five years ago.

Bert Scaife DCM, the Sapper Sergeant who with his AVRE swung the victory at Le Hamel, was commissioned in October 1944. He fought throughout the campaign in North West Europe, including the Rhine Crossing, and in 1945 returned home to his wife Charlotte in York, where they had married a month before D-Day. He also returned to the ironmongers where he had been apprenticed and worked for them throughout his long career, rising to be shop manager and a director. A keen tennis player, he captained his local club. Although he seldom spoke about his part in D-Day, he remained in touch with the crew of *Loch Leven*, his AVRE, and he called his house *Le Hamel*. He died, aged ninety, in 2010.

The Gunners

Sergeant Bob Palmer MM of the Essex Yeomanry, who had helped destroy the 77mm gun on the beach at Le Hamel, returned to Hertford after the war. He spent a long career in the Police Force and reached the rank of Chief Inspector. He returned to Le Hamel on the 50th anniversary of D-Day.

Lance-Corporal Denis *Danny* Bowstead MM, who was a Signalman attached to the 90th Field Regiment, was wounded later in the campaign, and carried shrapnel in his leg for the rest of his life. A keen footballer and Arsenal supporter, he had joined the Territorial Army before the war to play soccer and instead found himself fighting in Iraq, Tunisia, Sicily and North West Europe. After the war he made a career in telecommunications in the Post Office and latterly British Telecom. He was at work in the BT Tower on the day the IRA bombed it. Married in 1948, he and his wife, Betty, had a daughter and a son. In 1957 they moved from Enfield to Rainham, where he spent the rest of his life. Although proud of his army career, he would never wear his medals because he said he had had to kill people. Nonetheless, he was delighted in later life to find his name on the board of honours and awards at the Royal Corps of Signals Museum at Blandford Forum. At ninety-two he had major heart surgery, from which he made a good recovery. He died, aged ninety-five, in May 2014.

The Sherwood Rangers

Having recovered from his wounds and served in Italy, John Anderson DSO ended the war as an Acting Brigadier and was appointed CBE. In the mid-1950s he commanded 11th Armoured Division as a Major-General, receiving a CB and becoming Royal Armoured Corps Director at the War Office. As a Lieutenant-General, he was Director-General of Military Training and Deputy Chief of the Imperial General Staff. He was appointed KCB in 1960, Military Secretary in 1963 and GBE in 1967. He retired in 1968, serving as Colonel of his own Regiment (the 5th Royal Iniskilling Dragoon Guards) and Colonel Commandant of the Ulster Defence Regiment. An accomplished horseman, he was also a gifted painter and one of his watercolours was exhibited at the Royal Academy. He died in 1988.

After Mike Laycock MC was killed, Stanley Christopherson MC and Bar assumed command of the Sherwood Rangers and led them throughout the rest of the war, winning a DSO. They were constantly in battle, suffered heavy losses and acquired a reputation as an armoured regiment second to none. Christopherson himself quietly carried the burden of responsibility and the sadness of the casualties among his command. At the end of the war, now thirty-three, he returned to South Africa, where before the war he had followed his father by working for Consolidated Goldfields. In the mid-1950s he returned to England and became a stockbroker. He was married – by Leslie Skinner – in 1959. He and his wife had a son and a daughter and turned their house in Kent into a pre-preparatory school. He died in 1990 and his extensive war diaries, edited by James Holland, appeared posthumously in 2014.

The Reverend Leslie Skinner returned to the Sherwood Rangers within a month of having been wounded in the head. He remained their Padre throughout the rest of the campaign and won his flock's respect and affection. He had vowed that no Sherwood Ranger should remain missing, that each should receive a Christian burial and that no families should be left uncertain as to what had happened to their soldier. Remarkably, with only one exception – where his Colonel forbade him to go off in search of the missing man – he kept his vow. The British mentioned him in Despatches while the French and Belgians gave him medals. After the war his Methodist ministry took him all over the country, but he continued to serve with the Territorial Army and became a Lieutenant-Colonel. He died, aged ninety, in 2001, having celebrated his sixtieth wedding anniversary with Etta.

Stephen Mitchell MC was wounded twice during the war. He returned to England in December 1944, returning to his pre-war employers, John Player and Sons in Nottingham, and retiring as Personnel Director in 1970. For twenty years he served as a general commissioner of taxation for Nottinghamshire. He died, aged ninety, in 2003.

Stuart Hills won the MC crossing the River Noireau at the end of the Normandy campaign. At Gheel his Sherman was hit by a Panzerfaust (German infantry anti-tank weapon) but he emerged almost unscathed and survived the entire campaign. After the war he served in the Malayan Civil Service during the Emergency before joining a subsidiary of Shell and spending a great deal of time travelling in the Far East. He retired to Tonbridge in 1986 and in 2002 published his thoughtful memoir, *By Tank Into Normandy*. He died, just past his eightieth birthday, in 2004.

Jimmy McWilliam, a farmer's son from Lanarkshire, had qualified as a solicitor before the war. Discharged from the RAF when found to be colour-blind, he was commissioned in the Sherwood Rangers and was wounded at Alamein and twice more in North West Europe. After the war he served as a Major in the Legal Branch of the Military Government in West Germany. For twenty years he was a magistrate in Singapore, where he was a member of the Turf Club and rode as an amateur jockey. Retiring to Weybridge, he died, aged ninety-three, in 2009.

Trooper Philip Foster, who was the gunner in Sergeant Bill Digby's Sherman, was wounded beside Digby when the tank was hit by an anti-tank shell soon after it had landed. Bill Digby died of his wounds but twenty-two-year-old Philip Foster survived. Ordained in the Roman Catholic Church after the war, in 1994 Father Foster published a memoir, *A Trooper's Desert War*, which was extensively quoted in his Regiment's history, published in 2016.

Despite the success of his accomplished memoir, *Alamein to Zem Zem*, Keith Douglas's posthumous reputation grew only slowly after the war until Desmond Graham published his biography in 1974. He is now remembered (with Alun Lewis) as one of the two foremost poets of the Second World War. Douglas's distinctive young voice speaks out from both his book and his poems, while his surviving sketches reveal a sharp eye and a promising talent.

The many others – Sherwood Rangers, Gunners, Sappers, Devons, Dorsets and Hampshires – whose loss was every bit as tragic as Douglas's but who left legacies that were less public, are remembered by their families and by those of us who are lucky enough to know their stories.

The grave of Sgt William Evans MM and Bar at Bayeux

A note on medals

Because citations for gallantry awards are often written some time after the event, like any evidence they need to be treated with caution. Detail – dates, places and even the sequence of events – can be wrong. Nonetheless, for anyone assembling a story of this kind, they offer a rich source of information because they describe a particular incident, or series of incidents, in the course of an often confusing battle. I have used many in this book. In 1944 there were six principal awards available for soldiers to reward bravery in the face of the enemy and there were a few subtleties about their use which it may be helpful to explain here.

Only the VC and the mention in Despatches could be awarded posthumously. A bar signified a second award of the same medal.

The Victoria Cross, only one of which was awarded on Gold Beach on D-Day, was the highest award and it was available to all ranks. By its nature, it was given infrequently and often posthumously. It was and remains highly prized.

The Distinguished Service Order was usually given to battalion (occasionally company) commanders who did an outstanding job leading and commanding their units. It usually also recognised a good deal of courage on their part, as did Lieutenant-Colonel Cosmo Nevill's award for D-Day. The DSO could, however, very occasionally be awarded to junior officers as a near-miss for a VC; this was the case for Captain Cecil Thomas.

The Military Cross recognised bravery and often leadership on the part of officers of the rank of major and below. Major *Horace* Wright won both his MC and his Bar rescuing wounded under fire while Major Willie Hayes won both his awards for gallant leadership in the attack.

The Distinguished Conduct Medal, for warrant officers, NCOs and soldiers, was the next down from the VC. It was sparingly awarded in the Second World War and any soldier wearing this ribbon was regarded with respect. Winning his DCM as a young Bandsman marked Denis Bounsall out for the rest of his army career.

The Military Medal again rewarded warrant officers, NCOs and soldiers for bravery in action. Anyone under the misapprehension that the MM was a minor award should read what Sergeant Clement Bisson did at Le Hamel to earn his.

Below these five awards was a sixth, the **Mention in Despatches**, which was signified not by a medal but by an oak leaf worn on the ribbon of a campaign medal. Like the VC, a mention was open to all ranks. There are many instances – one of them, Captain Terry Cousins, at Port-en-Bessin – of a recommendation for a posthumous VC translating into a mention in Despatches.

No system of rewards operated by fallible human beings will ever be entirely fair. However carefully it may be administered, there will always be people whose courage goes unrecognised. Several of the men mentioned in this book will have deserved but not received an award. But the currency had not been debased. The great majority who received them thoroughly deserved them; and some, like Major *Bubbles Duke* MC and Bar and Corporal Sam Thompson DCM MM, earned them several times over.

APPENDIX ONE

1st Battalion, the Hampshire Regiment Order of Battle 6th June 1944

(k), (w) or (dow) indicates killed, wounded or died of wounds received on D-Day

CO	Lt-Col David Nelson Smith MC (w)
2IC	Maj Charles Martin DSO (k)
Adjt	Capt Frank Waters
IO	Capt W J Hand
HQ Coy	Capt T G Wilmer
QM	Capt A B Stone MBE
MTO	Capt J H Arnett (w)
RSO	Lt F Veitch
MO	Capt Ivor Joseph MC RAMC
RSM	WO (1) W Burgess MM
RQMS	G Ford

A Coy
Maj Dick Baines (k)
Capt Anthony Boyd MC
Lt Jack Lauder (w)
Lt Alan Norman (w)
Lt K C Miller (w)
CSM M Pearcey

B Coy
Maj Tony Mott
Capt Cecil Thomas DSO
Lt Lionel Bawden (k)
Lt Charles Williamson MC (k)
Lt Graham Mason Elliott (dow)
CSM W Mayne DCM

C Coy
Maj David Warren MC
Capt Ronald Kidd
Lt Alan King
Lt Horace Wright MC
Lt G Davison-Lungley (w)
CSM H Bowers MM

D Coy
Maj John Littlejohns
Capt David Edkins (w)
Lt Peter Paul
Lt Gordon Layton (w)
Lt Malcolm Bradley
CSM C Parris MM

SP Coy
Maj James Wicks
Capt P A E Hughes (w)
Lt John Boys (w) - mortars
Lt David Hammond – Carriers
Lt Guy Westley (k)
Lt Topper Brown – pioneers
CSM R Shave

199

APPENDIX TWO

1st Battalion, the Dorsetshire Regiment Order of Battle 6th June 1944

(k) or (w) indicates killed or wounded on D-Day

CO	Lt-Col E A M Norie
2IC	Maj A E C Bredin
Adjt	Capt L G Browne MC
IO	Lt D D Youngs (k)
HQ Coy	Capt C R Whittington (w)
RSO	Lt R H S Stade
Pioneer Pl	Lt W F Scott
QM	Lt A W Hatchard
MTO	Capt J P Luff
RMO	Capt L P Lassman RAMC
Padre	Capt R Watt RAChD

A Coy
Maj A A E Jones (w)
Capt J H L Royle
7 Pl Lt R T Ellis (w)
8 Pl Lt H J Webb (w)
9 Pl Lt H G Dibben
CSM Howell (w)

B Coy
Maj P Chilton MC
Capt A L Harris
10 Pl 2/Lt E F Mayes
11 Pl Lt L J Morris
12 Pl Lt J Whitebrook (k)
CSM Balkwill (w)

C Coy
Maj R M Nicoll
Capt R W Tucker MC
13 Pl Lt C F Windebank
14 Pl 2/Lt T P Stratton (w)
15 Pl Lt J Hamilton (w)
CSM Robbins (w)

D Coy
Maj W N Hayes
Lt J A Thomas (w)
16 Pl Lt C Bradbury (k)
17 Pl Lt P J Robjohn (w)
18 Pl Lt T S Lancaster (k)
CSM N O'Connell

SP Coy
Capt R E Harris
3 Pl Lt L Shambrook
4 Pl Capt E Hannah
2IC 4 Pl Lt B Weekes
5 Pl Capt G G L Hebden
2IC 5 Pl 2/Lt E G Neal
Lt R E Jones (w)

APPENDIX THREE

2nd Battalion, the Devonshire Regiment Order of Battle 6th June 1944

(k) or (w) indicates killed or wounded on D-Day

Lt-Col C R E Nevill OBE
Maj G B Browne
Maj F G Sadleir MBE – OC A Coy
Maj M W Howard MC – OC B Coy (w)
Maj H V Duke MC – OC C Coy (k)
Maj J R H Parlby – OC D Coy (w)
Capt H J Crawley
Capt M Holdsworth
Capt A D Eteson MC
Capt T A Holdsworth – Adjutant
Capt D E Harris – OC HQ Coy
Capt J D Symes – Signal Officer
Capt P J G Anderson – OC 4 Pl
Capt P Clark – OC 3 Pl (Mortars)
Capt P F Cox – OC A/Tk Pl
Capt J T A Lloyd RAMC – RMO
Lt W G Wood – IO
Lt H D Shinn – QM
Lt J G Coles – Transport Officer
Lt W B Kemeys-Jenkin

Lt F H Pease
Lt L E R Bentall – att'd 231 Bde
Lt E Gamble – 2IC 4 Pl
Lt F A Pearson – OC 5 Pl (Assault Pioneers)
Lt H R Whalley – Pl Cmdr
Lt P Hosking – Pl Cmdr
Lt J C Candlin – Pl Cmdr
Lt R A R Pethick – Pl Cmdr
Lt R W Murphy – Pl Cmdr
Lt E Foy – Pl Cmdr (pow)
Lt H Heap – Pl Cmdr
Lt J G Morris – Pl Cmdr (w)
Lt R C J Davey – Pl Cmdr
Lt E E Mead – Pl Cmdr
Lt H F Pearce – Pl Cmdr
Lt D Holdsworth – Pl Cmdr
Lt D F Riordan – Pl Cmdr
Lt K J Bull – Pl Cmdr (w)
Lt E Smith – Pl Cmdr (k)

Ryes Cemetery

APPENDIX FOUR

1st Battalion, the Hampshire Regiment Roll of Honour 6th–9th June 1944

We will remember them.

6th June 1944

13070153 Pte L T Archer (Bayeux)
14224634 Pte W J Ayres (Bayeux)
62620 Maj R G T Baines (Bayeux)
5954730 Pte H L D Barnes (Bayeux)
5505038 Sgt E H E Bartlett (Bayeux)
288933 Lt L A Bawden (Bayeux)
6848398 Pte F C H W Beach (Bayeux)
14348116 Pte W H Bell (Bayeux)
5505944 Pte M Bishop (Bayeux)
14430379 Pte P J Bristow (Bayeux)
4978164 Pte F Britton (Bayeux)
14649399 Pte A E Brooks (Bayeux)
5502564 Pte R G Bulpitt (Bayeux)
5511910 Pte E W Bunn (Bayeux)
14406233 Pte A F Burnett (Bayeux)
14648127 Pte R A Butt (Bayeux)
5339710 Pte J D Callaghan (Bayeux)
6017584 Pte J Chatters (Belchamp St Paul Church, Essex)
6351679 Pte A E Christopher (Bayeux)
5501401 Pte H T Clark (Bayeux Memorial to the Missing)
6411162 Pte F W Clarke (Bayeux)
5505035 L/Cpl I D Cleft (Bayeux)
14311504 Pte A C Clifford (Bayeux)
4396231 Pte C W Collins (Bayeux)
5509914 Pte P R Costen (Bayeux)
5497092 L/Sgt C I Cowdrey (Bayeux)
5504934 Pte R L Curtis (Bayeux)
4398823 Pte C Dossor (Bayeux)
5511661 Pte L Dyer (Bayeux Memorial to the Missing)
268027 Lt G M Elliott (Durley Church, Hampshire) *died of wounds 9th June*
5504956 Pte J Elson (Bayeux Memorial to the Missing)
4617550 Pte A Farrar (Bayeux)
6013402 Pte L J Futter (Bayeux)
5505055 Pte C F B Gough (Bayeux)
5499327 Pte J P Hassett (Bayeux)
13061854 Pte L Hatfield (Bayeux)
5494206 Pte V R Hobby (Bayeux)
4534313 Sgt J T Jenson (Bayeux)
14414983 Pte H J Lanning (Bayeux)
5504995 Pte C E J Larby (Bayeux)
5511602 Pte E Loader (Bayeux)
6407940 Pte S G Marsh (Bayeux)
5497656 L/Sgt W H Marshall (Bayeux)
69156 Maj A C W Martin DSO, Dorset Regiment (Ryes)

5337856 L/Cpl K J Matthews (Bayeux Memorial to the Missing)
6406570 Pte W H C Moorton (Bayeux)
4387708 Sgt F Owens (Bayeux)
5500360 Pte G F Philpott (Bayeux Memorial to the Missing)
5506783 Pte G R Pullen (Bayeux)
421339 Pte A E Redhead (Bayeux)
5345894 Pte W A Redman (Bayeux)
5505032 Cpl D E Rose (Bayeux)
13037382 Cpl W T Saussey (Bayeux)
4986029 Pte H Shelbourne (Bayeux)
5500000 Pte C W Smith (Bayeux Memorial to the Missing)

4860585 Pte J W Stain (Bayeux)
5512517 Pte C A Taylor (Bayeux)
13117458 Pte A E Walton (Bayeux)
5497872 L/Cpl L J Webb MM (Portsmouth Milton) *died of wounds 14th June*
180302 Lt G N Westley, York & Lancaster Regiment (Ryes)
14275021 Pte O White (Bayeux)
5507143 Pte D A Williams (Bayeux)
14648182 Pte D F Williams (Bayeux)
253674 Lt C Y Williamson MC (Bayeux)
14219467 Pte K F Young (Bayeux)

APPENDIX FIVE

1st Battalion, the Dorsetshire Regiment Roll of Honour 6th–9th June 1944

We will remember them.

6th June 1944

6016672 L/Sgt E E Abell (Bayeux)
5735659 Pte G Adams (Bayeux)
14356651 Pte C A Beard (Bayeux)
287835 Lt J Bradbury, Hampshire Regiment (Bayeux)
14650055 Pte E T Breden (Bayeux)
6353843 Pte L R Brice (Bayeux)
5728866 L/Sgt L W Bunning MM (Bayeux)
14679122 Pte G J Canning (Bayeux)
5735714 Pte L Carpenter (Bayeux)
5350162 Pte J E Carter (Bayeux)
6099074 Cpl P Carter (Bayeux)
5726315 Pte S R Curtis (Bayeux)
5725714 Pte J F Denning (Bayeux)
1590685 Pte M G Dixon (Bayeux)
1836912 Pte R Doran (Cambuslang, Lanarkshire) *died of wounds 8th June*
3907199 Sgt W J Evans MM & Bar (Bayeux)
6029379 Pte S F Gallant (Bayeux)
6399434 Pte L J Gazey (Bayeux Memorial to the Missing)
14299617 Pte Y G Gummerson (Bayeux)
1405157 Pte H J Hamblin (Bayeux)
811400 L/Cpl F C Hewett (Bayeux)

321716 Pte T P Homer (Bayeux)
5724419 Sgt A Horlick (Bayeux)
6107796 Pte F Ireland (Bayeux)
14392169 Pte W L Johnson (Bayeux)
212762 Lt T J Lancaster (Bayeux)
4539952 Pte H Lawson (Bayeux)
6098618 Pte E F C Martin (Bayeux)
5831843 Pte A J Morris (Bayeux)
5889337 Pte P Nugent (Bayeux)
6408787 Pte W G Piddock (Bayeux)
1576221 Pte G A Pierce (Bayeux)
4197815 L/Cpl J R Roberts (Bayeux)
5724979 Pte H C Satchell (Bayeux)
5728781 Pte A W Scrivens (Bayeux)
5735086 Pte H Sherriff (Bayeux)
5724571 Pte W Stevens (Bayeux Memorial to the Missing)
5728399 Pte P W Taylor (Bayeux)
233287 Lt J Whitebrook, King's Shropshire Light Infantry (Bayeux)
5724622 Pte T Wood (Bayeux)
5727747 Pte G G Youd (Bayeux)
201413 Lt D D Youngs, Royal Norfolk Regiment (Bayeux)

7th June 1944

14671216 Pte L Hann (Ryes)
284965 Lt E F Mayes (Ryes)

8th June 1944

14650048 Pte D F Blosse (Ryes)
14663589 Pte W J Bowl (Brouay)
5728832 Pte C Jeffery (Brouay)
14433597 Pte W March (Bayeux)

5725390 Sgt V B Marsh (Bayeux)
5723656 Cpl G A Pearce (Brouay)
121129 Capt R W Tucker MC (Brouay)

9th June 1944

5726991 Pte C Gollop (Tilly-sur-Seulles)

APPENDIX SIX

2nd Battalion, the Devonshire Regiment Roll of Honour 6th–9th June 1944

We will remember them.

6th June 1944

14687995 Pte J R Ball (Bayeux)
5625061 Pte H E Beer (Bayeux)
1110263 Pte E J R Bennett (Bayeux Memorial to the Missing)
5616314 L/Sgt H Cotton (Bayeux)
5616397 Pte J Dempsey (Bayeux)
5951893 L/Cpl R W Double (Bayeux)
85611 Maj H V Duke MC & Bar (Bayeux)
14622430 Pte J H Furze (Bayeux)
6012440 Cpl R G G Gannon (Bayeux)
14599635 Pte W R Hall (Bayeux)
6468366 Sgt W H Hallett (Bayeux)
14610273 L/Cpl E Iles (Bayeux)
5729122 Pte W E Jennings (Bayeux)
14435007 Pte W F Jevons (Bayeux)
5623626 Pte J E McDonald (Bayeux)
5623651 Pte M W Matthews (Bayeux)
5616950 Cpl L Neno (Bayeux)
14612006 Pte C Newall (Bayeux Memorial to the Missing))
14656022 Pte C J E Oldridge MM (Bayeux) *died of wounds 8th June*
14630721 L/Cpl F G Peart (Bayeux)
5627017 Pte B H Read (Bayeux)
14600856 Pte D G Rees (Gosport Ann's Hill) *died of wounds 9th June*
5625828 Pte A J Reeves (Bayeux)
5672102 Cpl L J W Roe (Bayeux)
5623074 Cpl A E Selfe (Bayeux)
277665 Lt E C S Smith, Hampshire Regiment (Bayeux)
14660997 Pte F G Southam (Bayeux)
5626059 L/Cpl A J Steffe (Bayeux)
5501971 Cpl H W S Stiff (Bayeux)
14625051 Pte B J Stone (Bayeux)
5624472 L/Cpl T H Theobald (Bayeux)
5444942 Pte F Trembath (Breage New Church, Cornwall) *died of wounds 9th June*
5616825 Pte G R Whewall (Bayeux)
5624777 Pte F A Wills (Bayeux)
14648607 Pte J E Wormald (Bayeux)

7th June 1944

140100 Capt P E Clark (Bayeux)
2571359 Pte S C Oliver (Bayeux)
5616858 Pte C R West (Bayeux)

8th June 1944

14567603 Pte E King (Bayeux)
6402825 Pte R F Rolf (Bayeux)

9th June 1944

14660924 Pte G H V Head (Ryes)

APPENDIX SEVEN

47th (Royal Marine) Commando Roll of Honour 6th–9th June 1944

We will remember them.

6th June 1944

PLY/X103334 Mne C Bainbridge (Bayeux)
PO/X106733 Mne H W Bedworth (Bayeux)
PO/X100001 Sgt E E Bee (Bayeux)
CH/X103608 Mne K C Bunyan (Bayeux)
7346931 L/Cpl A J Chatfeld, Royal Army Medical Corps (Bayeux)
Maj J R Feacey (Bayeux)
PLY/X106565 Mne P B Fellows (Bayeux)
PLY/X112746 Mne C H Fewtrell (Plymouth Naval Memorial)
CH/X103631 Mne J Flaherty (Bayeux)
EX/1222 Sgt D Hughes (Bayeux)
PLY/X102749 Mne W C D Kinloch (Bayeux)
PO/X117207 Mne J Lumsden (Bayeux)
CH/X106948 Mne G Norie (Bayeux)
CH/X107831 Mne W Redman (Bayeux)
PLY/X111491 Mne W D Sambrook (Bayeux)
PO/X105848 Mne F L Scott (Bayeux)
CH/X107029 Mne B G Smith (Bayeux)
PO/X105847 Mne J Smith (Portsmouth Naval Memorial)
PO/X105867 Mne E J Sweeney (Bayeux)
CH/X103820 Mne S H R Turner (Bayeux)
CH/X107580 Mne L T Waygood (Bayeux)
6305466 Pte E G Webster, The Buffs attached 47 (RM) Commando (Bayeux)
PO/X119052 Mne R M Wilkinson (Bayeux)

7th June 1944

CH/X104134 Mne G H Baxter (Bayeux)
PO/X4118 Sgt A J Bradley (Bayeux)
PO/X113949 Mne E T L Breach (Bayeux)
PO/X2367 Mne A E Carter (Bayeux)
PLY/X3877 L/Cpl J H Catts (Ryes)
PO/X105862 Mne D J Clark (Bayeux)
PO/111269 Mne J W Collins (Bayeux)
Capt T F Cousins (Bayeux) – mentioned in Despatches
PLY/X111698 L/Cpl E N David (Bayeux)
PO/X106964 Mne C Dutton (Bayeux)
PLY/X108771 Mne J E M Evans (Bayeux)

209

EX/1895 Mne A Fleet (Bayeux)
PO/X4497 Sgt T P Fletcher (Bayeux)
PO/X118564 Mne M H Goude (Bayeux)
PLY/X101844 Cpl A A Jenkins (Bayeux)
PO/X105351 Cpl N Jones (Bayeux)
PO/X110891 Mne G W F Mills (Bayeux)
PLY/X109015 Mne B Oates (Bayeux)

CH/X 109679 Cpl G Robertson (Portland Naval Cemetery) *died of wounds 14th June*
PLY/X103401 Mne W H Towle (Bayeux)
CH/X104128 Mne A F P Tull (Bayeux)
PLY/X103183 Mne R Walker (Bayeux)
PO/X120713 Mne J V Withington (Bayeux)

APPENDIX EIGHT

The Royal Armoured Corps Roll of Honour 6th–9th June 1944

We will remember them.

The Nottinghamshire Yeomanry (Sherwood Rangers)

6th June 1944

323418 Cpl W Digby (Bayeux) *died of wounds 8th June*
14527539 Tpr W G Geen (Bayeux)
403450 Tpr W J Hewlett (Bayeux)
194124 Lt M B Horley (Bayeux)
5053468 Tpr A J Jackson (Bayeux)

3458625 Tpr J T Lowe (Bayeux)
5053790 Tpr G R Percy (Gosport Ann's Hill) *died of wounds 9th June*
14363470 Tpr H W Powis (Bayeux)
14376364 Tpr S Pownall (Bayeux)
5054355 Tpr J A Worboyes (Bayeux)

8th June 1944

259283 Lt L H Verner (Ryes) *died of wounds 9th June*

9th June 1944

170611 Capt K C Douglas, Derbyshire Yeomanry (Tilly-sur-Seulles) – mentioned in Despatches
265521 Lt P Pepler (Tilly-sur-Seulles)

B Squadron, The 22nd Westminster Dragoons

6th June 1944

7886809 Tpr L C Birch (Ryes)
7934724 L/Cpl F Johnson (Bayeux Memorial to the Missing)

APPENDIX NINE

The Royal Artillery Roll of Honour 6th–9th June 1944

We will remember them.

6th June 1944

912132 L/Bdr K W Blanchard. 90th Field Regiment (Bayeux)
914849 Bdr N H Bottoms, 147th (The Essex Yeomanry) Field Regiment (Bayeux)
229051 Lt N D R Calkin, 90th Field Regiment (Bayeux)
935233 Bdr L F J Gates, 90th Field Regiment (Bayeux)
943201 Gnr F H Leopold, 90th Field Regiment (Bayeux)
913871 Bdr S R Prince, 90th Field Regiment (Bayeux)
955355 Gnr A Wyatt, 90th Field Regiment (Bayeux)

8th June 1944

1127335 Gnr D Delaney, 90th Field Regiment (Ryes)
955364 L/Bdr A E Duke, 90th Field Regiment (Bayeux)

9th June 1944

1136475 Gnr A E Gillott, 147th (The Essex Yeomanry) Field Regiment (Tilly-sur-Seulles)

APPENDIX TEN

The Royal Engineers Roll of Honour 6th June 1944

We will remember them.

14202086 Spr C G Boynton, 73rd Field Company (Bayeux)
2129982 Spr R Campbell, 295th Field Company (Bayeux)
1894117 Spr L Crawford, 295th Field Company (Bayeux)
2020507 Cpl H A Doleman, 73rd Field Company (Bayeux Memorial to the Missing)
44867 Maj H G A Elphinstone, 82nd Assault Squadron (Bayeux) – mentioned in Despatches
1872529 L/Sgt E George 82nd Assault Squadron (Bayeux)
2074403 Spr W Grant, 295th Field Company (Bayeux)
14419999 Spr W Heatley, 73rd Field Company (Bayeux)

276467 Lt D W Lofts, 73rd Field Company (Bayeux)
14213636 Spr S M McDermid, 73rd Field Company (Bayeux)
14213663 Spr J B McTaggart, 73rd Field Company (Bayeux)
1876923 Spr H R Preston, 295th Field Company (Bayeux)
132795 Capt P W Smith, 73rd Field Company (Bayeux)
2111014 Cpl J Sullivan, 73rd Field Company (Bayeux)
2119439 Dvr G E Williams, 295th Field Company (Bayeux Memorial to the Missing)

APPENDIX ELEVEN

The Royal Army Medical Corps Roll of Honour 6th June 1944

We will remember them.

7369977 Pte W Armstrong, 200th Field Ambulance (Bayeux)

APPENDIX TWELVE

Gallantry Awards won by 231 Malta Brigade and by Officers and Men of Supporting or Associated Units 6th-9th June 1944

Distinguished Service Order

Maj P M Donnell, 47 (Royal Marine) Commando
Lt-Col C A R Nevill OBE, 2nd Devonshire Regiment (attached from Royal Fusiliers)
Lt-Col E A M Norie, 1st Dorset Regiment (attached from King's Own Royal (Lancaster) Regiment)
Lt-Col R A Phayre, 147th (Essex Yeomanry) Field Regiment, Royal Artillery
Lt-Col C F Phillips, 47 (Royal Marine) Commando
Maj D J Warren MC, 1st Hampshire Regiment

Military Cross

Lt J N Austin, 295th Field Company, Royal Engineers
Capt N J D Bishop, 90th Field Regiment, Royal Artillery
Lt J N Boys. 1st Hampshire Regiment
Lt A G B Buckley, 73rd Field Company, Royal Engineers
Lt F S Cooper, 200th Field Ambulance, Royal Army Medical Corps
Capt E C B Edwards, 147th (Essex Yeomanry) Field Regiment, Royal Artillery
Lt I Goldstein, 47 (Royal Marine) Commando (attached from South African Defence Forces)
Lt I F S Greenaway, Sherwood Rangers Yeomanry
Capt P A Hamilton, 90th Field Regiment (attached from 74th Field Regiment), Royal Artillery
Maj W N Hayes, 1st Dorset Regiment
Lt A L King, 1st Hampshire Regiment (attached from Sherwood Foresters)

215

Capt B W M Lindon, 522nd Company, Royal Army Service Corps
Maj J L G Littlejohns, 1st Hampshire Regiment
Lt K A Munro, 147th (Essex Yeomanry) Field Regiment, Royal Artillery
Maj R M Nicoll, 1st Dorset Regiment
Maj F D Sadleir MBE, 2nd Devonshire Regiment
Maj C J Sidgwick, OC 413th Battery, 147th (Essex Yeomanry) Field Regiment, Royal Artillery
Capt D B Taylor, 147th (Essex Yeomanry) Field Regiment, Royal Artillery
Capt C Thomson, Sherwood Rangers Yeomanry
Capt D H Walton, 47 (Royal Marine) Commando
Capt C R Whittington, 1st Dorset Regiment (attached from Queen's Royal Regiment (West Surrey))
Capt J M C Wicks, 1st Hampshire Regiment
Lt I C T Wilson, 73rd Field Company, Royal Engineers
Capt W G Wood, 2nd Devonshire Regiment
Maj L E Wyatt, 73rd Field Company, Royal Engineers

Distinguished Conduct Medal

L/Sgt H M Scaife, 82nd Assault Squadron, Royal Engineers
Cpl S Thompson MM, 1st Dorset Regiment

Military Medal

Sgt C F Bisson, 1st Hampshire Regiment
L/Cpl D A Bowstead, Royal Corps of Signals (attached to 90th Field Regiment, Royal Artillery)
Sgt W Bracegirdle, Sherwood Rangers Yeomanry
L/Sgt F B Bradshaw, 295th Field Company, Royal Engineers
Cpl R W Burns, 295th Field Company, Royal Engineers
Sgt T Burt, 522nd Company, Royal Army Service Corps
Pte W R Butt, 1st Hampshire Regiment
Cpl V E Carter, 1st Dorset Regiment
Spr A Close, 73rd Field Company, Royal Engineers
Cpl G E Dyer, 200th Field Ambulance, Royal Army Medical Corps
L/Sgt W E Ellis, 47 (Royal Marine) Commando
Mne R Emsley, 47 (Royal Marine) Commando
L/Cpl C W Farrow, 200th Field Ambulance, Royal Army Medical Corps
Spr J M Fitzgerald, 73rd Field Company, Royal Engineers
Mne D R Gadsden, 47 (Royal Marine) Commando
Sgt D H G Gardner, 47 (Royal Marine) Commando
Mne J A Griffin, 47 (Royal Marine) Commando
Cpl W E Hawkins, 1st Dorset Regiment
Cpl G C Hockley, 1st Dorset Regiment
L/Cpl J A L Jesney, Royal Army Medical Corps, 47 (Royal Marine) Commando

Pte A G Keenor, 2nd Devonshire Regiment

L/Cpl P G Kendrick, 47 (Royal Marine) Commando

L/Cpl R Kingswell, 231 Brigade Defence Platoon (attached from Hampshire Regiment)

Mne W MacDonald, 47 (Royal Marine) Commando

Sgt D S McKenzie, 231 Brigade HQ (attached from Royal Electrical & Mechanical Engineers)

L/Cpl J W Miller, 1st Dorset Regiment

Cpl D J Oakley, 90th Field Company, Royal Engineers (No 10 Beach Group)

Pte C J E Oldridge, 2nd Devonshire Regiment

Sgt R E Palmer, 147th (Essex Yeomanry) Field Regiment, Royal Artillery

L/Cpl A J Perkins, 2nd Devonshire Regiment

Cpl A L Pymm, 47 (Royal Marine) Commando

Cpl J Redpath, 1st Dorset Regiment

L/Sgt F Rotherham, 2nd Devonshire Regiment

Sgt J T Sear, 2nd Devonshire Regiment

L/Sgt A E C Sippetts, 1st Hampshire Regiment

Cpl G J B Slade, 1st Hampshire Regiment

Sgt A W Talbot, 1st Dorset Regiment

L/Cpl V L Waller, 1st Hampshire Regiment

L/Cpl L J Webb, 1st Hampshire Regiment

Spr N Wint, 295th Field Company, Royal Engineers

APPENDIX THIRTEEN

OFFICIAL COPY

Crown Copyright Reserved

SPECIAL ARMY ORDER

The War Office,
28th November, 1946

20/Miscellaneous/2708   A.O. 167/1946

Regimental Honours

In recognition of their past services His Majesty the King has been graciously pleased to approve that the following regiments and corps shall in future enjoy the distinction of " ROYAL " :—

    The Lincolnshire Regiment.
    The Leicestershire Regiment.
    The Hampshire Regiment.
    Army Educational Corps.
    The Army Dental Corps.
    Corps of Military Police.
    Pioneer Corps.

These regiments and corps will henceforth be designated :—

    The Royal Lincolnshire Regiment.
    The Royal Leicestershire Regiment.
    The Royal Hampshire Regiment.
    Royal Army Educational Corps.
    Royal Army Dental Corps.
    Corps of Royal Military Police.
    Royal Pioneer Corps.

2. His Majesty has further been pleased to approve that the facings of these regiments and corps shall be as follows :—

The Royal Lincolnshire Regiment	To change from White to Royal Blue.
The Royal Leicestershire Regiment	To retain Pearl Grey.
The Royal Hampshire Regiment	To retain Yellow.
Royal Army Educational Corps	To change from Cambridge Blue to Royal Blue.
Royal Army Dental Corps	To change from Emerald Green to Royal Blue.
Corps of Royal Military Police	To retain Scarlet.
Royal Pioneer Corps	To adopt Royal Blue.

Bibliography

Aggett, W J P, *The Bloody Eleventh: History of The Devonshire Regiment Volume III 1915–1969*, The Devonshire and Dorset Regiment, 1995

Bailey, Roderick, *Forgotten Voices of D-Day: A New History of the Normandy Landings*, Random House, 2010

Barnes, B S, *The Sign of the Double 'T'*, Sentinel 1999

Bellows, Jim, *When in Doubt, Brew Up*, ELSP, 2002

Bredin, Lt-Col A E C, *Three Assault Landings: The Story of the 1st Battalion, The Dorsetshire Regiment in Sicily, Italy and NW Europe*, Gale & Polden, 1946

Brooks, Stephen, *Montgomery and the Battle of Normandy*, History Press, 2008

Daniell, David Scott, *The Royal Hampshire Regiment 1918-1954*, The Royal Hampshire Regiment, 1955

De Bolster, Marc, *47 Royal Marine Commando: An Inside Story 1943-1946*, Fonthill Media, 2014

Douglas, Keith,

Alamein to Zem Zem, Editions Poetry London, 1946

Collected Poems, Faber & Faber, 1966

The Letters, Carcanet, 2000

Forfar, Prof John, *From Omaha to the Scheldt: The Story of 47 (Royal Marine) Commando*, Tuckwell Press, 2001

Gilchrist, Maj R T, *Malta Strikes Back: The Story of 231 Infantry Brigade*, Gale & Polden, 1945

Graham, Desmond, *Keith Douglas*, OUP 1974

Hamilton, Nigel, *Monty: Master of the Battlefield 1942-1944*, Hamish Hamilton, 1983

Hills, Stuart, *By Tank Into Normandy*, Cassell, 2002

Holborn, Dr Andrew, *The D-Day Landing on Gold Beach*, Bloomsbury Academic 2015

Holdsworth, David and Diana, *One Day I'll Tell You*, Heraldry Today 1994

Holland, James, *The Wartime Diaries of Stanley Christopherson DSO MC TD*, Bantam 2014

Hunt, Jonathan, *Hard Fighting: A History of the Sherwood Rangers Yeomanry 1900-1946*, Pen & Sword, 2016

Jary, Christopher,

They Couldn't Have Done Better: The Story of the Dorset Regiment in War and Peace 1939-67, Semper Fidelis 2014

Yells, Bells & Smells: The Story of the Devons, Hampshires & Dorsets in the Siege of Malta 1940-43, Semper Fidelis 2017

Jary, Sydney, *18 Platoon*, Sydney Jary Limited, 1987

Miller, Russell, *Nothing Less Than Victory: An Oral History of D-Day*, Michael Joseph 1993

Neilland, Robin, and De Normann, Roderick, *D-Day 1944: Voices from Normandy*, Cassell 2001

Pearce Smith, Brig Kenneth, *Adventures of an Ancient Warrior in Peace, War & Revolution*, privately published, 1984

Picot, Geoffrey, *Accidental Warrior*, Penguin 1993

Saunders, Tim, *Gold Beach – Jig, June 1944*, Leo Cooper, 2002

Shaw, Frank & Joan, *We Remember D-Day*, Ebury Press 2014

Skinner, The Rev Leslie, *Sherwood Rangers Casualty Book 1944-45*, privately published 1996

Speakman, Nick, and Jary, Christopher, *Devotion to Duty: Gallantry Awards Won by the Devonshire Regiment and the Dorset Regiment 1919-58*, Semper Fidelis, 2016

Stanier, Sir Beville, *Sammy's Wars: Recollections of War in Northern France and Other Occasions of the late Brigadier Sir Alexander Stanier Bt DSO MC*, privately published 1998

Sullivan, Bernard, *Sullivan's Stories*, privately published 2007

Taylor, Jeremy, *The Devons: A History of The Devonshire Regiment, 1685-1945*, Bristol, 1951

Trew, Simon, *Gold Beach*, Sutton Publishing 2004

Twiston Davies, David, *Books 1 and 2 of Military Obituaries*, Grub Street 2003 and 2006

Winter, Paul, *D-Day Documents*, Bloomsbury 2014

Unpublished sources

The testimony of the following D-Day participants has helped bring this, their story, to life

(Ranks and any decorations are those held or earned on or before D-Day and regiments shown are those they served with on D-Day.)

Agnussen, Grenadier, 726th Infantry Regiment (Wehrmacht)
Aldred, Pte Jim, Hampshire Regiment
Baker, Sgt Bill, Devonshire Regiment
Bellows, Sgt Jim, Hampshire Regiment
Bethell-Fox, Lt John, Sherwood Rangers Yeomanry
Blanchard, L/Seaman Wally, RN
Booker, Lt Jack, RNVR
Bounsall, L/Cpl Denis, DCM, Dorset Regiment
Bowers, CSM Harry, MM, Hampshire Regiment
Bowstead, L/Cpl *Danny*, MM, R Corps of Signals attached 90th Field Regiment, RA
Bredin, Maj *Speedy*, Dorset Regiment
Brown, BSM Jack, 147th (Essex Yeomanry) Field Regt, RA
Browne, Maj Guy, Devonshire Regiment
Bushell, Pte David, Dorset Regiment
Chalk, Pte John, Hampshire Regiment
Chalk, Pte Stanley, Hampshire Regiment
Curton, Pte Sam, Hampshire Regiment
D'Anselme, Mme A
Douglas, Capt Keith, Sherwood Rangers Yeomanry
Dudley-Ward, Pte Tim, Hampshire Regiment
Eastman, Pte Ron, Hampshire Regiment
Edkins, Capt David, Hampshire Regiment
Forfar, Capt John, RAMC attached 47 (RM) Commando
Foster, Tpr Philip, Sherwood Rangers Yeomanry
Gardner, Sgt Donald, 47 (RM) Commando
Gosling, Maj Cecil, 147th (Essex Yeomanry) Field Regt, RA
Hargreaves, Lt Harold, DSC, RNVR
Harris, Able Seaman Norman, RN
Hawes, Pte Dennis, Hampshire Regiment
Hayes, Maj Willie, MC, Dorset Regiment
Hayles, L/Cpl Ron, Hampshire Regiment
Hills, Lt Stuart, Sherwood Rangers Yeomanry
Holdsworth, Lt David, Devonshire Regiment
Holdsworth, Maj Mike, Devonshire Regiment
Holdsworth, Mrs Diana
Holley, Pte Ivor, Hampshire Regiment
Holman, Lt Jack, Sherwood Rangers Yeomanry
Jackson, Pte Victor, Dorset Regiment

221

Johnson, Capt Peter, RAMC
Laity, Pte George, Devonshire Regiment
Lauder, Lt Jack, Hampshire Regiment
Lawrenson, Tpr Edgar, Westminster Dragoons
Marshall, Howard, BBC War Correspondent
Martin, Maj Charles, DSO, Hampshire Regiment
Martin, Maj Peter, Cheshire Regiment
McWilliam, Lt Jimmy, Sherwood Rangers Yeomanry
Minogue, Tpr Joe, Westminster Dragoons
Mott, Maj Tony, Hampshire Regiment
Nelson Smith, Lt-Col David, MC, Hampshire Regiment
Nevill, Lt-Col Cosmo, DSO OBE, Devonshire Regiment
Norman, Lt Alan, Hampshire Regiment
Page, Gnr Percy, 147th (Essex Yeomanry) Field Regt, RA
Palmer, Sgt Bob, MM, 147th (Essex Yeomanry) Field Regt, RA
Parker, Cpl Terry, Dorset Regiment
Pearson, Lt Frank, Devonshire Regiment
Phillips, Lt-Col Cecil, DSO, 47 (RM) Commando
Powis, Pte David, Devonshire Regiment
Prior, Pte John, Border Regiment
Richards, Cpl Taffy, R Corps of Signals
Roland, Pte Joe, Dorset Regiment
Russell, Cpl Jock, MM, Devonshire Regiment
Scaife, Sgt Bert, DCM, 82nd Assault Sqn, RE
Shepperd, Pte Ernie, Hampshire Regiment
Skinner, Capt The Rev Leslie, RAChD, Sherwood Rangers
Smith, Midn Stan, RNVR
Stanier, Brig Sir Alex, DSO MC, late Welsh Guards
Stone, Lt John, MC, 274th Field Coy, RE
Sullivan, Sub-Lt Bernard, RNVR
Travett, L/Cpl Norman, Devonshire Regiment
Vigour, Pte Ted, Dorset Regiment
Warburton, Capt Arthur, 147th (Essex Yeomanry) Field Regt, RA
Warren, Maj David, DSO MC, Hampshire Regiment
Wetjen, Mne John, 47 (RM) Commando
White, Pte Ron, Hampshire Regiment
Wills, Sgt *Ginger*, Devonshire Regiment
Wilson, Gnr Charles, 147th (Essex Yeomanry) Field Regt, RA
Wilson, Lt Ian, MC, 73rd Field Coy, RE
Wilson, Pte Jim, Devonshire Regiment
Wiltshire, Cpl Frank, Hampshire Regiment
Winter, Lt Peter, 47 (RM) Commando
Wright, L/Cpl Frank, 47 (RM) Commando
Wright, Lt *Horace*, MC, Hampshire Regiment

Index

Page numbers shown in bold indicate pictures. (n) indicates a footnote.

Aam 179–80
Abel, Maj 69
Abell, L/Sgt E E 121, 162
Absence Without Leave 25–6
Adair, Maj-Gen Alan 178
Agnussen, Grenadier 132
Ajax, HMS 42–3, 150–2
Aldred, Pte Jim 56–7, 165, 182, 188
Amos, Cpl G 156, 158–9
Anderson, Lt-Col John 16, 33, 77, 176, 194
Armstrong, L/Smn 76–7
Armstrong, Pte William 84
Arnhem 177–9, 182
Arromanches, liberation of 138–41
Asnelles, fighting in 93, 104–7
Audrieu 166, 168
Austin, L/Smn Allisder 51
Austin, Lt Neil 92
AVREs, description of 19–21

Baines, Maj Dick 9, **10**, 36, 42, 51–2, 55–7, 71, 125, 181–2
Baker, Sgt Bill 134–5
Balkwill, CSM 61
Barnes, L/Cpl Henry 174
Bawden, Lt Lionel 11–12, 93
Baxter, Spr Jim 130
BBC 38, 83
Beach mines and obstacles 1–2, 19, 31–3, 40, 43, 46–8, **50**, **58**
Beale, Capt 63
Beddows, Capt Ian 139

Bellows, Sgt Jim 25, 28, 73–5, 89, 94, 107, 144–5, 188
Bemmel 179
Benbow, CSM 78, 85, 147
Bethell-Fox, Lt John 167
Bevin, Rt Hon Ernie 35
Biddle, Maj Laurence 81
Birch, Tpr Leslie 131
Birchall, L/Cpl 76
Bishop, Capt Neville 44, 110, 119, 123
Bishop, Pte Monty 55
Bisson, Sgt Clement 93, 106, 125, 126, 128, 133, 141, 145, 188, 197–8
Blanchard, L/Bdr Ken 110
Blanchard, L/Smn Wally 41, 43
Blyth Ogilvie, Sgt Forbes 1–2
Bollam, CSM Reg **103**, 164
Booker, Lt Jack 47–9, 51
Bottoms, Bdr Norman 64
Bounsall, L/Cpl Denis **iv**, v, xvii–xviii, 12, 14, **60**–61, 121, 142, 191, 197
Bowers, CSM Harry 130
Bowstead, L/Cpl Denis 25, 36, 62, 110, **111**, 123, 194
Boyd, Capt Tony 52, 54–6, 63, 90, 173, 181
Boys, Lt John 73, 126, 145, 147
Bracegirdle, Sgt William 133, 176
Bradbury, Lt Joe 7, **24**, 120
Bradley, Lt Malcolm 140, 175
Bradshaw, L/Sgt Fred 68
Brameld, Lt 136
Brandon, Pte John 166

223

Bredin, Maj *Speedy* 21, 23, **24**, 28, 41, 120, 146, 168–9, 171–2, 175, 180, 182–3, 188, **189**

Brett, Pte Jimmy **53**, 182

British Army

Divisions

Guards Armoured 177–8

1st Airborne 177–9

6th Airborne 30

7th Armoured 182

43rd Wessex 177–8, 182

50th Northumbrian *passim*

Brigades

56th 30, 32, 124, 243

69th 30, 32, 99, 146, 179, 183

151st 32, 161, 168, 179

231st Malta *passim*

Armoured Regiments

4/7th Dragoon Guards 166

Irish Guards Group 168

24th Lancers 17, 161, 172

Royal Tank Regiment 25

Sherwood Rangers, introduction 16–17

Westminster Dragoons, 22, 31, 46–8, 55, 72, 130–1, 143

Royal Artillery Regiments

21st Anti-Tank 179

90th Field, introduction 16

102nd (Northumbrian Hussars) Anti-Tank 124

147th (Essex Yeomanry) Field, introduction 16

Royal Engineers

82nd Assault Squadron 31, 41, 46, 131. 143–4

73rd Field Company 31, 42, 46–7, 50, 68–9, 125–6, 130–1, 144

90th Field Company 86

274th Field Company 1–2

295th Field Company 31, 42, 68–9, 92, 131, 144

Infantry

Cheshire Regiment 69, 119, 121, 136, 151–2, 172

Commandos (for RM Commando see Royal Marines)

Devonshire Regiment *passim*

Dorset Regiment *passim*

Durham Light Infantry 5, 12, 32, 123, 161, 168–9, 179

East Yorkshire Regiment 5, 30, 44

Essex Regiment 124, 143

Gloucestershire Regiment 32, 124

Green Howards 5, 12, 30, 44, 119

Hampshire Regiment *passim*

King's Liverpool Regiment 159, 192

King's Own Malta Regiment 3

King's Own Royal Regiment 12, 175

King's Shropshire Light Infantry 7, 61

Middlesex Regiment 162, 167, 179

Parachute Regiment 178

Queen's Royal Regiment xvii, 7, 11, 87, 105, 182, 185, 190

Royal Fusiliers 14, 38, 82, 192

Royal Norfolk Regiment 7

Royal Warwickshire Regiment 174

South Wales Borderers 7, 32, 143

Welsh Guards 5, 183

Services

Military Police 84

Royal Army Medical Corps 83, 84, 118, 155–6

Royal Army Service Corps 25, 154, 166

Royal Corps of Signals 25, 104, 110–11, 123, 194

Britton, Pte Frederick **53**, 181–2

Brown, BSM Jack Vilander 22, 45, 80–1

Brown, Lt *Topper* 70, 173–4

Browne, Capt Graham **24**, 174

Index

Browne, Maj Guy 26, 34, 175
Buckley, Lt George 69
Buhot 93, 105–6, 110–12, 124, 133, 142–3, 144
Bull, Lt K J **27**, 135
Bulolo, HMS 38, 43
Bunning, Cpl Len 40, 147
Burgess, RSM *Jimmy* 9, 144–5
Burns, Cpl William 68
Burt, Bdsmn *Snowy* 61
Burt, Sgt Tom 154
Bushell, Pte David 68, 93, 113
Butt, L/Cpl Roy 107, 115, 132–3, 145

Cabane 31–2, 48, 90, 114–18, 126, 127, 173
Calkin, Lt Nigel 109
Canning, Pte G J 121
Carter, Cpl Percy 121
Carter, Cpl Vic 105–6, 112–**114**, 123, 190
Centaur tank 31, 49, 63
Chalk, Pte John 107, 115–16
Chalk, Pte Stanley 176
Chapman, Gnr George 88
Chateau Maisons 154, **163**–4
Chilton, Maj Pat 12, **13**, **24**, 60–1, 64, 90, 93, 99, 142, 159–61, 166, 189
Christopherson, Maj Stanley 16–**17**, 90, 166–7, 176, 194
Churchill, Rt Hon Winston 35
Clark, Capt Philip 152–3
Clarke, Pte Frederick **53**, 181–2
Close, Spr Alec 69
Coleman, Roger 37–8, 185
Collins, L/Sgt 106,
Cook, Capt 44
Cooper, 2/Lt Frank 156–7
Cousins, Capt Terry 156–7, 158–9, 198
Crabs – see Flails
Crawley, Capt H J 135
Curton, Pte Sam 117
Curley, Sgt Robert 174

d'Anselme, Mme A 40
Davey, Pte George 68, 113

Davis, L/Cpl 180
DD Tanks **20**, 21, 44, 46, 59, 77, 94, 143
De Guingand, Maj-Gen Freddie 2
Delap, Mne A 158
Digby, Cpl Bill 77–8, 195
Donnell, Maj Patrick 98, 157
Dorset, training in 23
Dossor, Pte Cecil 58–9
Douglas, Capt Keith 16–**17**, 29, 89, 143, 167–8, 196
Dudley Ward, Mrs Eileen 70, 173–4
Dudley Ward, Pte Tim 70, 173–4
Duke, Maj Hugh 14, **15**, **27**, 108, 136, 147, **148**, 153, 174, 198
Duplex Drive Tanks – see DD Tanks
Dupont, Capt 134–5
Dyer, Cpl Graham 156–7
Dyer, L/Cpl Leonard **53**, 181

Eastburn, Col-Sgt 12, 141, 144
Eastman, Pte Ron 132
Edkins, Capt David 9, 64, **116**, 140, 147
Edwards, Capt Eric 87
Eisenhower, Gen Dwight 3, 26
Elgie, CSM Norman 179
Ellis, L/Sgt W E 159
Ellis, Lt (Dorset) **24**, 61, 122
Ellis, Lt (RE) 133
Ellis, Mne 158
Elphinstone, Maj Harold 47–8, 50, 55, 131
Empire Arquebus, HMS 34, 36
Empire Crossbow, HMS 35, **43**, 144
Empire Spearhead, HMS 35
Empire Sword, HMS 34
Emsley, Mne Roy 157, 159
Enderby, Capt Bill 76, 90
Eteson, Capt Arthur 18, **27**, 175
Evans, Sgt William 7, 61, 147, **196**

Farrar, L/Sgt Jonah **53**, 54, 180–2, 188
Farrar, Pte Arthur **53**, 54, 182, 188
Farrow, AB *Geordie* 86
Farrow, L/Cpl Cyril 156–7

225

Feacey, Maj James 96
Fewtrell, Mne Charles 96
Fitzgerald, Spr John 69
Flails, description of 19, 21, **58**
Fletcher, Sgt Teddy 156
Force G 35, 38, 65
Forfar, Capt John 97
Fortescue, 5th Earl **27**
Foster, Tpr Philip 77–8, 195
Foy, Lt Edward 135
Freeman, Capt 155
Fritz 140–**141**
Frost, Lt-Col John 178
Funnies – see AVREs and Flails and DD tanks

Gadsden, Mne Derek 158–9
Gardner, Sgt Donald 97, 157, 159
Gates, L/Bdr Leonard 119
Geen, Tpr W G 44
George Leygues 150
George, L/Sgt Eli 48–9, 131

German Army
    352nd Division 33, 135
    716th Division 33
    916th Grenadier Regiment 100, 134
    59th Engineering Construction Battalion 112

Girling, Maj 44
Glenroy, HMS 34, 38, 41
Goldstein, Lt Isaac 156, 59
Gosling, Maj Cecil 62–3
Graham, Maj-Gen Douglas 5, 18, 163, 177
Greenaway, Lt Ian 113, 176, 180
Greene, Lt 48
Gregson, Lt 81
Griffin, Mne J A 159

Haines, Cpl 166
Haking, Gen Sir Richard 27
Hamilton, Lt John 67, 105, 112

Hammond, Capt David 173–4
Hand, Capt Bill 175
Hann, Pte Leonard 161
Hannah, Capt Eric 161, 174
Hanson-Lawson, Maj John 17, 76, 107, 117, 139, 167, 180
Hardie, Lt-Col Ian 16, 45, 109–10
Hargreaves, Lt Harold 46
Hargrove, Lt Charles 38, 82
Harris, AB Norman 85–6
Harris, Capt Arthur xx, **24**, 177
Harrison, Bdmsn *Slim* 61
Harvey, Pte 120
Hawes, Pte Dennis 109
Hawkins, Cpl Bill 120–1, 123, 162
Hayes, Maj Willie 12, **13**, **24**–5, 35, 37, 64–5, 93, 110–12, 119–23, 166, 171, 177, 179, 182, 190, 197
Hayles, L/Cpl Ron 56
Heap, Lt Harry **27**, 175
Heath, Cpl K **53**, 182
Hedgehogs – see Beach mines and obstacles
Heuvel 179
Hewlett, Tpr W J 44
Hills, Lt Stuart 75–6, 180, 195
Hobart, Maj-Gen Percy 21
Holdsworth, Capt Mike **18**, **27**, 103, 136, 151–2, 163–4, 168, 172, 183, 192
Holdsworth, Capt Tyrrell 25, **27**
Holdsworth, Lt David **18**, **27**, 79, 102–3, 135–6, 151–2, 192
Holdsworth, Mrs Diana 18, 28–9
Holley, Pte Ivor 54, 59
Holman, Lt Jack 143
Horley, Lt Monty 77–8, 124, 131
Horlick, Sgt Arthur 37, 120, 162
Howard, Maj Mike 14, **15**, 78, 84–5, 103, 136, 147, 192
Howe, Mne D E 158
Howell, CSM 61
Howie, Lt-Col Charles 159, 173, 175
Hudspeth, Lt Ken 65(*n*)

226

Index

Inverary, training at 19
Irwin, Lt 155, 158

Jackson, Pte Victor 68
Jackson, Tpr A J 44
Jary, Lt Sydney 8
Jesney, L/Cpl John 156, 159
Johnson, Capt Peter 83, 118
Johnson, L/Cpl Fred 131
Jones, Maj Tony 12, **13, 24**, 50, 60–1, 121, 166, 175
Joseph, Capt Ivor 132, 175

Keenor, Pte Aubrey 134, 137
Kendrick, L/Cpl *Shock* 155, 159
Kershaw, Lt Leslie 119
Kidd, Capt Ronald 89
King, Lt Alan 107–8, 125, 145, 175, 186
Kingswell, L/Cpl Roy 82–3

Labett, Capt *Titch* 25
Laity, Pte George **91**
Lancaster, Lt Turlogh 35, 120–1, 162
Landing Craft, description of 19
Landing Ships, description of 19
Lassman, Capt Laurance **24**, 142, 171
Lauder, Lt Jack 7, 25, 45–6, 51–2, **53**, 54, 56, 132, 165, 180–2, 186, 188
Laurence, AB 77
Lawrence, Pte Reg 89
Lawrenson, Tpr Edgar 55
Laycock, Maj Mike 16, 77, 167–8, 176, 194
Layton, 2/Lt Gordon 44, 139–40, **187**
Le Patourel, Major Bert 11
Leopold, Gnr Fred 110
Lindon, Capt Bryan 154, 156
Lindsay, Sgt 72
Lipscombe, Lt-Col Christopher 8
Littlejohns, Maj John 9, **10**, 64, 89–90, 115–18, 126–7, 138–40, 145, 173, 175, 185
Lloyd, Capt John **27**, 84, 115, 176
Lofts, Lt Donald 125
Longues Battery 34, 149–53
Lowe, Tpr J T 44

Mabbott, Maj 49
MacDonald, Mne William 158–9
Madden, Mne J 158
Manvieux 32, 159
Marsh, Maj 98
Marshall, Howard 38, 83
Martin, Maj Charles 7, **8**, 89, 94, 106, 147
Martin, Maj Peter 172
Martin, S/Ldr John 7–8, 94
Mason Elliott, Lt Graham 12, 93, 106–7, **169**–70
Matkin, Tpr 76
Mattock, Sgt Richard 179–80
Mawdesley, Jane 18, 108
Mayes, Lt Ernest **24**, 161
Mayne, CSM William **11**, 12, 42, 175, 187–8
McKenna, Mne G L 158
McKenzie, Sgt David 82
McWilliam, Lt Jimmy 77, 131, 180, 195
Medway, Sgt 179, 181
Miller, L/Cpl Joe **120**–1, 123, 172
Miller, Lt K C 55
Minogue, Tpr Joe 22–3, 49, 51, 52(*n*)
Mitchell, Maj Stephen 17, 28, 77–8, 119, 133, 195
Mohan, Pte 86
Montgomery, Gen Sir Bernard 2, 3–5, 176
Morgan, Lt-Gen Sir Frederick 3
Morris, Capt 44
Morris, Lt J G **27**, 135
Morris, Lt L J **24**, 166
Mott, Maj Tony **10**–12, 28, 36–7, 42, 44–6, 57–9, 90, 93–4, 100, 105–8, 124–8, 133, 139–41, 144–5, 159, 175, 185, 188
Mountain, Stoker William 47
Munro, Capt Kenneth 63–4

Nelson Smith, Lt-Col David 6, 9–**10**, 19, 26, 28, 59, 62–3, 71, 89, 140, 147, 184
Nevill, Lt-Col Cosmo 9, 14–**15**, 19, 21–2, 25–6, **27**–8, 34, 38–9, 84–5, 99–104, 134–7, 146, 149–53, 156, 162–3, 172, 176, 192, 197

Nicoll, Maj Bobby 12, **13**, 65–7, 90, 93–4, 96, 100, 105, 111–13, 119, 122–3, 166, 171–2, 177, 189–90
Nijmegen 178–80
Nith, HMS 35, 38, 42
Norie, Lt-Col Evelyn 9, 12–**13**, 19, 21, **24**, 26, 45, 64, 119, 121–2, 146, 166, 169, 171–2, 175
Norman, Lt Alan 51(*n*), 52, 54–**56**, 63, 90, 132, 174, 186–7
Nyburg, Lt-Cdr Arnold 47, 49

O'Connell, CSM Nick **111**, 174
Oakley, Cpl Douglas 86
Oldridge, Pte Cyril 135, 137

Page, Gnr Percy 80–1
Palmer, Sgt Bob 128–**129**, 130, 193
Parker, Pte Terry 19, 35, 37, 121, 162, **191**
Parlby, Maj John 14–**15**, 25, **27**, 79, 85, 103, 136, 147
Paul, Lt *Peter* 7, 140, 173
Pearce, Cpl George 166
Pearson, Lt Frank **27**, 91–2, 94, 99, 152
Pease, Lt Frank **27**, 126, 136, 149–51, 174–5
Pepler, Lt Peter 167–8
Pepper, Brig *Peter* 32
Peskett, Lt-Col Victor 31
Petard – see AVRE
Phayre, Lt-Col Robert 16, 108
Phillips, Lt-Col Cecil 23, 96, 99, 101, 154–6
Pinfold, Sgt 180
Playford, Pte Robert 172
Point 54 32, 90, 110–13, 122
Point 72 154–5, 158, 162–4
Port-en-Bessin 23, 30, 32, 96, 99, 153–9
Powis, Pte David 78, 100–1
Prince, Bdr Stephen 119
Prior, Pte John 86
Prouton, Pte R **53**, 182
Puits d'Herode 32, 117–21, 123, 136, 142, 146, 166, 168, 172
Pymm, Cpl Arthur **97**

Ramsay, Admiral Sir Bertram 2
Ratnage, Cpl John 172
Rawlinson, Spr 48–9
Ray, Lt-Col Broke 19
Raybould, S/Ldr Arthur 150
Redpath, Cpl James 168–9
Richards, Cpl *Taffy* 104
Robinson, Lt-Col 84
Robjohn, Lt Peter **24**, 121
Robson, SSM 76
Roland, Pte Joe 105
Rose, Cpl Dennis **53**, 57, 181–2

Royal Navy and Royal Marines
   1st RM Armoured Support Regiment 31, 49
   47th (RM) Commando 23, 30–2, 96–9, 101–2, 153–9, 162–4, 169
   Landing Craft Obstacle Clearance Units 31, 41–2, 46, 50–1

Royle, Capt John **24**, 61–**62**, 121–2, 168
Russell, Cpl Jock 14, **108**, 153, 192
Ryes 32–3, 85, 95, 101–4, 134–7, 142, 146
Rymer, Sgt 107

Sadleir, Maj Franc 6, 14–**15**, 18, 25, **27**, 29, 78, 85, 134–5, 137, 163–4, 175
Scaife, Sgt Bert 40–1, 47–8, 50, 55, **127**–8, 130–1, 133, 138, 144, 193
Scrivens, Pte Bill 121
Sear, Sgt James 156
Senior, Brig Ronald 161
Sexton SP Gun 21
Shepperd, Pte Ernie 50–1
Shinn, Lt Harry 25, **27**
Sidaway, Sgt 76
Sidgwick, Maj Christopher 45, 48, 64
Sippetts, Sgt Arthur 52, 56, 132–3, 145, 174
Skinner, Capt The Rev Leslie 29, 81–**82**, 90, 124, 143, 167–8, 176, 180, 194–5
Slade, Cpl *Bert* **53**, 72, 132–3, 145–6, 179
Smith, Capt Peter 69, 125

Smith, Lt Edward 7, 135–6
Smith, Midshipman Stan 76
Smith, Mne John 96
Smith, Sgt 93
Spencer, Lt-Col Bill 19
Stanier, Brig Sir Alex 5–**6**, 9, 18–19, 23–**24**, 26, 35, 38, 82–3, 85, 94, 98–9, 101, 103–4, 144, 146, 150–1, 153, 163–4, 182–4
Stanyon, Capt Harold 47
Stevenson, Sgt E 175
Stone, Capt Freddie 182
Stone, Lt John 1–2, 19, 193
Stone, Pte 84
Storey, Tpr Geoff 75
Stratton, Lt 67
Stroulger, Pte J 181
Sullivan, Sub-Lt Bernard 65–7

Tagg, Sgt 76
Talbot, Sgt *Alby* 86–7, 93–4, 123, 142, 190
Taylor, Capt 55
Taylor, Capt Derek 63–4
Teller mines – see Beach mines and obstacles
Terry, Sgt 61, 122
Thomas, Capt Cecil **11**–12, 133, 140, 159, 174, 197
Thomas, Lt J A **24**, 111
Thompson, Cpl Sam 14, 105–6, 111–12, 122–3, 166, 175–6, 198
Thomson, Capt Colin 78, 92, 106, 133, 180
Tomlinson, Mne J E 158
Travett, L/Cpl Norman 79
Tucker, Capt Bob 6, **121**–2, 166
Turner, Lt-Col A J D 176

Urquhart, Maj-Gen Roy 4, 177

Valentine, Lt-Col *Cupid* 19
Vandeleur, Lt-Col J O E 178
Verner, Lt Victor 166
Vigour, Pte Ted 61
Vine, Capt 44, 176

Waller, L/Cpl Victor 132–3, 145
Walsh, Lt G H D 180
Walton, Capt Dennis 155, 159
Warburton, Capt Arthur 128
Ward, Pte 166
Warren, Maj David **10**–11, 33, 35–6, 42, 63–4, 71–3, 89, 91, 94, 106–7, 118, 125–8, 139–40, 145–6, 175, 185
Waters, Capt Frank 73, 115, 182
Watt, Capt The Rev Robert **24**, 161–2
Webb, L/Cpl Leslie 117–18, 145–6
Wells, Maj 44, 176, 180
Wetjen, Mne John 98
Wharton, Lt 44
Wheaton, Capt 104
White, Pte Ron 73, 147
Whitebrook, Lt John 7, **24**, 61
Whittington, Capt *Dick* 7, **24**, **87**, 123, 190
Wicks, Maj James 9, **10**, 89, 125–6, 140, 145, 173
Wilford, Capt Ken 47
Wilkinson, Mne Robert 96
Williams, AB *Taffy* 85–6
Williams, Capt Bill 151
Williams, Lt 69–70
Williams, Sgt Sam 172, 180
Williamson, Lt Charles 12, 93, 147
Wills, Sgt *Ginger* 22, 41, 83–4
Wilmer, Capt Tom 182
Wilson, Gnr Charles 87–8
Wilson, Lt 158
Wilson, Lt Ian 44, 46–7, 50, 68–9, 125–6, 131, 193
Wilson, Pte Jim 156
Wiltshire, Pte Frank 70
Windebank, Lt Colin **24**, 67, 105, 175
Wint, Spr Norman 68
Winter, Cpl Bill 55
Winter, Lt Peter 96–7
Wood, Capt Bill 26, 85, 100, **137**
Wood, Pte T **121**
Woodcock, Sgt Tom 180
Woodgate, Mne B 97

229

Worboyes, Tpr Jesse 77–8
Wright, L/Cpl Frank 101
Wright, Lt *Horace* 11, 71–**72**, 73, 141, 173, 177, 179, 185–6, 197
Wyatt, Gnr Alfred 119
Wyatt, Maj Leslie 69

Youngs, Lt Donald 7